# Through the Bible, Chapter by Chapter

# Through the Bible, Chapter by Chapter

**Amos R. Wells**

**BAKER BOOK HOUSE**
Grand Rapids, Michigan

Copyrighted 1955
COPYRIGHTED 1933

© 1933, 1955 by Amos R. Wells
Formerly published under the title,
*The Living Bible, Chapter by Chapter.*
Paperback edition issued 1977 by
Baker Book House
ISBN: 0-8010-9583-2

*All rights reserved*

Made in the United States of America

# WEEK 1

### Sunday   *Read Genesis 1*   **My Creator**

It is God who made all things, and God is good. I need not fear anything God has made.—Christ was with God in the beginning, and "without Him was not anything made." I must read all the New Testament into the first chapter of Genesis.—God saw that it all was good. As I go forth into the beautiful world I also shall see it to be good, if I have God's Spirit within me, and am taught of Him how to see. Lord, open Thou mine eyes.

### Monday   *Read Genesis 2*   **My Edens**

What made Eden? The presence of God. That presence will make my home an Eden today; my school, my shop, my office. Lord, help me to bring it about.—What did God's presence do for Eden? It gave to mere dust the breath of life and the glow of intelligence. It created eye-pleasantness and body-food. It established society and love. It will do all that for my life, however bare and lonely it may be.

### Tuesday   *Read Genesis 3*   **My Sins**

I must keep my desires in hand, for it is through them I shall fall, if I fall at all.—Let me watch my "little" temptations, and remember that the smallest of them may be my undoing.—If any Eden is shut against me, it is because of my sin, and it will be opened to me because of my Saviour. What is my besetting sin? Lord, help me to overcome it.

### Wednesday   *Read Genesis 4*   **My Brother**

Envy and murder are twin iniquities. If there is a man I envy, I am in the pathway of Cain.— When I begin to ask, "Am I my brother's keeper?" I begin to be his murderer. There is only one safe rule of conduct with reference to any man, and that is the Golden Rule. What brother has God sent me whom I am not "keeping"?

### Thursday  Read Genesis 5  My Old Age

Am I preparing a vigorous old age for myself? Health is a duty, because health alone makes it possible to perform well my other duties.—Long life is a duty — as long a life as God designs for me. The longer I live, if I live well, the more valuable will I be to God's work.—Let me prepare for myself Enoch's splendid epitaph. Oh, may I walk with God to-day. Have I any habit of body or mind that will prevent it?

### Friday  Read Genesis 6  My Separation

There is evil in the world around me, a terrible mass of evil; but I can at least see to the purity of the world within me.—Death is the doom of the wicked. Let me realize their fate, and shun it.—"I will establish my covenant with thee," says God to me. "Come ye out from among them, and be ye separate." Lord, I will have no more communion with evil!

### Saturday  Read Genesis 7  My Ark

Sure as God's word is the destruction of the wicked; and sin is so easy! I dare not at any minute hold myself safe from it.—If I trust in my own wisdom, or resolution, or holiness, they fall to dust, and let in the black waters upon my soul. —One ark I have, and one alone, sufficient and unfailing. It is Christ's righteousness. "He sent from on high, he took me, he drew me out of many waters." Lord, am I hid with Thee in Thy pavilion?

## WEEK 2
### Sunday  *Read Genesis 8*  **My Safety**

How many times, when the floods raged around me, has my God lifted me safely above them! And not a flood but has gone down at last.—So many doves of hope have come to my ark, with the olive leaves of good cheer! I will praise the Lord for His protecting care.—And I will praise Him for the future as for the past, for the promise that seed time and harvest shall continue, and His love clothe the world with blessings. O my God, how endlessly good art Thou!

### Monday  *Read Genesis 9*  **My Covenant**

God has made a compact with me, and I with God. He has given me commandments, as He gave them to Noah; and a bow of promise, as He gave it to Noah.—I will remember my covenant; God will remember His. I will not enter the church without remembering it, nor kneel in prayer, nor open the Bible. It shall overarch my life with rainbow splendors.—My Father, help me this day to be true to Thee, as Thou wilt surely be true to me.

### Tuesday  *Read Genesis 10, 11*  **My Pride**

Am I building a Babel tower in the face of heaven? Am I rearing my ambitions over against God's desires? Am I forgetting heaven in the allurements of earth? Do these dangers await me this day? Lord, overthrow my high tower of pride! Give me, O God, as the most blessed of Thy gifts, a wise and healthful humility.

### Wednesday  *Read Genesis 12*  **My Migration**

I dwell in Ur of the Chaldees. Idols are all about me; in my home, in my heart. I hear a great voice, bidding me leave familiar scenes of the soul, break with old habits of sin, go

## WEEK 2

forth, over whatever deserts, to Canaan and to God. O Abraham, for thy courage and faith! Give it to me, my Father, the God of Abraham! And give it to me to-day.

### Thursday  *Read Genesis 13*  **My Choice**

Every day I am tempted by the Plain of Jordan. It is rich and fair. Every day God holds up before me the heights of Hebron. The soil is poorer there, the work is harder. But God is there, and calls me. Ah, let who will choose Sodom and Gomorrah! My choice, this day and all days,—God grant it!—shall be the hills.

### Friday  *Read Genesis 14*  **My Nine-tenths**

Has Melchizedek, King of Salem, come yet to me? Has the priest of the Most High met me? Has he spread before me a table of delights? Ah, yes, yes! Every day is such a priest, and every event such a table! And what am I rendering unto the Lord for all these benefits? As much as Abraham? Surely it shall be no less. I would be Thy steward to-day, O my God.

### Saturday  *Read Genesis 15*  **My Promise**

How full is my life of fear! And has not God promised to be my shield, and my exceeding great reward? Has he not come to me, in all horrors of great darkness? Has he not promised me all things,—height, depth, things present, things to come? Simply and trustingly, I will take the great gift; and I will walk to-day in the joy of it.

# WEEK 3

**Sunday**   *Read Genesis 16*   **My Protection**

How often I am proud, as Hagar was, when God gives me a gift or a grace He does not give to others! And how often that pride drives me to the wilderness! But Thou dost find me there, O God, and dost bring me back with promises of safety. So protect me to-day, my God; and above all protect me from myself!

**Monday**   *Read Genesis 17*   **My New Name**

Thy covenants with me are many, my Father. Every morning multiplies them and every evening sees their fulfilment. Thou hast bought me with blessings; I am Thine, and proudly Thine! Change my name, in token of Thine ownership of me. I would be called by Thy name. And I would not forget, a moment of this day, whose I am, and whom I serve.

**Tuesday**   *Read Genesis 18*   **My Intercession**

Souls all around me are going down into the pit. I see it, I note their descent, now slow, now rapid. What is it to me? Am I my brother's keeper? Oh, for Abraham's brotherhood! Oh, for his passion of intercession! Lord, I am ashamed of my prayers. Help me henceforth to take self out of them, and fill them with love.

**Wednesday**   *Read Genesis 19*   **My Peril**

Am I in Lot's plight? Have I chosen the city of the plain, the ways of the world? Let me recognize the danger of all worldliness—a danger far more terrible than any volcanic outburst. God will send His angels, yes, this very day, to lead me out of Sodom, up on to high land. And may I have the wisdom to follow!

*WEEK 3*

**Thursday** *Read Genesis 20* **My Temptation**

I shall be tempted to-day, as Abraham was, to put expediency in the place of truth and right. Whenever I do this, I bring others into peril, but myself far more. Lord, there is only one safety, and that is the truth. Help me to be true to-day, outwardly and inwardly, and in all things. Amen.

**Friday** *Read Genesis 21* **My Wilderness**

Not Hagar alone wanders in the wilderness of Beer-sheba. Many days have I spent there, and am likely to spend there again, because of my sins and the sins of others. But God has a well for me in that wilderness, and a voice to call me, and He is ready to cause the wilderness to blossom as the rose. Praise the Lord, O my soul!

**Saturday** *Read Genesis 22* **My Obedience**

Dost Thou ask my best, my dearest? Thou dost not ask in tyranny, but in love; not to despoil, but to enrich; not with the knife, but with the outstretched hand of blessing. Let me do God's will, however dark the way. Let me pursue His purpose, however threatening. For His will is life.

# WEEK 4

**Sunday**   *Read Genesis 23*   **My Dead**

Ah, yes, Abraham; I too have my Machpelah, and it is becoming ever more crowded, as the years go by, with the mortal remains of the dear departed. How often my thoughts turn to Machpelah, and the tears rush to my eyes! O Thou resurrection Lord, help me to remember that they are not there, in the ground, but that my true Machpelah is heaven. How blessedly crowded heaven is getting to be! May this day's living draw me nearer that abode of the obedient.

**Monday**   *Read Genesis 24*   **My Alliances**

Such care as Abraham took that his house should not be allied with the Canaanites, and that his son should have a proper wife,—be this my care for my life alliances. Guide Thou my friendships, O God! Enter Thou all my associations and partnerships! May I go nowhere this day but Thou shalt go with me, nor embark in any enterprise in which Thou wilt not share.

**Tuesday**   *Read Genesis 25*   **My Birthright**

Am I, like Esau, selling my birthright? Alas, yes! For my birthright is power, and I sell it by sloth. And joy, and I sell it by sin. And peace, which I sell by ambition. And love, which I sell by selfishness. And God, whom I sell for a beggarly bit of this world. Let me hold on to my birthright, what remains of it; and, O God, help me through obedience to increase it to what it was!

**Wednesday**   *Read Genesis 26*   **My Peace**

It is so hard to turn the other cheek! So hard to be driven from well to well, and patiently to

*WEEK 4*

dig new ones! So hard to be reviled and answer not again! O Christ, impart to me Thy meekness, Thy forgiveness, Thy divine forgetfulness of injury. To-day and forever let me forgive those that trespass against me, that Thou also mayest forgive my trespasses.

### Thursday  *Read Genesis 27*  **My Deceptions**

How simple and clear would be my life, were I only content with what my God sends me and plans for me! Let me no longer be a Jacob, scheming to get more than my share, to thrust myself into my brother's place. Let me know that I can have no real blessing except in the place Thou hast prepared for me, O my Father!

### Friday  *Read Genesis 28*  **My Bethels**

Nearer, my God, to Thee! Though a cross raises me. Though, like the wanderer, I make a Bethel out of my stony griefs. Whatever draws me to Thee,—misfortune, failure, sickness, loss, ignominy, loneliness, fear,—all shall be bright and blessed; they shall be angels ascending and descending a golden stairway. May every hour of this day be a Bethel, my Father. Amen.

### Saturday  *Read Gen. 29*  **My Postponements**

Does the world cheat me, Laban-wise? Does it promise a reward and require double payment? Is joy deferred, and fruition? Let me be patient, and rather set my affection on things above. For God is a just master. His promise is sure. His reward is certain. His payment is prompt and generous. What matter the postponements of earth? I have a present God.

# WEEK 5

### Sunday     Read Genesis 30     My Craft

Jacob was shrewd, but he had no good from his shrewdness. He was a witty bargainer, but he often left God out of the compact. Let me not imitate him in this, nor envy wealth that is got without God. Let my craft be of unselfishness, and let me plan how others may increase.

### Monday     Read Genesis 31     My Wrongs

Men wrong me sometimes, as they wronged Jacob. Let me choose Christ's manner of redress rather than Jacob's. Let me love my enemies, and heap coals of fire on their heads. Thy way is best, O Christ, though it is hardest. Thy way is not hardest, O Christ, because Thou dost walk it with me.

### Tuesday     Read Genesis 32     My Peniels

Not the Angel of Jehovah wrestling with me can prevail against my hardness of heart, the intensity of my sinful will. Not the fierceness of my desire wrestling with God can prevail against God's inevitable laws. I will cling! Oh, I will cling, as Jacob clung, to the heavenly messenger. And I will not let him go. And he will bless me.

### Wednesday     Read Genesis 33     My Brother

Why do I not fear to meet my brother men? Have I not wronged them? In what I have failed to do, if not in what I have done. Let me not blame Jacob. Let me rather pray for a conscience as sensitive as his, and as righteous a fear of retribution! And, O God, let me be to-day a true brother to men!

### Thursday     Read Gen. 34     My Friend's Wrong

I am too little troubled by the wrongs done to thers, and too much troubled by the wrongs

*WEEK 5*

done myself. When sorrow is brought mountain-high upon another, I bear it complacently; when it is so much as dusted upon my head, I am frantic. Let me live more in the lives of others, for their defence and upbuilding. Oh, I would be unselfish to-day!

**Friday**  *Read Genesis 35*  **My Memorials**

How often has God answered me in the day of my distress! He has been good to me, even when I have been most evil. Yet I do not set up memorials to His loving kindness, either outwardly or in my memory. I will think of Thy kindness more steadily, my Father; I will praise Thee with readier lip. And I will record Thy goodness where I and all men may know it.

**Saturday**  *Read Genesis 36, 37*  **My Envy**

God does not love all men alike, though He would like to, because not all men love Him alike. To His Josephs He gives coats of many colors. Shall I repine when I see another more richly blessed of God? Shall I envy him and seek his hurt? That would be to defeat my very desire. For I, too, may become a Joseph. Let me only be what God would have me be, and I shall have all I should like to have.

# WEEK 6

**Sunday**  *Read Gen. 38, 39*  **My Temptations**

How many wiles has the devil! I cannot steel myself against them by philosophy, or custom, or regard for men's opinion, or even my own self-respect. There is but one resource against temptation, and that is Thy presence, O Thou who wert tempted in all points as I am, yet without sin! Oh, wilt Thou walk with me to-day!

**Monday**  *Read Genesis 40*  **My Insight**

Truly Joseph was right. Not dreams and interpretations alone, but all hidden things belong to God. There are many dark mysteries in life,— mysteries of sorrow, of fate, of pain, of sin, of the future. I will not try to interpret them, for God will show them to me, all I need, as I go on. God will be my vision and my understanding.

**Tuesday**  *Read Gen. 41*  **My advancement**

I perceive that all real progress in life comes like Joseph's, by God's appointment. Let me therefore stand still and labor, and trust God for advancement. It is He that must bid me "Come up higher." Let me cease to consider where I am with respect to others, but only whether God is with me where I am.

**Wednesday**  *Read Gen. 42*  **My Repentance**

God grant that I may repent early and easily, not needing the spurs of affliction and danger! God grant that I may repent at once! Why should I need a famine and a long journey Egyptward to remind me of the brother I have wronged, and convict me of my sin? Lord, that I may make reparation this very day!

*WEEK 6*

### Thursday   Read Gen. 43   **My Magnanimity**

In dealing with my brothers who have wronged me, am I, like Joseph, magnanimous, great-minded? When I withhold forgiveness, is it always for their growth in grace, and never for my own vindictiveness? Is my chief desire not to humiliate them, but to better them? Am I *parv*animous or *magn*animous?

### Friday   Read Gen. 44   **My Self-Sacrifice**

When my brother is in danger, do I play the part of Judah? Am I as ready to plead for him with my life as with my tongue? Am I eager to take his yoke upon me, wear his chains, enter his cell? This would be taking Thy nature, O Christ, and entering into the joy of Thy spirit.

### Saturday   Read Gen. 45   **My Reconciliation**

When my brother sins against me, let my forgiveness be contemporary with his sin. For his good I may withhold the expression of it, but for my own good let me not postpone an instant the feeling itself. For to hate my brother is murder—murder not alone of him, but of myself, my joy, my peace, my power.

# WEEK 7

**Sunday**  *Read Genesis 46*  **My Goshens**

What a sad journey for Jacob, down to Egypt, away from the land of promise, away from the hopes of the future! I have often taken just such journeys. But God knows best. His Goshens, when He sends me there, are bettter than Canaan. They are lands where my hopes, seemingly frustrated, become a victorious multitude. I will trust Him wherever He leads me.

**Monday**  *Read Genesis 47*  **My Dignity**

If God go with me, I shall not fear, like Jacob, to stand before kings. Little though I am among the children of men, yet both I and they are as dust before the Almighty. When one looks off to Arcturus, what matters a few inches difference in height on our tiny earth? So shall I walk through life with erect head, if my God walks with me.

**Tuesday**  *Read Genesis 48*  **My Blessing**

No old man has ever laid his hand upon my head in blessing, or given me a portion of his goods, or foretold my destiny. But a greater blessing may be mine, an infinitely greater. Let me feel this day upon my head the hand of the Ancient of Days, and let the words of His blessing ring in my ears.

**Wednesday**  *Read Genesis 49*  **My Fortune**

These fates of the sons of Jacob were not selected at random, but were built up slowly through the years by themselves, and only announced by the wise patriarch. What future am I now constructing for myself and for posterity? Would I shrink from having it proclaimed? Nay, every word and deed of mine proclaims it!

*WEEK 7*

**Thursday**  *Read Genesis 50*  **My Memory**
What a train of power, of glory, of blessings, Jacob left behind him! And that in spite of his many faults. I have faults enough,—more than his. What is the balance of my life? How will men remember me when I am gone? Oh, my God, help me to think of that to-day. Help me to live as, on my death-bed, I shall desire to have lived.

**Friday**  *Read Exodus 1*  **My Tasks**
When my tasks seem more than I can bear, I shall remember that after Pithom comes Elim, after Raamses comes Sinai! The burdens are sure to slip off, if they are borne with Christian grace. The chains are sure to fall away, if I am a bond-slave of Christ. God will lay upon me no weight too heavy for my back; nor will He allow men to overburden me.

**Saturday**  *Read Exodus 2*  **My Safety**
Though kings plot against me, and an empire is in arms to my hurt, a barrier of bulrushes will be sufficient protection, if God is with me. He will fashion a fort for me out of the palaces of my enemies, and a guard for me out of their tallest soldiers. No harm can befall me, while God befalls me, in this world or in any world. O my Father, I will trust Thee to-day and forever!

# WEEK 8

**Sunday**   *Read Exodus 3*   **My Commission**

No burning bush for me? Why, my God surrounds my life with burning bushes! Wherever I turn, they blaze up before me. Appeals, warnings, exhortations, promises, guidances, providences, glories, rewards, powers,—the world is crowded with radiant beckonings to service! Forbid, O God, that I should pass by unheeding, to herd my selfish sheep!


**Monday**   *Read Exodus 4*   **My Reluctance**

"O Lord, send, I pray Thee, by some one else!" Have I ever prayed that faithless prayer? Ah, have I not prayed it many, many times? Let me rather say: "Here am I, O Lord; send me! However hard and perilous the task, send me! But let me go nowhere, though I ascend a throne, except where Thou dost go with me."


**Tuesday**   *Read Exodus 5*   **My Difficulties**

"Bricks without straw!" How much of my life is like that! Tasks, tasks, tasks, lacking health, and strength, and wisdom, and courage, and perseverance, and grace! But it was not bricks without—God; nor is it ever tasks without God. Let me remember that this very hour.


**Wednesday**   *Read Exodus 6*   **My Hope**

Is not Jehovah my God as well as the God of Israel? Has He ever been more to any man than He will gladly be to me? Did He ever bring a soul out of his distresses and will not bring me out of mine? I will appropriate every promise, every assurance, every fulfilment, in all the history of the world. It all belongs to me, to me!

*WEEK 8*

### Thursday   *Read Exodus 7*   **My Authority**

Behold, the Lord has given to me, as to Moses, a wonder-working rod! I bear about with me the symbol and assurance of God's presence and power. Lo, He is with me alway. Yet how often, alas! I use the rod as a walking-stick, and think no more about it!

### Friday   *Read Exodus 8*   **My Hard Heart**

Pharaoh hardened his heart before God hardened it! The king repulsed the plea of pity until God could no longer pity him. God fixed him in evil, but only after he had proved his unalterable will for evil. Oh, Almighty Judge, may no such fate be mine! May I fix my heart on Thee, that it may not be fixed in wickedness!

### Saturday   *Read Exodus 9*   **My Obstinacy**

Alas for my folly, in which I join Pharaoh and all the long line of fools! I sin, and misfortunes come. I think they will pass, and continue to sin. They do not pass, but increase. I refuse to connect them with my sin. How must God grieve, when even His wisest and best-contrived penalties do not move His rebellious child!

# WEEK 9

**Sunday**   *Read Exod. 10*   **My Last Chance**

God's warnings will not continue forever. To me, as to Pharaoh, will come a final message. How do I know when it will come? How did Pharaoh know? He did not know, nor do I. He was gratified, like a fool, by the removal of each plague, and went on in his folly. Let me not scorn him till I am sure I am not doing the same.

**Monday**   *Read Exodus 11*   **My Death**

I do not fear the death of the body. That, I know, is only an incident, a passing incident, in my continuing career. I look forward to it with equanimity. But my dread is of the death of the soul, a death that may come upon me at any time if I do not break with sin. What was the horror of that Egyptian midnight, what that carnival of woe, compared with this death of the soul?

**Tuesday**   *Read Exodus 12*   **My Passover**

Has the death angel passed over my soul? Has only the dark shadow fallen upon me with its warning, and then hastened away? Do I stand again in the safe sunshine of God's love? It is no grace of mine, but all of Another. It is no merit of mine, but Another's sacrifice. Oh, endless praise be to Him who has delivered me from this death!

**Wednesday**   *Read Exod. 13*   **My Guidance**

Not only has the shadow passed by me, but I am given leadership for my safety, day and night. Fire and cloud—fire which I fear because of its power, cloud which I dread for its darkness—these awful omens God has transformed into the symbols of my salvation. By His very terrors I am guided, by His flaming omnipotence I am led!

*WEEK 9*

### Thursday  *Read Exodus 14*  **My Red Sea**

Many a time it has stretched out before me, some sea of discouragement, difficulty, danger. The waves run high, the wind blows, the enemy press on behind; I hear their rattling chariot wheels, their shouts of triumph. And then the sea has become a cloistered pathway, and I have passed through untouched by a wave, while all my foes have been swallowed up. This has happened, all this, yet still I fear for the future!

### Friday  *Read Exodus 15*  **My Marah**

Lo, God has changed all my bitter springs to sweet water, and all my Marahs to Elims! There is no sorrow that has not issued in joy, no failure He has not transformed to success. That has been when I gave my life into His keeping, as I shall do to-day.

### Saturday  *Read Exodus 16*  **My Manna**

Is this world a desert? I know men say it is, but where's the proof? I am housed beneath the covering of God's protection, I am abundantly fed with the manna of God's love, I am led by the pillar and cloud of God's providences. With shelter, food, and a highway, where is the desert? O my God, how endlessly good art Thou!

# WEEK 10

**Sunday**  *Read Exodus 17*  **My Meribahs**

My rebellion is often hot against God. I do not acknowledge it to myself, but God understands! He hears my complaints: "Why didst Thou bring me into this hard place? Wilt Thou slay me with thirst?" And then, perchance, my Father opens for me a fountain out of the very rocks that hem me in. He would have done it anyway; how much better had He done it without my complaints!

**Monday**  *Read Exodus 18*  **My Over-work**

Surely I am indispensable! Surely no one else can do the work! Surely the Lord rests upon me, and His Kingdom is established on the rock of my faithfulness! Thus I talk with myself. Oh, let my better sense be the Jethro. Let it show me how well the world progressed before I was born and will progress after I die, and bid me toil with a less immodest frenzy. Let me work with others, gladly sharing with them the toil, the praise, and the reward.

**Tuesday**  *Read Exodus 19*  **My Preparation**

God does not speak to me as He spoke to Moses and Moses' people. With good reason, too, for I do not make ready to hear Him. I have not purified my heart and life. I have not expected Him and been attent. Every day is a possible Sinai. Oh, let me go softly, waiting for the trumpet peal!

**Wednesday**  *Read Exod. 20*  **My Decalogue**

Part of the Commandments are easy for me; God forbid that my obedience there should satisfy me, as certainly it does not satisfy God. For part of them are terribly hard. *That* part is my Decalogue. Over *that* part I must pray and groan. There is my test, and by that obedience or disobedience I stand or fall.

*WEEK 10*

**Thursday**  *Read Exodus 21*  **My Slavery**

Let me count it my pride and joy to be a bond-slave of the Lord! Not for six years shall my service be, and a glad release on the seventh; but gladly for all years, and release to be counted the most terrible of disasters. My ear to Thy door post, O Thou Most High!

**Friday**  *Read Exod. 22*  **My Responsibility**

My hands are heavy with fate. Fortunes of friends, of neighbors, of children, of other dear ones, of the community, the state, the farthest tribe, are in my keeping. My life is not well lived unless through me their lives are well lived or better lived. Who, without divine help, is equal to these things? But the help always comes.

**Saturday**  *Read Exodus 23*  **My Angel**

Surely as for His people of old, God sends His angel before me,—ready to punish, ready to praise; ready to rout my adversaries, ready to guide me in any gloom. Am I living my life without this supernatural aid? Then it is not my life, but only the pitiful shadow of the life that is rightfully mine!

# WEEK 11

### Sunday   Read Exodus 24   My Covenant

Not at the foot of a literal Sinai, awful with the presence of a visible Deity, have I made my covenant with the Almighty. No; but beneath the sublime arch of heaven, and before the unseen throne of the Infinite One! I am His. My life is His. I am not my own. Shall I consider this day as mine? Shall I be false to my solemn vow? And how then can I expect my God to bestow His covenanted blessings?

### Monday   Read Exodus 25   My Offering

There are so many millions of Christians, wealthy, strong, zealous, and wise. They do not need me, or my small offering. Ah, but do I not need, all the more, to give it? Do I not need to identify myself with this great task, and the more because it is so great and prosperous? Yet how do I know they do not need me? And do I not know that God—even God Himself—does need me?

### Tuesday   Read Exodus 26   My Tabernacle

What sanctuary am I fashioning for my God? I know the temple He desires. My body—ah, wonderful thought!—He has deigned to seek as His temple. Could higher honor come to me, among all earth's crowns and kingdoms? Lord, for purity of heart! Lord, for obedience of will!

### Wednesday   Read Exodus 27   My Altar

Upon what shall I lift up my sacrifice to Thee, O Thou Most High? Thou dost not seek stones heaped up, though of beryl or chrysolite. Thou dost wish rather the altar of my affections. Thou art best pleased with my prayers when they lie

*WEEK 11*

upon my heart and are founded upon my life. Such shall be my communing with Thee henceforth, O my Father.

**Thursday** *Read Exodus 28* **My Raiment**

Why should not I, as well as Aaron, wear upon my heart the names of those dear to me,—yes, of all those, to the ends of the earth, who are dear to my Lord? And why should I not wear upon my very forehead, "holy to the Lord"? Be my vesture day by day a sacred robe, however commonplace to the eye of men; and in it may I walk as becomes a priest of the Most High.

**Friday** *Read Exodus 29* **My Consecration**

Not Aaron, not any of his sons, was more a priest of God than I am. Some share have I in the worship of the church and my home; and I alone minister in that sacred temple of my heart, where God enters and dwells. I would live worthily of this exalted dignity. Shall a priest profane himself?

**Saturday** *Read Exodus 30* **My Incense**

What incense shall I offer Thee, most glorious, most bountiful, most loving One? My words; Thou delightest even in my stammering praise. My life; with all its failures, it is dedicated to Thee. My prayers; halting, stumbling, mistaken, yet they climb to Thee. My love,—ah, that is best of all, and includes them all, and—wonder of wonders!—it but reflects Thy love for me!

# WEEK 12

### Sunday   *Read Exodus 31*   My Sabbaths

They are to be "a perpetual covenant," it seems. A token of my fidelity to God. A token of God's love for me. Days of communion, days of partnership, days of friendship. If I break away from them, am I not breaking away from God? Ah, let me make my Sabbath a delight! Let me love its every hour, because I love its God!

### Monday   *Read Exodus 32*   My Golden Calf

Too often my ideals go up on a mountain, and a cloud removes them from sight, but I stay down on the lower levels of life, where the base memories are, and the pressures of trivial needs. It is so easy, there, to make an idol of my folly, and bow down before it. Gold? Fame? Ease? Pleasure? Oh, my God! whatever it is, help me to grind it to powder!

### Tuesday   *Read Exodus 33*   My Vision

O God, show me Thyself! If I can see Thee, I can look all enemies in the face. If I can see Thee once, I will henceforth see Thee everywhere. If I can see Thee, life will become a long, glad journey toward the vision of Thee forever. But a glimpse of Thee, even of the gesture of Thy hand, even of the corner of Thy robe, O my Father!

### Wednesday   *Read Exod. 34*   My Communion

Up in the mount with God! Oh, may no triviality detain me, no obstacle bar me, no sin, basely cherished, unfit me for that high privilege. That my face shall shine from the glory of it I care not, as I shall not know, though others will know; but my heart will shine, and the sun will dwell in all my life. Yes, "early in the morning," up in the mount with God!

*WEEK 12*

### Thursday  Read Exodus 35  **My Offerings**

Is my heart willing for its gifts? What I set apart for the Lord, of time, or money, or strength, do I set apart gladly, or grudgingly? Do I long for chances of service, or shrink from them? Is my heart in the work, or only my calculating head? Let me learn from these ancient builders of the tabernacle, and let to-day be a divine temple on which I shall lavish myself lovingly for the Lord.

### Friday  Read Exod. 36  **My Workmanship**

I should take more pride in my work for the Lord. When I speak, the words should be my choicest. When I plan, I should be ambitious, prudent, courageous. When I execute, I should be indefatigable. I must not allow my secular work to be better done than my religious work. Sockets and clasps and "fine twined linen"—let my work for God be perfect and praiseworthy!

### Saturday  Read Exodus 37  **My Ark**

I need—oh, how I need to find God! Whether the blessed Presence flames forth from between golden cherubim, or speaks invisible in the quiet of some morning hour, I need the mercy seat! The ark has perished, but the reality it embodied has not perished. The mercy seat of gold is gone, but mercy remains, at my very hand, ready to forgive me and bless me at a word.

## WEEK 13

**Sunday**   *Read Exodus 38*   **My Gold**

To what uses do I put my gold? Am I most interested in weighing it out for the Kingdom, or for my own pleasures, or for hoarding it in the bank? Do I really believe that the money I use as God would have me use it is the only money I really have? And if I believe this, do I really act on that belief?

**Monday**   *Read Exodus 39*   **My Breastplate**

What do I take as the breastplate of my life, my defence against the darts of the evil one? Is it such steel and hammered brass as the world furnishes, masses of money, solid force, aggressive ambition? or is it such breastplate as God furnishes,—twelve precious stones, engraved with the names of His people, the tokens of His church? Is love for God and man the safety in which I confide? Ah, it will never fail me!

**Tuesday**   *Read Exod. 40*   **My Tent of Meeting**

As often as I go to church, do I meet my God? Do I go confidently expecting to meet that dread, that beloved, Presence? I know I shall see my friends there; am I as sure that I shall see Him there? Ah, let me find myself in a true "tent of meeting" next Sunday!

**Wednesday**   *Read Lev. 1*   **My Burnt Offering**

What wilt Thou have for a burnt offering, O my God? Thou hast given Thyself for me as a burnt offering. Thou wert consumed in fiercest fires— and for me. Can I give Thee anything less than my life, myself, my ambitions, loves, longings, the best and strongest I am? And I cannot give it less than completely. It shall be laid upon the altar, and purified by the divine fire, till it is all Thine, and worthy of Thee.

### Thursday     *Read Lev. 2*     **My Firstfruits**

Shall not the Lord have first place in all my enterprises? And this cannot be if they are first for myself and only secondarily for Him. How shall I subordinate my interests? I cannot. I will identify them with His! I in Him and He in me,—then the firstfruits and the lastfruits shall be all His, and all mine.

### Friday     *Read Lev. 3*     **My Peace Offering**

I would dedicate to God my hours of rejoicing. My recreations shall be His, my festivals. I will not go to Him with my griefs alone, but with my happiness. Why should He, who has given me all my pleasures, every one, be left out of them?

### Saturday     *Read Lev. 4*     **My Sin Offering**

Day and night the remembrance of my sins weighs me down. O God, for relief from the burden of them! Nay, but Thou hast placed relief at hand. O Thou who wert taken without the camp, Thou upon whose head were laid the sins of the world, Thou my Sin Offering, how I bless Thy holy name!

# WEEK 14

### Sunday   *Read Lev. 5*   **My Unintended Sins**

When I do wrong, let me not say, "I did not mean it," "I did not know it." What if I might have known it? What if I should have known it? O God, forgive me for my unwitting sins! Forgive me for the carelessness that does not keep close to Thee, so that I may know Thy will and do it in all things.

### Monday   *Read Lev. 6*   **My Restorations**

If I have harmed my neighbor, my brother,— as I have by many deeds or failures to do,—let me not rest content until I have restored all he has lost by me, and more. Yes, even if I stole only (*only!*) some brightness out of his sky, or whispered against him a half-justified reproach. Let me not go to sleep a single day in debt.

### Tuesday   *Read Lev. 7*   **My Freewill Offerings**

Shall I give Thee only what is commanded? O Thou that givest me so much more than I ask! Should I spend my day in petitions, I could not name over Thy benefactions of the day. Let me imitate Thy liberality, though it can be but feebly. Let the measure of my gifts overflow, and let my willingness still surpass my giving.

### Wednesday   *Read Lev. 8*   **My Consecration**

Have I felt upon my head the sacred oil? Am I set apart to holy use and service? If not, then why not? For we are all to be kings and priests unto God. Let me realize my consecration. Because of that holy anointing from the hands of the Spirit, let me walk purely all my days.

### Thursday   *Read Leviticus 9*   **My Obedience**

Is my obedience such—so exact, so ready— that as the result of it "the glory of the Lord" appears to "all the people"? Is my labor crowned with the crown of God's manifest presence? Ah, no. And yet it may be. And by God's grace it shall be.

**Friday** *Read Leviticus 10* **My False Fire**

The thing was good, in itself. I spent time and thought upon it, and men praised me. Ah, but God did not praise me! It was not His good. My own will impelled me to do it, my own selfish ambition. False fire! false fire! and justly might the flame of God's anger devour me.

**Saturday** *Read Leviticus 11* **My Food**

Do I "make a difference between the unclean and the clean"? Do I recognize the great truth that my body is not my own, that it with all its powers and functions is the Lord's? The dish too much is unclean. The food or the drink that befogs my brain or chokes any conduit of my body is unclean. All gluttony, all intemperance, is unclean. And the desire for what is unclean is as unclean as the thing itself. O God, keep me pure!

# WEEK 15

### Sunday   *Read Leviticus 12*   **My Birth**

How wonderful that I am to live forever! How much more wonderful that I ever came to live at all! Thou who art the Life, to Thee shall the gates of life be consecrated. Let every thought that concerns the sacred entrance into existence be a hallowed thought; for in that Thou hast shared with us Thy creative powers, and deigned to place us nearest to Thyself.

### Monday   *Read Leviticus 13*   **My Leprosy**

Why do I not dread sin as the most horrible of diseases? It is indeed a leprosy. It makes its approach in secret, it advances stealthily. It eats, corrodes. It is foul, disgusting. It separates from men. I will lay my hand upon my mouth. I will cry, "Unclean! Unclean!"

### Tuesday   *Read Leviticus 14*   **My Cleansing**

Only Thou canst cleanse me, O Purity! Only Thou canst touch the foulness of my sin with healing efficacy, stay the mad riot of my blood, bid the hideous impulses depart, restore the torn and bleeding life. I fall at Thy feet. My tears run like rain. I can do nothing but beg for recovery. And at length—with what transports of joy!—I hear Thy tender words: "I will; be thou clean."

### Wednesday   *Read Leviticus 15*   **My Body**

In what a casket hast Thou placed my soul, my Creator! How marvellously contrived, with what powers, what adaptations, what beauties; and also with what possibilities of evil! It shall be Thy temple; yea, in all its functions and acts it shall be held meet for Thy abode.

*WEEK 15*

### Thursday  *Read Lev. 16*  **My Approach to God**

What sense have I of the vastness of Deity, His terrible power, His awful majesty? In Christ I may come close to Him; but let me never be carelessly familiar. Let me never draw near to God but with reverence. Let my heart be bowed, with my head.

### Friday  *Read Leviticus 17*  **My Sacrifices**

My day is filled with a myriad tasks, my mind with a myriad designs. I would enter upon no task, adopt no plan, without Thee, O my God! Let me carry it before Thy altar. Let me present it to Thy wisdom. Let me offer to Thee the life-blood of it. Let me, if I receive it at all, receive it from Thy hands.

### Saturday  *Read Leviticus 18*  **My Relations**

My kindred, to whom I am bound by so many sacred ties,—I will cherish them, and they shall be as my own life! Sooner may I harm myself than them. More gladly may I seek their joy than my own. For what has God set us together in families, but to love one another, and help one another, and lead one another nearer to our one Father in heaven?

# WEEK 16

**Sunday**  *Read Leviticus 19*  **My Duties**

How many relationships I have, and how many duties they all bring with them! How many persons there are to whom I must be kind and helpful, just and loving and true! Yet God requires of me only one duty at a time, and in that one duty He is present to help. Therefore I shall not be confused, but I shall go peacefully all my days.

**Monday**  *Read Leviticus 20*  **My Separation**

Of me, of me also, my God hath made "a peculiar people." Mine are not to be the laws of the world, the laws of greed, of a carnal desire, of fierceness and selfishness. And when they allure me with their bait, O God, give me strength to say, "No, no! I am not yours; I am apart from you, happily, and forever!"

**Tuesday**  *Read Leviticus 21*  **My Perfection**

I must be perfect. As of old, so now, God would have only perfect men standing in His holy presence. And what a cripple I am, how blind, how broken, how full of blemishes! Yet to my joy, a fountain of perfectness is open for me, the Perfect One shares with me His perfections, and through Him I dare to enter even the Holy of Holies. Praise His name!

**Wednesday**  *Read Lev. 22*  **My Profanations**

When I pass from my vileness to Thy purity, O Infinite Whiteness! when out of the midst of my sins I approach the Most Holy; when, spotted and unworthy as I am, I take in my hand Thy instruments and enter Thy temple,—how shall I not be consumed? Only as I enter with Thy Son, O God! Only as He invites me, only as He leads

*WEEK 16*

me, only as He wraps around me the mantle of His purity. With Him, I shall not be afraid, even before Thee.

**Thursday**  *Read Leviticus 23*  **My Festivals**

Have I no time from my labor to think of the time when that labor must cease? Am I too busy with the present to consider the past, to which the present is owed, and the future, by which the present is significant? This day shall be the Lord's! Though I may labor in it, it shall be a festival! I will fill it with thanksgiving. I will fill it with prayer.

**Friday**  *Read Leviticus 24*  **My Lamp**

Let the thought of my Saviour burn ever in my heart. Let its tender light illuminate my life continually. Let it plead for my darkness before the Mercy Seat. Let it be fed with the pure oil of holy thoughts. Let it be raised upon the standard of brave deeds. Let it be a lamp that never goes out.

**Saturday**  *Read Leviticus 25*  **My Jubilee**

A fresh start! I need it sorely. Not only every seventh year, but every seventh day. Not only every fiftieth year, but all the time. I need to begin again. I need to forget my sinful past. I need a new grip on myself and my duty. I need a clean slate, a new sheet of paper. And I can get it all from Thee, O most indulgent Father!

# WEEK 17

**Sunday**   *Read Lev. 26*   **My Alternative**

Blessings, or cursings! Joys, or sorrows! The Lord's face with me, or against me! It must be one or the other. Which is it? Which shall it be? Which am I preparing for my eternal existence? Awe-filled alternative! God help me to cleave to the right!

**Monday**   *Read Leviticus 27*   **My Oblations**

Let me take in turn each thing that I possess, however valueless, however precious, and consider whether I have consecrated it to the Lord. If not to Him, then it is Self's and Satan's. If His, then it endures and is fruitful. But let me be honest; is it really a devoted thing? is it really His?

**Tuesday**   *Read Numbers 1*   **My Family**

Suppose the people of God—the true people—were numbered to-day; where should I be enrolled? Am I certain that I should be enrolled at all? Just what is my place in the church?—not as men see, but as God sees. For the numbering is going on. Day by day the entries are making in the Great Book.

**Wednesday**   *Read Num. 2*   **My Life Centre**

How gloriously was that tent-city laid out! It did not centre about Moses' tent, or Aaron's or Joshua's. It did not centre about the commissary department or the military. Judah was not made the rallying point. No; its heart was the tent of meeting, and the heart of that tent was the presence of Jehovah. Thus let me order my life, with all its interests; and let me permit no other centre.

*WEEK 17*

**Thursday**   *Read Num. 3*   **My Church Work**

We have no Levites, but we have Levitical work. Who is to do it, but me, and my like? What is my task as a Levite? Have I recognized it? Am I about it? What particular share in God's house have I? what part in Christ's kingdom? However small, let me adopt it, and train for it, and do it, for Christ's dear sake.

**Friday**   *Read Numbers 4*   **My Burden**

Wrapped in blue or in purple, what burden has the Lord laid upon me or given in my charge? Does it seem a heavy weight, or a proud delight? Is it a load, or a crown? Beneath that wrapping is some golden vessel of the sanctuary. See! light and blessing radiate from it. I will walk happily all the day, for very joy of my burden.

**Saturday** *Read Numbers 5* **My Hidden Sins**

I need no "water of jealousy" to bring them out. They are bitter within, and ugly already to the eyes of men. My sins find me out. The world soon finds them out. Let me no longer hide them from myself, since they are not hidden from God and His creatures. Let me know myself; but first, O Christ, let me know Thee!

# WEEK 18

**Sunday**    *Read Numbers 6*    **My Blessing**

The benediction of Aaron upon his people is a benediction upon me also, for is not their God my God as well? And He has promised to bless me and keep me. His shining face is graciously turned upon me. In the light of His countenance I find my peace. Oh, let me never wander away from it!

**Monday**    *Read Numbers 7*    **My Altar**

It has been set up by the Almighty. It is dedicated to Him. As the flame and smoke ascend from it, they shall be the bond between earth and heaven. But how are they the bond between me and my God? Only as I give my life for the altar; my life,—that is, my time and interest and strength, and the gold and silver that measure these and represent them.

**Tuesday**    *Read Numbers 8*    **My Light**

Where is the sacred seven-branched candlelabrum? Has the light of the sanctuary gone out? Is it dark in the Holy Place? Ah, no! For we, even we Christians, are to shine as lights in the world. Oh, not to let my light go out! Oh, not to hide it under a bushel! Oh, to tend it daily, with prayer and with a song!

**Wednesday** *Read Num. 9* **My Guiding Cloud**

It is indeed a cloud, dark and ominous, and it has settled down upon my life, forbidding progress. Why will the Lord hold me in this place? Why may I not break through, and speed on to the promised land? Ah, the Lord is in the cloud! If I break through it and go upon my way, it is my way alone, and His no longer.

*WEEK 18*

### Thursday  *Read Num. 10*  **My Silver Trumpet**

If God is with me, my voice shall be like the silver trumpets of Moses. By my words shall men come together and move forward. In the days of gladness and on solemn festivals men will take up the note I sound. And it will not be because it is I, but because it is God; and God will speak through any one else as gladly as through me.

### Friday  *Read Numbers 11*  **My Grumbling**

Whatever my lot, it is of the Lord. As direct as the manna from the sky, my fortune falls from the hand of my loving Father. And shall I complain? Shall I not rather rejoice? Whatever the day brings me, shall I not rejoice, since it brings me God? Shall I wish to exchange it for anything that will not be God?

### Saturday  *Read Numbers 12*  **My Jealousy**

When I envy another his ability or position, or anything that is his, surely it is as a leprosy, eating both body and soul. Pray for me, O Thou Second Moses, Thou Deliverer of Thy people, first that I may see my plague, and then that it may pass from me.

# WEEK 19

### Sunday  *Read Numbers 13*  **My Giants**

My Promised Land lies before me. It is mine, because God has promised it to me; and yet not mine, because I have not yet seized it. I have looked longingly at it. I have made faint-hearted excursions into it. But ah, the giants are there! They are big and strong, and I am weak and little; I am as a grasshopper. Alas, I forget Him in whose eyes all men, giants and pygmies alike, are but grasshoppers!

### Mon  *Read Num. 14*  **My Tardy Repentance**

There is a "too late." There has been many a "too late" in my life. "To-day," when I might have heard His voice, has become "yesterday." What is left for me? To batter my head against the closed doors, the doors closed by my own folly? No; but to walk with the Lord all the rest of my days, past or into whatever doors He may choose.

### Tuesday  *Read Numbers 15*  **My Blue Cord**

Men no longer wear on their garments that cord of blue, but should they not all the more wear it on their hearts? Do I keep in perpetual remembrance God's known will for me? How distinct are His commandments in my view? How do I go about the firm remembrance of them?

### Wednesday  *Read Num. 16*  **My Rebellion**

When the Lord sets others over me, in authority, position, influence, or ability, am I not as Korah, Dathan, and Abiram? Do I not forget that men are nothing, to stand high or sink low, but God is all in all? Let me live my life to Him alone, in humility and self-distrust, and so let me escape the pit, the fire, and the plague.

*WEEK 19*

### Thursday   *Read Numbers 17*   **My Rod**

May my life blossom and bear fruit! Though dry now, and withered, send Thou the sap through its dead veins, quicken it without roots, vivify it without life, and make of it an almond-tree, O God! Then will I lay up the marvel in my Most Holy Place, that I may give Thee praise forever.

### Friday   *Read Numbers 18*   **My Portion**

Be the Lord my portion and my inheritance! He will not be, while I seek any other portion or inheritance. All such seeking is an affront to His graciousness. It is proof that He does not suffice. But Thou dost suffice, O Father.

### Saturday *Read Numbers 19* **My Cleanness**

By how many rules, and what minuteness of parable, did God's own people need to be taught the necessity of purity! Not by their road, but by some road, however hard and long, I must reach the same end. My God is spotless purity, and I cannot reach Him while a hint of defilement rests upon me.

# WEEK 20

### Sunday  *Read Numbers 20.*  **My Meribah**

Almost daily, almost hourly, I smite the rocks in my own strength. Every time I do this, I affront the Lord Almighty, I toss aside the teachings of my past, I play the fool. For if I should have learned anything from my life, it is that in myself I am nothing. Thus it is that I keep myself out of my Canaans.

### Monday  *Read Num. 21*  **My Fiery Serpents**

They surround me, stinging worries, poisonous doubts, crafty temptations, crawling iniquities, glittering sins. They assail me by day and night. They come up against me from the east and the west. I have no help but from the cross, and Him that was raised upon it. Oh, I will look to Him, and then I shall live indeed!

### Tuesday  *Read Numbers 22*  **My Utterances**

My words are my self. As they are spoken or withheld, I live—to the Lord of heaven, or the demons of hell. Let me watch the doors of my mouth. Before I speak, let me look to the Lord. Let me not at any time utter my words, but His. So alone can I live not my life but His.

### Wednesday  *Read Numbers 23*  **My Courage**

Let me speak what pleases men or what displeases them, and let me not care, if only it pleases God. I will not harshly disregard my fellows, but I will not fear them. I will be kind, but not servile. One is my Master, and they are my brethen.

### Thursday  *Read Numbers 24*  **My Insight**

I, even I, may be such a prophet as Balaam, if I am such a hero as he was. To obedient hearts come inspirations. To worshipping eyes

*WEEK 20*

come visions. To courageous tongues come revelations. Thou dost know all mysteries O God, and I may know Thee!

### Friday      Read Numbers 25      My Zeal

I would be red-hot for God! No half-hearted service shall be mine, no luke-warm enmity of evil. It shall be war to the knife, and the knife to the hilt. Oh, my carelessness, my lackadaisical sloth, my languid indifference, when the battle of eternal issues is on, and my Captain calls every soldier to the field!

### Saturday   Read Num. 26   My Continuance

None left for the second numbering, save only Caleb and Joshua! Would *I* have had a place in that little roll of honor? Shall I have a place on the vast muster roll of the divine Moses? Let me meet my giants daily with that thought ever before me.

# WEEK 21

**Sunday**  *Read Numbers 27*  **My Successor**

I should care less for my fame in my work than for the work's success. Let me not seek to be remembered after death, but that my work may be continued; let me be more eager for my successor than for my eulogy. For what am I, O Lord, that Thou dost deign to employ me at all?

**Monday**  *Read Numbers 28*  **My Offerings**

What reminders did the Israelites need of the sacrifices, what earnest repetitions! Not because Jehovah needed to receive the sacrifices,—His are the cattle on a thousand hills,—but because they sorely needed to give them. And *my* offerings? Ah, do not I also need a myriad of reminders, and even then go to them languidly? Why should not my longing desires be my only law-book?

**Tuesday**  *Read Numbers 29*  **My Set Feasts**

Shall I say that every day is to be a sacred festival? Yes; but only as at stated times I observe due days of worship and thanksgiving. Consecration is born of habit, and habit is born of practice, and practice is born of system. I must be bound before I can be free.

**Wednesday**  *Read Numbers 30*  **My Vows**

What are my vows to God? Are they only the words I take upon my lips? Are they not also the mercies I receive from His hands, the situations in which I allow myself to be placed, the whole tenor of the life I so gladly accept? And shall I hold myself only to the few petty obligations I seal with my tongue?

**Thursday**  *Read Numbers 31*  **My Midians**

I will have implacable hostilities. I will set my face like a flame against all that God hates.

*WEEK 21*

My war shall be endless and greedy against them. I will be a raging lion, a ravening wolf. There shall be no compromise, no quarter, for that which my God hates.

**Friday** *Read Num. 32* **My Brotherhood**

Is my dwelling apart? Has my inheritance fallen in solitude? None the less does my duty lie in the crowd. The solitude is pleasant, but selfish. It will be a hell to me, though a Gilead, if I cannot carry to it the spirit of brotherhood.

**Saturday** *Read Numbers 33* **My Journeys**

Well that the Israelites did not know, before they set out, how long was the way, how many were the stages! Well for us also that we have no prospectus of the coming years. God knows them all, and, if we let Him, will guide us safely through them all, giving us daily strength for the daily road.

# WEEK 22

**Sunday**  *Read Numbers 34*  **My Inheritance**

What an inspiring thought that God has laid out for me an inheritance as broad, as rich, and as accurately measured as this He ordained for His chosen people! I have only to walk in His ways, and at the end of the road I shall find my estate. It is already surveyed. Its fields stretch far and beautiful. And in the centre is the "mansion prepared."

**Monday**  *Read Num. 35*  **My City of Refuge**

Praise God, I do not live in a time when men need an earthly city of refuge, with stone walls and an open gate! My refuge is always at hand, and needs no running to it. There is no doubt of my reception. Entered in, I am safe from all pursuers. For my city of refuge is the heart of Jesus Christ.

**Tuesday**  *Read Numbers 36*  **My Tribe**

How much of my life is not mine! How much has come to me without my toil or thought, from my father and mother, from neighbors and friends, from the patriots and saints who have built my church, my college, my nation! And my life is due in turn, in great measure, to these persons and institutions that have done so much for me. May I not alienate their right in me!

**Wednesday**  *Read Deut. 1*  **My Retrospect**

It is good to take such a review of the past as Moses took. Let me dare to reckon up my disobediences. Let me count God's kindnesses. Let me see the good way He has led me hitherto. Let me bow in contrition and in prayer. Let me say to my God, "Henceforth I am Thine; do Thou lead me."

*WEEK 22*

**Thursday** *Read Deuteronomy 2* **My Sihons**

I know them! I make them fair offers, but they refuse. I will not harm them, but they scout me. I offer commerce, they draw the sword. I, even I, have my enemies. But they are God's enemies, too, if I am God's, as Moses was; and they shall not stand before me.

**Friday** *Read Deut. 3* **My Forbidden Canaan**

It looks so fair, across the Jordan! For so long a time I have been journeying to it, and now to be shut out! Ah, but who shuts me out? It is not God; it is my sin. Let me not blame God, but rather praise Him, that He is a God of justice, and not of weak yielding.

**Saturday** *Read Deuteronomy 4* **My God**

Who has a God like my God? I will exult in Him, as Moses exulted. Verily, He is high and lifted up! I will rejoice in His power. I will comfort me in His wisdom. His love shall overshadow me in the heat. Oh, who has a God like my God?

# WEEK 23

**Sun** *Read Deut. 5* **My Ten Commandments**

Some of them are easy for me; but they are all for me, the hard as well as the easy. And some are very hard. Lord, let me not rest in the easy ones! Lord, let me not rest in the easy observance of any of them by the letter! Lord, engrave Thy Ten Words upon my heart!

**Monday** *Read Deuteronomy 6* **My Memory**

There is enough in my past to furnish ample warning for the future, would I only keep it before me. There is enough encouragement to fill with power all my remaining years, and enough happiness to irradiate them with joy. Let me not throw away the life I have lived.

**Tuesday** *Read Deuteronomy 7* **My Enemies**

My friends shall not be found among God's foes. Those that are against God shall find me against them. There shall be no compromise, no alliance, no breach of my loyalty. I shall not wish to be held "liberal," where God is not "liberal."

**Wednesday** *Read Deuteronomy 8* **My Pride**

In this chapter I see myself. God makes it all possible for me. God gives me the opportunity and the power. I grasp the opportunity, fill up its waiting measure, and then boast within myself, "My power has done it." Oh, to know my littleness! Oh, for a sane and humble heart!

**Thursday** *Read Deut. 9* **My Past Sins**

Had I a faithful Moses, to rehearse my evil past, to paint it in black, to push it ever before my eyes! I remember my good deeds very well, but my memory is poor for my sins. Lord, be

*WEEK 23*

Thou the daily quickener of my conscience. My Father, mercifully remind Thy erring son of his many wanderings.

### Friday   *Read Deuteronomy 10*   My Duty

What does God require of me, more than of His ancient people? What, save to fear Him, and love Him, and serve Him? And my fear—is forgetfulness; and my love—is heedlessness; and my service—is perfunctory. O heart, my heart, arouse thee! Think how it will be with thee at the sight of the King in His glory!

### Sat   *Read Deut. 11*   My Treasure of Truth

How material is my life, how bound to the things of sense! The treasures I lay up with satisfaction,—are they of wisdom? The richness of my house, the stores I value, the aims I set before others in my conversations,—are they of this world, or another? Let me turn from all this folly. Let me lay up God's words in my heart.

# WEEK 24

**Sunday**   *Read Deut. 12*   **My Pleasures**

Let me never fancy that my Father wishes for me anything less than my delight. "After all the desire of thy soul"—that is His word to me, as to His people of old. He is not satisfied that I am dutiful; He wants me to be joyful.

**Monday**   *Read Deut. 13*   **My Temptations**

In many ways I am enticed away from the Lord. False voices allure me, false gods attract me, false friends beckon me. I have no safety but the way Moses pointed out. Let me kill my temptations! Let me hate them with a deadly hatred! Yes, though they spring from my own household, from my own bosom!

**Tuesday**   *Read Deuteronomy 14*   **My Food**

Shall I say that these Mosaic laws regarding food are abolished? that Christ has made "all meats clean"? That is true; and yet God cares as much as ever that I should eat only what is healthful. He has written His law in my members, and I can read it there, as the ancient Hebrews could not. Let me not wilfully neglect it.

**Wednesday**   *Read Deuteronomy 15*   **My Poor**

Are they not the Lord's poor? Did I make them poor? Do I keep them poor? Why should I be impoverished because of them? Ah, I shall not be impoverished! Giving does not impoverish, nor does withholding enrich. It is withholding that impoverishes; for they are God's poor, and my wealth is God's, and I am His!

**Thurs**   *Read Deut. 16*   **My Commemorations**

On such a date God saved me from a great sin. On such another date, He raised me from a

*WEEK 24*

severe illness. Again he answered my agonized prayer for a loved one. What were those dates? Why do I allow them to slip from memory? Why are they not become annual festivals?

**Friday** *Read Deuteronomy 17* **My Kings**

I have set over me many earthly authorities,— my rulers, my friends, my employers, my elder relatives, my pastor. Let them all be subordinate to the King of kings! I will choose them by His guidance. I will obey them in His fear.

**Saturday** *Read Deut. 18* **My Prophet**

I sorely need a prophet, one who shall guide me with wisdom, encourage me with confidence, comfort me with praise, rebuke me with fidelity. How rare are these qualities, even among friends! But such a Prophet has God raised up, for me and for all men. And I will be His son.

# WEEK 25

### Sunday  *Read Deut. 19*  My Unplanned Sins

So much harm I do unwittingly! Yet am I not to blame? My speech was not malicious; yet it cut, because it was careless. My neglect was not premeditated, just heedless; so, perhaps all the more, it stung. Lord, I need Thy forgiveness, the refuge of Thy mercy, for these unplanned sins, quite as much as for those of intention.

### Monday  *Read Deut. 20*  My Confidence

The Lord is with me. His omnipotence. His omniscience. His eagerness to give me of His almightiness and His unfailing guidance. Yet I cower and tremble. Yet, oh, paltry wretch that I am! I run to the rear in the battle.

### Tuesday  *Read Deuteronomy 21*  My Justice

There is much in my life that is like "the son of the hated," much that has a claim upon me, a righteous claim, but inclination runs averse to it. Let me learn to set justice far above inclination. Let me learn how shallow are my fancies, and discover the delight of duty. Let my choice be never my own till it is also my God's.

### Wed  *Read Deut. 22*  My Brother's Loss

I am to help my brother recover his property, his cattle when they stray, his purse when it is lost. How, when his conscience goes astray? How, when his honor is lost?

### Thursday  *Read Deuteronomy 23*  My Vows

What the Lord wishes of me, that I must do, and I am not free to vow it or not vow it. Let me do more than is required. Let me add a heaping measure. Let me vow freewill offerings. And then let me sedulously perform my vows.

### Friday  *Read Deut. 24*  **My Charities**

A poor man is such a sorrow to my God, such a grief to wealthy heaven! And I am made so rich by the Father! Is it not that I may make others rich also? How shall I enjoy anything by myself, until all men abound?

### Saturday  *Read Deut. 25*  **My Measures**

Before gain, let me value honesty, and before applause, let me honor sincerity. May every weight and measure of my life be just,—what I give others for what others give me, of money, or praise, or position, or love. Let me remember that there are many ways of being a thief.

# WEEK 26

**Sunday**  *Read Deuteronomy 26*  **My Tithe**

Surely God would have all my gifts to be freewill offerings. He sets up no counter before Him. And surely God would have all my gifts liberal ones. Surely, too, God would have His people grow in liberality, and in love of His Kingdom. Surely He would have me give to His cause more than the tithe of the ancient Hebrew!

**Monday**  *Read Deuteronomy 27*  **My Curses**

The curses that come upon me have not been imposed upon me by another man, still less by God. My own heart has recited them. My own conscience has said Amen to them. As they are my sins, so are they my curses. Fool that I am!

**Tuesday**  *Read Deut. 28*  **My Blessings**

When I do God's will, when I observe His commandments, the blessings that follow are part of the deeds, as light is part of heat. This is not because I bring the blessings, any more than because I do the deeds. Ah, no! Both deeds and blessings are of God.

**Wednesday**  *Read Deut. 29*  **My Covenant**

I am in a league with the Most High! I am allied with the Almighty! Were such an honor mine from an earthly king, how proud I should be to hold it untarnished! Much more, then, since the honor has come to me from the King of kings.

**Thursday**  *Read Deuteronomy 30*  **My Word**

The Word that is to guide me in every perplexity, that is to comfort me softly in every grief, that is to arouse me in every despondency, and warn me in every error, and encourage me

*WEEK 26*

in every faltering, and praise me in every achievement,—is not far off, hard to reach; it has been placed by my loving Father in my own heart. Dear God, I thank Thee.

**Friday** *Read Deuteronomy 31* **My Joshua**

I am not Moses, but I have a work that I have been doing, and that needs to be continued. I am doing it only for to-day and not for to-morrow unless I provide for its continuance. Let me seek out my Joshua. Let me instruct him and train him.

**Saturday** *Read Deuteronomy 32* **My Rock**

As I look back over my life, I see God more and more as a Rock. My Rock of shadow from the sun, of defence from the enemy, the home of springs, the foundation of my abode. I will have no other Rock. Upon it I will rest my eternity.

# WEEK 27

**Sunday**   *Read Deut. 33*   **My Blessings**

I do not need a Moses to declare my blessings on his death-bed, for a living God, my Father in heaven and earth, has declared them. They are as many as His thoughts for me, as happy as His love for me, as firm as His arms beneath me. They are my goods, and in them alone will I rejoice.

**Monday**  *Read Deuteronomy 34*  **My Pisgahs**

Let me not, like Moses, see the promised land afar, and be forbidden to enter it. My sins rise up before me, O my God! They are high as heaven, but not so high as Thy mercy. Upon Thy loving kindness, as a golden stairway, I will surmount my sins, and so shall I reach my Canaan.

**Tuesday**   *Read Joshua 1*   **My Success**

I am assuming heavy burdens, borne by the giants that went before me; but their God is my God. I am facing perils that even they did not face; but the strength on which they drew is at my disposal. Before me is this Jordan; yes, but the Lord goeth before me!

**Wednesday**   *Read Joshua 2*   **My Safety**

In the destruction that will come upon all things, what is the scarlet cord that I may find in my window? Is it the good deeds that I have done? Ah, no! for where are they? I have done less than my duty. It is the scarlet cord of the atonement, the token of my Saviour's mercy. In that sign I shall be safe.

**Thursday**   *Read Joshua 3*   **My Jordan**

The river rolls threateningly before me, overflowing all its banks. My foes are ranged on the

*WEEK 27*

other side. How shall I advance against these difficulties? I need not mind the how, but only advance. The Ark goes before me. The difficulties turn aside, and leave a firm path for my feet. There are no difficulties to him that walks with God.

### Friday  *Read Joshua 4*  **My Memorial**

Where in my life have I set up a monument to God's goodness? Where in my life is there not such goodness to commemorate? Let me bring words, as the Israelites brought stones, and let me rehearse the loving kindness of God, and let me say to all men, "He is my God, faithful and true. Serve ye Him!"

### Saturday  *Read Joshua 5*  **My Gilgal**

Whatever is of Egypt, let me purge it from my life! Let me put off the old man, and put on the new! Let me cease to look backward, and look forward! At whatever cost, I am now for the Lord's land, and the Lord's work, purely and altogether!

# WEEK 28

**Sunday**     *Read Joshua 6*     **My Jericho**

I will trust in the Lord's way, and not in my own. My way may be with cannon and shot and all the munitions of war. His way may seem absurdly inadequate to the gigantic task. But it is His way, and before it Jericho will fall; while for my way, however the cannons roar, not one stone will topple.

**Monday**     *Read Joshua 7*     **My Ai**

My only strength is in obedience. When I disobey, I faint. When I touch what the Lord bids me not to touch, and keep what He forbids my keeping, and seek what He would have me avoid, I am as water before my foes, and all my power is emptiness. O my God, every day let me remember Ai.

**Tuesday**     *Read Joshua 8*     **My Recovery**

If there is in my life an Ai defeat, there may be as well an Ai victory. God is as able to lift me up as to cast me down. If disobedience brings defeat, as certainly will obedience bring the victory. Obedience is a philosopher's stone that will transmute all my life to gold.

**Wednesday**     *Read Joshua 9*     **My Gibeon**

What mistakes I make, when I "ask not counsel at the mouth of the Lord"! My foes are very crafty. The devil has a thousand wiles. There seem so many reasons why I should make my peace with the world. Many of these reasons will present themselves to-day. Lord, at every such appeal let me turn to Thee, and seek counsel of Thy wisdom alone.

**Thursday**     *Read Joshua 10*     **My Triumphs**

Let me have no enemies but the Lord's enemies, for those are the only ones I shall conquer.

*WEEK 28*

Let me have all the Lord's enemies as my enemies, for not one of them shall remain. If I seem to be victorious without God, let me run in terror, for all disaster is impending.

**Friday** *Read Joshua 11* **My Conquests**

How great is the land the Lord designs for me? As great as my enemies are! As large as my obstacles are! As extensive as my difficulties! Shall I grieve, then, because I meet opposition? I am meeting my kingdom!

**Saturday** *Read Joshua 12* **My Kings**

These were the kings, thirty and one, that the Hebrews conquered, and they with no king among them! Ah, but they had a king among them, even the King of kings! Who am I, that I should envy rank, or seek a worldly station? Am I not the son of the only King?

# WEEK 29

### Sunday  Read Josh. 13  My Remaining Work

So much left undone! So much land remaining to be possessed! The command was large and the accomplishment discouragingly small. Yet let me not be despondent, if I have done my best. All eternity is yet before me, for results. On earth is only a beginning of obedience.

### Monday  Read Joshua 14  My Hebron

Let me be a Caleb! Let me choose the hard things, mountains rather than plains, rocks rather than loam! Even in old age, may the same sturdy spirit remain in me. For the Lord dwells among the hills.

### Tuesday  Read Joshua 15  My Anakim

For me, as for Caleb, the hills are full of Anakim. I must drive them out, for my inheritance lies there. I must not heed their height, nor the fierceness of their faces, not their battle-cries and brandished spears. I must only remember my Ally, and my inheritance.

### Wednesday  Read Joshua 16  My Servants

The Canaanites were not driven out from Ephraim,—ah, slowly knelling prophecy of all the woe to come! They were held as servants. They were doubtless useful. What danger from servants? The danger that always lies in disobedience. Those were the servants that mastered Israel.

### Thursday  Read Josh. 17  My Enlargement

God does not hem in the children of Joseph, nor the children of any one else. If we are great people, we may hew out for ourselves a great inheritance. There is no holding back in the plans

*WEEK 29*

of Providence. As fast as I am able to move forward, God opens the way before me.

**Friday**  *Read Joshua 18*  **My Entrance**

The blessings may be mine. God has given them to me. I have broken down the barriers before them, and driven out the enemies. Yet I do not hold them till I enter in and possess them. How strangely slow am I to seize upon and enjoy the Christian delights that are rightfully mine!

**Saturday**  *Read Joshua 19*  **My Surplus**

Judah's portion was too much for Judah, therefore Simeon had a share in it, dwelling in the midst of Judah's inheritance. Do I ever stop to consider whether God has not given me more than I need? Perhaps the inheritance He designs for some one else is right in the midst of the inheritance I am holding as wholly mine. Lord, keep me from the damning sin of selfishness!

# WEEK 30

**Sunday**     *Read Joshua 20*     **My Safety**

What matter how many pursue me? If I am innocent, I am safe. Though men misunderstand me, and even though my deed seems to condemn me, God understands me, and His voice in my conscience acquits me. The law is my city of refuge against fleshly harm, but I need no human law to give me peace of soul.

**Monday**     *Read Joshua 21*     **My Enemies**

As God delivered into the hands of the Hebrews all their foes, so He will never allow an enemy to stand before me, if I am His. All my foes shall fall, and their cities shall fall, strongholds material and spiritual. I have only to be on the side of the Omnipotent.

**Tuesday**   *Read Joshua 22*   **My Altar of Ed**

When I am farthest from the privileges of God's house, still let the thought of it be very near. Let me rear in my heart an altar of witness. Let my life be a moving tent like the tabernacle, with its holy place and its holy of holies. I love the courts of the Lord's house, but it is because they symbolize that country in which there is no temple save the Son of God Himself.

**Wednesday** *Read Joshua 23* **My Retrospect**

I do not often review my past. As often as I do, I am encouraged, and warned. I am encouraged by perceiving God's constancy. He has always fulfilled His word. He has always rewarded obedience. He has always put to flight my foes. And I am warned. For as I look back I am sure that all my good is from God, and as I am God's. Without Him, it will all be evil.

*WEEK 30*

**Thursday**  *Read Joshua 24*  **My Covenant**

It is hard to serve the Lord, for He is a holy God; He is a jealous God. It is easy to serve the Lord, for He is a merciful God; He is a loving God. By its difficulty and its ease, by my duty and my delight, by my fear and my love, I will serve the Lord!

**Friday**  *Read Judges 1*  **My Tributaries**

The Lord would have me drive from my life all servants of Satan, all evil fancies, all doubtful ambitions, all worldly lusts. Shall I retain them as tributaries? Shall I think to make gain of them? There is no gain to be got from them. There is no gain but in obedience to the Lord.

**Saturday**  *Read Judges 2*  **My Forgetfulness**

Continually, like the Hebrews, I forget the conditions of prosperity and joy. Continually I am basing my life on worldly policy. Continually I am neglecting my charter, and disregarding my patent, and forfeiting my title. No wonder I lose my kingdom!

# WEEK 31

**Sunday**  *Read Judges 3*  **My Deliverances**

"The Lord raised up a deliverer for me"—how many sentences like that must I insert in my life story! And every time the necessity for the deliverer is my own folly and sin. How endless is God's patience, how tireless are God's resources, how active is God's love!

**Monday**  *Read Judges 4*  **My Glory**

I am to go out against the foes of my God. I am to move at God's command and not at my own desire. I am not to fight for my own glory. The glory may go to a woman, to a child! I am not striving for glory, but for obedience.

**Tuesday**  *Read Judges 5*  **My Praise**

It is not I that fight, when I go out before the Lord. The stars in their courses fight for me. All nature, all men, all subtle influences of heaven, fight for me. I will praise the Lord for my victories, since they are not mine. I will shout aloud. I will leap with joy. I will not be a churl with my thanksgiving.

**Wednesday**  *Read Judges 6*  **My Signs**

God has given me more tokens of His presence and power than ever He gave Gideon; for I have Gideon's, and mine also. God has proved Himself to me whenever I sought proof. He has not failed in any test. He has surpassed all His promises. He has given me every cause to trust Him, and every warrant to engage in His cause.

**Thursday**  *Read Judges 7*  **My Sword**

I call it my sword—my intellect, and strength, and opportunities, and talents. And it is my sword, as it was Gideon's; my task, as it was Gideon's. But it is also the sword of the Lord.

*WEEK 31*

Because it is His also, I shall venture to wield it, and I shall not dare to let it lie idle. Because it is His also, it will prevail.

**Friday** *Read Judges 8* **My Authority**

When God places me in power, though it be only power over a servant, or an assistant, or a little child, let me refuse to rule over my subordinate. Let me nobly say, as Gideon said, "I will not rule: the Lord shall rule." Power is a trust from Him, as money is a trust, or any ability. And He shall do His will with His own.

**Saturday** *Read Judges 9* **My Requital**

Be it verily known to me that every least sin of mine shall return upon my head. Not only the great sins, terrible as Abimelech's, but the sins of heedlessness, the little sins I have forgotten. They are not forgotten by God. If I do not procure forgiveness, they will not be forgotten by me.

# WEEK 32

**Sunday**  *Read Judges 10*  **My Monotony**

Though my life be humdrum or diversified, I find in it a sorrowful monotony of evil. I am like the ancient Hebrews, after each deliverance returning again to my sin. How many, many times I have done this! Surely at some time God will say to me, "I will save you no more." And my heart cannot blame Him.

**Monday**  *Read Judges 11*  **My Sacrifices**

The Lord wants nothing from me to my hurt, or the hurt of any one dear to me. The Lord is not purchased by my pain. I need not buy His favors by my loss. I need not in any way make myself a Jephthah.

**Tuesday**  *Read Judges 12*  **My Shibboleth**

Let me be very sure that my shibboleth is a wise one. Let it truly separate between friends and foes,—not mine, but God's. Let it be no trifling test, but one piercing to the root of the matter. For tests are needed, only let them accurately testify of wrong and right.

**Wednesday**  *Read Judges 13*  **My Offspring**

Whether children, or deeds, or words, or the silent influence of character, every one gives birth to some offspring whereby the world is better or worse. To every one, therefore, comes the divine warning that came to the wife of Manoah: Keep away from all uncleanness, for the sake of your offspring and the world.

**Thursday**  *Read Judges 14*  **My Jesting**

My sport shall be such as becomes a man,— frank and gallant, innocent and gay, tender as a woman, yet sturdy as a hero. It shall be original,—no other's way, but my own. It shall be

*WEEK 32*

thoughtful, not such as ever to shame me. By my play as by my work I am to be judged.

### Friday  *Read Judges 15*  **My Weapon**

If the spirit of the Lord comes upon me, I shall seize whatever lies nearest, and I shall find it a tool of conquest. I will not fret for means; I will only strive for the spirit of the Lord. I will not seek out a way; I will seek Him who is the Way.

### Saturday  *Read Judges 16*  **My Delilah**

What is it that weakens me for the service of the Lord? That is my Delilah. It will be something I love, something that fascinates me, something that draws me continually to itself. And I have no safety except by flight. I may not play with it, palter with it, try how near I can go to it. Soon the sharp razor, soon the sapped power, soon the blindness and the prisonhouse.

# WEEK 33

## Sunday. Read Judges 17  My Home Worship

I must not be outdone by idolaters, or by men that groped in the darkness of ancient times. If they sought God for their homes, how much more should I? If they would have household priests, how much more should I be a priest in my household? Let my house be a true temple of God, and let every room be a holy place.

## Monday  Read Judges 18  My Counsel

I cannot live close to God without helping all men around me to live closer to God. I cannot make for myself a household of God without leading others to seek God for their own households. Piety is blessedly contagious, and the fruits of holiness are desirable even in the eyes of worldlings.

## Tuesday  Read Judges 19  My Hospitality

At all cost, I must entertain strangers, for in so doing I am entertaining Christ. What matter though the strangers are aliens? though they are disagreeable, and diseased, and their coming will expose me to ridicule and abuse? All this is only a disguise of my Lord, and my reward will be the greater if I pierce though the disguise and welcome Him.

## Wednesday Read Judg. 20  My Punishment

For every deed of churlish selfishness, for every act of cruelty, for every curt indifference and neglect, my punishment is sure. I may delay it, but it will come. I may hold off the armies of revenge, but they will be in wait against me, and take me unaware. There is no cheating Jehovah

## Thursday.  Read Judges 21  My Pity

After punishment, what? Forgetfulness and sorrow! After a man is deservedly cast down, what? Help him up again! O God, who art daily obliged to forgive me so much, guard me from censoriousness toward others! Let me not remember their sin, as I would not have Thee remember mine, and let me restore them as I would be restored.

**Friday**  *Read Ruth 1*  **My Fidelity**

Am I a friend for all times? Is mine a fair-weather love? Do I cleave to others while they are above me and can uphold me, but cast them off when they fall into sorrow? Oh, for the faithfulness of Ruth! It is better than a crown of gold, and all the diamonds that ever shone.

**Saturday**  *Read Ruth 2*  **My Friends**

I am not afraid, if I am friendly, but God will raise up friends for me. My faithfulness will inspire fidelity in others, and my considerateness will make them thoughtful of me. I would not do good deeds in order to get a return of good, but that return is pleasant none the less!

# WEEK 34

## Sunday  Read Ruth 3  My Righteousness

There is a dearer than delight, and that is honor. There is a more precious thing than joy, and that is uprightness. If my pleasure ought to be another's, it shall be no pleasure in my life, its name for me shall be aversion.

## Monday  Read Ruth 4  My Reward

For every good deed I do with the Lord's strength, the Lord Himself recompenses me many fold. I am almost ashamed to take it, for the strength was not mine, nor was the deed mine. How good is my God to me!

## Tuesday  Read 1 Samuel 1  My Petitions

How much I ask of the Lord, that He is not able to grant! He longs to grant it, I know, but He cannot, because I am not able to receive it. His gifts must be used in His way. He will not give to my hurt, or the hurt of His world. Let me cease asking for the gift, and begin to ask for readiness for the gift.

## Wed  Read 1 Samuel 2  My Responsibilities

I have to live, not my own life alone, but the lives of all whom I may influence. Are any dependent upon me for guidance? Am I an Eli, and where are my Hophni and Phinehas? Let me see to my children and friends, my pupils and acquaintances and servants. These are in my keeping, and as I keep them the Lord will keep me.

## Thursday  Read 1 Samuel 3  My Listening

Have I the hearing ear? In the night or the daytime, in solitude or the crowd, am I ready to catch the messages of Jehovah? Am I quick to say, with Samuel, "Speak; for Thy servant

*WEEK 34*

heareth"? Lord, quicken my spirit. Lord, make me sensitive to the least whisper from Thee.

**Friday** *Read 1 Samuel 4* **My Retribution**

The ark of the Lord will not remain with the unfaithful. God's protection and love cannot enwrap the disobedient. Death is in failure to do God's will, and the death begins with the failure. Alas, for those that are the Lord's in name, but do not the things that He says!

**Saturday** *Read 1 Samuel 5* **My Reverence**

If I will not revere the Lord through love, He will see that I revere Him through fear. He is merciful, but He is also majestic; tender, but also terrible. He will have no false gods in my life. He will whirl them from their pedestals. Fortunate am I if I am not sent whirling after them.

# WEEK 35

### Sunday  Read 1 Sam. 6  My Guilt Offerings

When I have sinned against God, wherewith shall I return to Him? He is not in need of my gold or silver. He does not lack for my strength. What have I to fill my hands, when I return to the Lord? I need not ask that question. The guilt offering has been made, it has been laid at the foot of the throne, it has been found worthy. Oh, endless praise to Thee, Thou Sacrifice of the world!

### Monday  Read 1 Samuel 7  My Ebenezer

If I should raise stones of help wherever the Lord has helped me, I should be walled all about with gratitude. Why should I not do this? Not in crude material, perhaps, but in thoughts and in words. For Thou art my defence, O God, forever.

### Tuesday  Read 1 Samuel 8  My Kings

All my tyrants I have myself set over me. I have not only assented to their harsh sway, but I have urged them to their thrones, I have bent my neck spontaneously under their yokes. Oh, for the yoke, the one yoke, that is easy, the one burden that is light!

### Wed  Read 1 Samuel 9  My Humble Duty

It is not only Saul that, seeking his father's asses, has found a kingdom. Men and women innumerable, while trudging painfully along life's common way, have lifted their foreheads to the anointing oil, have stretched out their hands to the sceptre. All good things for me—let me never forget it—lie along the path of God's will for me.

*WEEK 35*

### Thursday  Read 1 Sam. 10  **My Coronation**

If God intends a crown for me, and I do God's will, let me never worry about the crown! Upon all the waves of chance it will be borne to me. Amid all the apparent lotteries of the world I shall find it. There is no chance, there is only a regal certainty, to one that does God's will.

### Friday  Read 1 Samuel 11  **My Gilgal**

Who are they that reject me and despise me? Are they men? I shall laugh, if God is on my side. I shall hold my peace, and let events speak for me. I shall stay my arm, and let God's providence be my revenge. For every Mizpah of His servants, God will make ready a Gilgal.

### Saturday  Read 1 Samuel 12  **My Honor**

When men turn aside from me, let me solace my honor in caring for the Lord's. It boots not what they think of me. I shall be proud in His renown, and by His glory alone shall I be exalted. Oh, may my plea never be for myself!

# WEEK 36

**Sunday**   *Read 1 Samuel 13*   **My Obedience**

Though God's command seem unreasonable, it is to be obeyed, for it is not unreasonable. It is to be obeyed in the letter, for the Spirit is in the letter. It is to be obeyed in the spirit, for the letter without the spirit is dead. It is to be obeyed altogether and always, and with all my soul.

**Monday**   *Read 1 Samuel 14*   **My Salvation**

When I am in peril, let me not even reckon up the force on my side and the power of my enemy. "There is no restraint to the Lord to save by many or by few." I am an army, with God. I outnumber all my foes, with God.

**Tues**   *Read 1 Sam. 15*   **My Half-Obedience**

God will have all or none. When He asks for a ram He will not accept a sheep; when He asks for my money He will not accept my time. When He wants my heart He will not take my hand. He has no delight in sacrifices, when they are not the sacrifices of a contrite heart.

**Wednesday**   *Read 1 Samuel 16*   **My Choice**

Let me learn to select as God selects, among men, and occupations, and powers, and possessions. Let me learn the wealth of the childlike soul, the strength of purity, the invincible valor of holiness. In all my choices let me set the youthful David above all the taller sons of Jesse.

**Thursday**   *Read 1 Samuel 17*   **My Goliath**

It may be some natural weakness or defect. It may be some sickness. It may be poverty or loneliness. It may be a terrible temptation. Whatever my Goliath is, let me remember David's great word, that "the battle is the

Lord's." God can make a pebble from the brook more powerful than a spear-head of six hundred shekels.

**Friday** *Read 1 Samuel 18* **My Popularity**

Have I many friends? Let me enjoy them and bless God for them, but let me not rest my life in them. Woe unto me when all men speak well of me! Human praise breeds enmity in others and vanity in myself. Let me seek God's praise alone.

**Saturday** *Read 1 Samuel 19* **My Jealousy**

What would it avail me to have the greatness of Saul, if I also have his littleness? And what is smaller than jealousy? What is more dwarfing? Lord, may I learn to exult in my friend's good fortune, to rejoice in his skill, and count myself happy when he is praised. So shall I be richer in all the riches of my friends.

# WEEK 37

### Sunday  Read 1 Samuel 20  My Friendship

If I am a friend to another, let my friendship prove itself. It will find its proof not in prosperity but in adversity. If I am a friend from the heart, I shall grieve with my friend's sorrow, and meet his enemies as if they were my own. I shall not shrink before any foe, nor fear any danger save that I prove false to friendship.

### Monday  Read 1 Samuel 21  My Privileges

All that the Father has is mine. His house is mine. His table is spread for me. No Holy Place too holy for me to enter, no shew bread too sacred for me to take, no consecrated weapon too precious for me to wield. God keeps open house and open heart for all His children.

### Tuesday  Read 1 Sam. 22  My Recompense

When I do a good deed, as Ahimelech did, shall I meet Ahimelech's fate? Perhaps; God does not guarantee worldly rewards for unworldly acts. But Ahimelech's death was not Ahimelech's reward. His reward was in David's love, and the everlasting record of the Book, and the approval of the King of kings forever.

### Wednesday  Read 1 Samuel 23  My Escape

If not by my arm, then by another's; if not in my way, then in a better way I had not thought of; if not with glory to me, then with better glory to Himself; somehow, at any rate, the Lord will save me from all my foes. It is mine to do my best, and to trust, and wait. It is mine also to praise, for I am safe, and I shall be saved.

### Thursday  Read 1 Samuel 24  My Revenge

Ever be my revenge such as David's! As persistently as my enemy shows himself a foe, so per-

*WEEK 37*

sistently let me show myself a friend. Let my warfare be of kindness, and all my weapons be forged in the fire of love.

**Friday**     *Read 1 Samuel 25*     **My Anger**

There is a rough handle and a smooth handle whereby to grasp each circumstance. May I seize upon the smooth handle! Be my speech gentle, my acts courteous, and let my thoughts move peacefully. So shall I be ever the stronger, and so shall my ways be prosperous.

**Saturday**    *Read 1 Samuel 26*    **My Patience**

When others persist in wronging me, what is my hurt compared with theirs? They are not slaying me, they are slaying their own souls. They are not destroying my happiness, but their own, and forever. Is not pity due them, rather than wrath?

# WEEK 38

**Sunday**  Read 1 Samuel 27  **My Flight**

It is not always best for me to contend against my difficulties and troubles. Sometimes God's way is the way of flight. Sometimes it is best to go away from them altogether and forget them for a season. I shall return against them all the stronger, when God bids me return.

**Monday**  Read 1 Samuel 28  **My Fate**

It rises up from the earth, it rides upon the air, it breathes in every zephyr, it shouts in every thunderclap. There is no escaping God's decree. Soon or late, the doom will fall. My sin will find me out. There is only one escape, and that is first to find out Christ.

**Tuesday** Read 1 Sam. 29  **My Partisanship**

God will ever preserve me from blunders, if I am His. He will bring me up to the very point, perhaps, of some great calamity, such as David's fighting against his own, and then, in some unexpected way, He will save me from it. I need not fear, if my hand is in His, to march on through the most treacherous wilderness. Thy ways, O Father, are ever kind.

**Wednesday**  Read 1 Sam. 30  **My Victory**

I will strengthen myself in the Lord my God. I will pursue my foes. I will not heed their power or my weakness. I will fall upon them, even in their hour of triumph. I will turn all my defeats into victory. For my God knows no defeat, nor need His children ever know defeat.

**Thursday**  Read 1 Samuel 31  **My Gilboa**

If I sin, and persist in sin, the Philistines will come upon me in force, and I also shall find my Gilboa. It may be when I have forgotten my

*WEEK 38*

sin, and think that God has forgotten; but God does not forget. It may be when I think I am stronger than all the Philistines, but I am not at any time stronger than God.

**Friday** *Read 2 Samuel 1* **My Dirge**

I would mourn over the grave even of an enemy. If he died in his enmity, so all the more let me mourn. How are the mighty fallen! How are the lovely brought to the dust! Let me mourn for all sin, and for the wages of sin, which is death.

**Saturday** *Read 2 Sam. 2* **My Need of Tact**

Like David with the men of Jabesh-gilead, I may with a word turn an enemy into a friend. That is better than slaying him with a sword. I will learn of Thee, Thou Meek and Lowly, how kindness conquers men. Thy way is strongest, and needs most strength. Arm me with power for it, I pray.

# WEEK 39

### Sunday  Read 2 Samuel 3  My Honor

If those near me do wrong, my relatives, friends, or associates, it is not my wrong, or it is my wrong. It is not my wrong if I try to hinder it, if I protest against it and boldly deplore it. It is my wrong if I remain silent and quietly look on. Lord, quicken my conscience for my friend's sins as well as my own!

### Monday  Read 2 Sam. 4  My False Friends

They are not friends to me who would aid my evil ambitions and not my good ones, nor those who would do evil that good may come to me. No one is my friend except along the way of righteousness. And I am friend to no man except as I do him good, and do others good in his name. O God, keep me from involving my friends in evil!

### Tuesday  Read 2 Samuel 5  My Prosperity

When I perceive my affairs doing well, let me not fail to look deeper, and perceive that it is God doing well for me. When my enemies encamp against me, let me not think to go out in my own strength, but let me await the sound of a going in the tops of the mulberry-trees. In joy or sorrow, in adversity or prosperity, Thou, O Lord, shalt be all in all.

### Wed  Read 2 Samuel 6  My Presumption

Shall I lay hands upon the ark of the Lord, to steady it? Shall I instruct the Omniscient and aid the Omnipotent? Shall I fear for God's success and bewail His failures? Alas, for my absurd conceit! How merciful is God, that I am not smitten like Uzzah!

*WEEK 39*

### Thursday  Read 2 Sam. 7  My Plans for God

It is well for me to plan large things to do for the Kingdom of God. Jehovah will be pleased with my desires, and will reward them, though He may not accept them. What He wants is not my deeds, but the will to do them. Let me humbly and gratefully submit to His ordering of my life.

### Friday  Read 2 Samuel 8  My Victories

I am victorious, but I will not be exalted. I conquer my foes, but I will not let myself be conquered by pride. No danger can assail me so great as pride. If I can know in my heart that it is the Lord alone that gives the victory, my victory will be safe for me.

### Saturday  Read 2 Sam. 9  My Kindnesses

Who has been kind to me? I must pass the kindness on. I am in debt for all the love bestowed upon me, all the helpfulness of my friends. I am a bankrupt unless I help others. O God, for the spirit of love,—not of necessity, but of eager free will!

# WEEK 40

### Sunday  Read 2 Samuel 10  My Kindnesses

Shall I cease to be kind because others are unkind? Shall I do no more good deeds because others misinterpret them? No! For my Father sends His rain upon the just and the unjust. Upon me, in my sins, He sends the sunshine of His grace. I shall not put it in the power of any man to make me a misanthrope.

### Monday  Read 2 Samuel 11  My Sin

When I learn of the evil in any man, let me never boast myself, "This is not in me." Let me rather say, "In that mirror see yourself, O my heart!" There is no sin, anywhere, to which I am not akin. There is no man needing God's mercy, if I do not need it.

### Tuesday  Read 2 Samuel 12  My Woe

What is my punishment? Is it not, in whatever penalty, the same as David's, that the Lord is become against me and not for me? That dear ones are sick of my sin, that dear ones die of my sin, that the sword enters my own soul, all this is only the exterior of my woe; its heart is this, that God is against me.

### Wed  Read 2 Sam. 13  My Present Moment

There is a life in the present that slays the future, and there is a life that enriches and vivifies it. There is a pleasure that ends in satiety and death, a love that ends in hatred; and there is a pleasure that is fruitful of living joy, and a love that is stronger than death. Which shall be mine?

### Thurs  Read 2 Sam. 14  My Reconciliation

I must not show to others a sternness I would not have God show to me. Are they sinners?

So am I. Have they persisted in sin? So do I. Are they slow to repent? How like me! Absalom had sinned. Ah, but so had David!

**Friday**  *Read 2 Samuel 15*  **My Ambition**

What harm has come to my soul, except through greed and selfishness? Is there not room on the earth for all men with me? Is there not work for all, and wealth and honor for all? Let me receive with gratitude the lot the Lord allows me, and let me not look at the fortune of others except to increase it for them.

**Saturday**  *Read 2 Sam. 16*  **My Dark Days**

I may not think to sit upon a throne all my days, and to dwell in a palace. I have provided an exile for myself. Out of my own life has sprung my punishment. There is no need for God to undo me, when I am so busy with undoing myself. Alas for David, and for us all! Why do we not let God guide us?

# WEEK 41

### Sunday  Read 2 Samuel 17  My Counsellors

I have two counsellors. One of them advises wisely, and one foolishly. One of them counsels according to my carnal nature, and the other according to my spiritual nature. One of them would have me seek pomp and show in the eyes of men; the other would have me seek the reality, the substance. To which shall I listen, to Hushai or Ahithophel?

### Monday  Read 2 Samuel 18  My Self-seeking

May I ride my selfishness under an oak, and may it be caught by the head and swung up to heaven! May it be thrust through the heart till it is dead! For if I do not slay my selfishness, it will surely slay me.

### Tuesday  Read 2 Samuel 19  My Friends

Some day I shall come to my own. Some day the Lord will cause me to triumph over my enemies. Some day I shall reign in my palace. Let me not reign there alone. Let me prepare for myself now a goodly host of friends, who will rejoice with me in that glad day.

### Wednesday  Read 2 Samuel 20  My Loyalty

Whether my friend is friendly or not, I will be a friend to him. Though he reject me, I will not reject him. Though he put another in my place, I will set no one else in his place. If he is my David, he shall be my David forever, though he prefer Amasa before me.

### Thursday  Read 2 Samuel 21  My Famine

How often the days of hunger come, the days of fainting and fear, the days when God is far away, and joy is far away, and the very memory of happiness is no more! In those days let me

*WEEK 41*

not be ignorant of the reason. The cause is my sin. The remedy is my repentance, and the fruits of repentance that I may bring forth. There is no other.

**Friday**   *Read 2 Samuel 22*   **My Rock**

When I seek other upholding than Thine, O God, let me fall to the earth! When I would be protected except with Thee, let the arrows find me! To rely on any other safety than Thy favor is to lean on a bubble.

**Saturday**  *Read 2 Sam. 23*  **My Mighty Men**

I cannot fight my battles alone. If I try, they will become defeats. Where are my strong helpers? Where are my mighty men? Where are my friends? I would be wise, and surround me with a cordon of them, for my enemies are many, and my wars are difficult.

# WEEK 42

**Sunday**  *Read 2 Samuel 24*  **My Payment**

I will not, even as David did not, offer sacrifices that cost me nothing. They would not then be sacrifices. My gifts to the Lord shall cost me money, and time, and thought, and strength. Yes, they may cost me health, and ease, and popularity, and other good things; for they are to obtain the highest good.

**Monday**  *Read 1 Kings 1*  **My Enterprise**

It would have been so easy for Solomon's succession to go by default! It is so easy for any good thing to go by default! The friends of the good must be ever alert to push that cause, as the friends of the evil are ever ready to further the ends of evil.

**Tuesday**  *Read 1 Kings 2*  **My Retribution**

All my wrongdoing shall return upon my own head. Not the barrier of many years shall shut it out. Not the gulf of long forgetfulness shall separate it from me. Punishment can bridge any gulf. Punishment can overleap any barrier. There is only one safety against it, and that is Thy bosom, O my Father!

**Wednesday**  *Read 1 Kings 3*  **My Choice**

The Lord has given me Solomon's choice; may I choose as wisely as he! Above wealth or fame or long life or any other good, may I choose the wisdom that is from above and that alone can go with me above! For with it shall come to me all other good things that could come to me in any wise.

**Thursday**  *Read 1 Kings 4*  **My Fame**

If I would win fame—and who would not?—let me know that the only way to win it and keep it

*WEEK 42*

is Solomon's,—to be wise. For what men want, after all, is wisdom; and whoever can give them that, may have their honor. Nay, they cannot long withhold it.

**Fri** *Read 1 Kings 5* **My Inherited Tasks**

There are many things the fathers could not do. The years were too short, or their strength failed, or the time was not ripe. These things, many of them, are my inheritance. They are better than an inheritance of wealth, or an earldom. They are a patent of true nobility, if I only lay hold upon them.

**Saturday** *Read 1 Kings 6* **My Temple**

I, even I also, will build a temple for God. It is my body, for He has said it. If it is pure and strong, if it shines in the beauty of holiness, then He will be as well pleased with this temple of mine as with Solomon's.

# WEEK 43

**Sunday**  *Read 1 Kings 7*  **My Temple**

Let me think of God's house as my house. What I would lavish upon my own house, of strength and riches and beauty, that let me rejoice to lavish upon the house of the Lord. No workmanship is too fine for it, no cost too great, no time too long. It shall be my pride. It shall be counted worth my whole life if I can add but one hewn stone to the house of the Lord.

**Monday**  *Read 1 Kings 8*  **My Prayers**

I pray many things. My life is one long prayer of many petitions. Every desire is a prayer. Every hope is a prayer. Every ambition is a prayer. And now I wish to centre my prayers upon God's house. I wish to build them up about God's Kingdom. I wish to remove their centre from myself and fix it upon Thee, my God and my King!

**Tuesday**  *Read 1 Kings 9*  **My Covenant**

God gives me no promise without a condition. He can give nothing without conditions. He will serve me, but only if I serve Him. He will enrich me, but only if I will use the riches in the best way. He will make me happy, but only if I am good. He will establish my throne forever, but only if I hold my sceptre in obedience to Him.

**Wednesday**  *Read 1 Kings 10*  **My Search**

There is one errand upon which it especially profits me to go, and that is the pursuit of wisdom. There is one prize best worth gaining of all prizes, and that is the prize of wisdom. There is one reward which is the crown of crowns, and that is to be wise. The Queen of Sheba was wise indeed before she started on her quest, and that was why she started.

*WEEK 43*

### Thursday   Read 1 Kings 11   **My Peril**

Solomon's enemy was not outside himself. Yes, though Hadad and Rezon and Jeroboam all should league themselves against him, Solomon's enemy was within his own breast. It was an enemy that alienated God, and no other enemy could do that. And failing to do that, no other enemy could make headway against him.

### Friday   Read 1 Kings 12   **My Choice**

I have two sets of councilors. Every one has two sets of councilors. I am counselled for God. I am counselled for Satan. I am advised for pride and for humility. I am urged toward prosperity and destruction. My life is saved or it is lost, according as I take the right counsel. Lord, direct my steps, that I wander not away from Thy commandments!

### Saturday   Read 1 Kings 13   **My Obedience**

I have obeyed God in this matter; may I therefore disobey Him in another matter? How easy it is to do God's will when I will it myself! how hard, when I do not will it! There is no safety for me in doing God's will unless I do it all; and I shall not do it all unless my will is God's will. There is therefore no safety for me, O God, until my will is Thine.

# WEEK 44

**Sunday**  *Read 1 Kings 14*  **My Disguises**

Like Jeroboam with his messenger, I try to disguise myself, and cheat the Lord. As if He who spells the stars, and pierces to the centre of the earth, cannot discern my soul, and comprehend my shallow concealments. I am naked before His eye,—my secret thoughts, my most hidden deeds, are to Him as if spread in the light of the market-place. O Lord, when Thou seest, forgive!

**Monday**  *Read 1 Kings 15*  **My Good and Bad**

The high places were not removed, "nevertheless" Asa's heart was perfect. He was wise, "but" he made that foolish alliance with Syria. He was prosperous, "nevertheless" he was diseased in his feet. What a tissue of good and bad is all life, is my life! Help me, my Father, to get rid of the bad, and make my life from end to end just what Thou canst approve.

**Tuesday**  *Read 1 Kings 16*  **My Jezebels**

I may fill my heart with Jezebels, though I keep Jezebel out of my house. Lustful thoughts are Jezebels, malice, passion, pride, are Jezebels. So are falsehood, and envy, and hypocrisy. Heaven preserve me from the fatal brood!

**Wednesday** *Read 1 Kings 17* **My Cruse of Oil**

The oil of gladness need never fail me, but God will renew my happiness day by day, my cup running over! What care I how it is done, with what gifts from God's bounty? I know He is my loving Father, more eager to give than I to receive. I know that there is no limit of His beneficence, and why should I fear?

**Thursday**  *Read 1 Kings 18*  **My Carmel**

I also, like Elijah, am confronted by priests of Baal. They swarm around me by the thousand, devotees of the gods of this world. What shall I do but what Elijah did,—rear my altar, lay upon it my sacrifice, and pray to my God? The fire will fall upon my offering, the sword will fall upon my enemies, the floods of blessing will fall from heaven! And every day I must ascend my Carmel.

**Fri** *Read 1 Kings 19* **My Revelation of God**

It may be in the whirlwind and the fire. It may be in the cake and the water cruse. It may be in the open desert. It may be in the cave. Wherever it is, and however it is, that Jehovah speaks to me, it will be with the still, small voice. And I shall know that the great things are the most gentle, and that the eternal things come most near.

**Saturday** *Read 1 Kings 20* **My Forbearance**

What God would have me devote to slaughter, against it may my sword be hot! Let not my anger cool nor my zeal grow slack. Let me make no parley. Let me hasten after it, and take no rest. Whatsoever the Lord hates will I hate, and there shall be no peace between me and it forever.

# WEEK 45

### Sunday  *Read 1 Kings 21*  **My Covetousness**

Naboth's vineyards all around me! Ahab's spirit ever in me! How can I drive it out? Shall I condemn myself to a life as barren as Elijah's? At any rate, I must mortify the flesh, and I must teach my soul to desire only the best gifts. For vineyards—for dirt and leaves and sweetened water—I must not sell my soul.

### Monday  *Read 1 Kings 22*  **My Truth-telling**

Though a king confront me, let me learn to look him in the eye, and speak in honesty. Be my words such as God would seal. They shall outlast granite. They shall march with the ages. They shall live with all eternal verities.

### Tuesday  *Read 2 Kings 1*  **My Dalliance**

Do I dally with the gods of this world? Do I wish to make friends of them and at the same time hold to Jehovah? Let me know Jehovah as a jealous God! Let me fear His lightning stroke. Let me count any converse with evil as worse than death.

### Wednesday  *Read 2 Kings 2*  **My Succession**

Some one of the Lord's prophets is ascending, and the Lord calls upon me to take up his mantle and fill his place. A humble place or a large one, it will be too large for me. I shall be Elisha to his Elijah. What of that? I shall be prophet of the same God.

### Thursday  *Read 2 Kings 3*  **My Vision**

What to one man is pure, clear water, to another is red blood, a treacherous snare. How do my eyes look upon this world? Do they see clearly, or is their vision full of scarlet passion? May the Lord grant me eyesight crystal-pure, to see His earth and His heaven!

*WEEK 45*

### Friday  Read 2 Kings 4  My Oil Jars

I shall bring them forth, receptacles of blessing, from all corners of my house, till there is no more! I shall go to my neighbors and gather them, and to the shop and buy them, till I have brought together as many as possible. For God's goodness is unstinted. Only let my faith be unstinted.

### Saturday  Read 2 Kings 5  My Jordan

It is the river of Christ's blood in which my soul must bathe. I have scorned it. I have sought the sparkling Abana and Pharpar of the world. But also I have tried it, and in it my leprosy has melted into health. Oh, the heavenly Jordan! Oh, the rewards of trust and obedience!

# WEEK 46

**Sunday**     *Read 2 Kings 6*     **My Allies**

Lord, open my eyes, that I may see the angelic host, Thy ministers of defence around me! Why do I go through the world fearful and troubled? Surely, though no one seems on my side, they that are with me are more than they that are against me. I will trust, and not be afraid.

**Monday**     *Read 2 Kings 7*     **My Discoveries**

I have looked, and I have seen that the enemies are no enemies. I have perceived that the Lord is mightier than them all. I have gathered rich spoil of faith and hope and glad fruition. Shall I be worse than a leper? Shall I not tell all men what I have found?

**Tuesday**     *Read 2 Kings 8*     **My Ambitions**

It is right for me to be ambitious; it was right for Hazael; only, let all my ambitions be such as God and His saints can look upon with delight. My eyes must not fall before the searchings of any man, or surely they will fall before the searchings of the All-seeing eye.

**Wed**     *Read 2 Kings 9*     **My Retribution**

Blood for blood, shame for shame, blackness for blackness! Sin and penalty are close as fire and light, weight and pressure, heat and consumption. Surely my sin shall find me out, and, finding me out, destroy me. There is only one safety; but, praise God, there is one.

**Thursday**     *Read 2 Kings 10*     **My Reform**

Root and branch, to the farthest rootlet, to the least twig, digging up and overturning and burning,—such be my attack upon sin! There shall be no remainder. There shall be no lurking place of evil. There shall be no new brood.

An utter destruction of iniquity,—grant it, O God!—that there may be a perfect reign of the good.

### Friday   Read 2 Kings 11   My Covenant

I need no Jehoiada to make a covenant for me that I will be the Lord's. I have been my own Jehoiada; I have made the covenant; now how am I keeping it? The Lord is mine, without reserve, all His wondrous self going out to me, for me. How much of my life is His? How much is basely and foolishly withheld from Him?

### Saturday   Read 2 Kings 12   My Church

Does my house of God need repairs? Are its walls dingy, its floors dirty, its cloths ragged, its windows broken? This house of God given me to tend, do I really regard it as a house of God? Do I cherish it as His house? It is for others also to care for it; yes, but it is also for me.

# WEEK 47

**Sunday**   *Read 2 Kings 13*   **My Arrows.**

Whatever I do for the Lord of Hosts must be done with all my might. Who am I, to be linked with His vast enterprises? It is an honor too great for me. And if I am lax and languid, if I am less than my best, I am false to the chief opportunity of my life.

**Monday**   *Read 2 Kings 14*   **My Own Sin**

I inherit much evil, through thousands of ancestors, generation back of generation, nation preceding nation, century on top of century. Some of my sins are theirs; but for them I shall not lose my soul. Alas, I have sins enough that are all my own! Alas, I have increased the fearful burden, under which the centuries groan! Lord, whom can we trust, they and I, except the Saviour of men?

**Tuesday**   *Read 2 Kings 15.*   **My Imitation.**

How often my life imitates the evil in others, when it might just as well imitate the good in them, even as the kings of Israel followed after the sins of Jeroboam, rather than his energy and sagacity! It is well to draw from the lives of others; no man liveth to himself; only, let me draw life and not death.

**Wed**   *Read 2 Kings 16*   **My Spoliation**

I would not do as Ahaz did; I would not despoil the Lord's house, and scatter its gold among its enemies. Ah, but do I not despoil it when I withhold its dues? Is it not the poorer by me? May not the Lord justly take my goods from me and give them to a more honest steward?

**Thursday**   *Read 2 Kings 17*   **My Captivity**

How speedily do my sins send me into exile! Away from all joys, out of all peace, into loneli-

## WEEK 47

ness and fear, into remorse and dishonor,—a captivity far worse than the Babylonian! Open the doors of my prison house, my Saviour, and bid me come forth. And keep me so close to Thee that I shall henceforth dwell in Thy Holy Land.

### Friday    *Read 2 Kings 18*    **My Debate**

The worldlings come up against me. They boast and threaten and sneer. Their words are large and lofty. Their claims and promises are alluring. But they are only words, empty air. One whisper of my Lord is worth them all.

### Saturday  *Read 2 Kings 19*  **My Deliverance**

I have called upon my God, and He has heard me. His hearing has been answering. His answering has been rescue. His words were deeds, His syllables were blessings. How mighty is this light-breathed instrument of prayer, since it can summon almightiness to my aid!

# WEEK 48

**Sunday**   *Read 2 Kings 20*   **My Recovery**

If I am sick, and pray to God, or if some holy man prays for me, shall I recover? I know not. In one sense, I care not. If I recover, the added years will be beautiful, for they will be God's gift. If I do not recover, the added eternity will be God's gift also; and ah, but it will be beautiful!

**Monday**   *Read 2 Kings 21*   **My Influence**

As I walk, so others will walk. I need not be a Manasseh, to draw an entire kingdom after me, and my own child. I need only be my ordinary, humble self to draw a kingdom after me,—my kingdom, as important to me, however small, as his to him. Lord, help me to live as for other lives!

**Tuesday**   *Read 2 Kings 22*   **My Bible**

Is it hidden in some rubbish heap, forgotten and mildewed? Though it lies in a conspicuous place, is it nevertheless virtually hidden, its covers being never opened? Yet this is to millions the bread of life, the fountain of life. How little I use of the power and peace that are right at hand!

**Wednesday**   *Read 2 Kings 23*   **My Reforms**

When I see a wrong, shall I shut my eyes to it, or turn my back to it, or leave it to others to correct? It is not their wrong, but mine, since I saw it! Seeing it is a mandate. Feeling its iniquity is a commission. God has sent me against it, with His authority. Shall I not be true to my trust?

**Thursday**   *Read 2 Kings 24*   **My Penalty**

There is no cheating the divine retribution. There is no hiding from it or parleying with it. Sure-footed and swift it approaches, steadily and inevitably. I may push back the planets in their orbits or wrench the sun from its place sooner than disturb its majestic course. If I am subject to it, I may not hope to escape it.

**Friday** *Read 2 Kings 25* **My Doom**

Shall my eyes be blinded, like those of Zedekiah? Shall love and peace and joy be slain before my eyes? Not unless my eyes were blinded already to the good and eagerly open to the evil. Not unless I had already spurned love and peace and joy, and stabbed them in my soul. Jehovah executes the doom, but I myself have chosen it.

**Sat** *Read 1 Chron. 1, 2, 3, 4, 5* **My Help**

Me also shall God help, as He aided His people of old (chapter 5:20). For I put my trust in God. I have no confidence in myself. I know that I am powerless; I know that He is almighty. I have proved my weakness. I have proved His strength. This knowledge and faith are my only strength. Indeed, what more do I need?

# WEEK 49

**Sun** *Read 1 Chron., chaps. 6, 7, 8, 9* **My Task**

To me, as to each of the Levites, is my "set office" (chapter 9). To me there is some little apportionment of the Lord's work, something that will not be done unless I do it; or, if done, it will be done at the expense of some one's over-work. I will have pride in my task. I will rejoice in my task. And, with God's help, I will be faithful to it.

**Monday** *Read 1 Chron. 10* **My Punishment**

"So Saul died for his transgression." Of course he did. Every one dies for his transgression. Sin is death, and death at once. What matters the death of the body? What avails to drag around, in a living body, a dead soul?

**Tuesday** *Read 1 Chron. 11* **My Friendships**

How sacred is it, all that my dear ones are doing for me! How precious is their self-sacrifice! How beautiful is their thoughtfulness! What a crown, passing an emperor's, is the honor they pay me! I will pour it all out, as David did, for a libation to the Lord. It is too holy a thing to be used in any way selfishly.

**Wednesday** *Read 1 Chron. 12* **My Helpers**

Little of my victories are my own, and little of my work is done by me. I have innumerable helpers. I cannot live alone or labor alone or fight alone in any battle. God has buttressed me round about with comrade toilers. They may not be called my comrades, but they are. And I will praise God for them day by day.

**Thurs** *Read 1 Chron. 13* **My Forwardness**

I to advise the All-wise! I to aid the Almighty! I to criticise the All-loving! I, a worm, an atom!

*WEEK 49*

And yet this inconceivable folly has been mine, as it was Uzza's; and not once only, but many times. How can I hope for pardon? And yet the Lord is All-merciful.

**Friday**  *Read 1 Chron. 14*  **My Victories**

Before I go up to battle, let me inquire always of the Lord. To whatever battle, against many or against few. In whatever place, when the advantage is with me, or against me. For I know not the issue, but God knows. And my victory, in any event, is in obedience to God.

**Saturday**  *Read 1 Chronicles 15*  **My Joy**

Over what do I rejoice? Is my singing, is my dancing, is my laughter, for the ark, for the church, for the Kingdom of God? or is it for the bank, for the finery, for the hand-clap? Let me know myself, even as God knows me, by the things that make me happy.

# WEEK 50

**Sunday**  *Read 1 Chron. 16*  **My Rejoicing**

David shows me in what I should rejoice. I should glory in the Lord. My thanksgiving should be for His kindness, my praise for His perfections, my prayer for His triumphs. As I lose myself in Him, then for the first time do I truly find myself.

**Monday**  *Read 1 Chron. 17*  **My Ambition**

It is when I seek to build a house for the Lord that He is enabled to build my house. When, in humble sincerity, I would exalt Him, His reply is to exalt me. Is any praise equal to His goodness?

**Tuesday**  *Read 1 Chronicles 18*  **My Spoil**

What I gain from my wars, let me, like David, dedicate to the Lord. It is He that quickened my mind to win victories in the realm of learning. It is He that strengthened my soul to overcome temptation. It is He that has turned my rout into a triumph on many a difficult field. His alone is the power, and His shall be the glory, forever.

**Wed**  *Read 1 Chron. 19*  **My Good Intentions**

When I am misunderstood, when my purposes are misjudged, when men suspect me wrongfully and make my good evil, what shall I do? Let me follow the example of Him who, when He was reviled, reviled not again. Let me do good, seeking for nothing in return. Let my reward be from God, and not from men.

**Thursday**  *Read 1 Chron. 20*  **My Giants**

They oppose me everywhere, horrible enemies, looming gigantic and frightful. They menace me with their hands,—dire temptations, manifest dangers, losses and failures, ridicule

*WEEK 50*

and opposition, a thousand uglinesses and perils. But I will do battle in the name of David's God. I will not fear them, or many more like them. For Jehovah is greater than all besides.

**Friday** *Read 1 Chron. 21* **My Census**

Forbid, O God, that I should repeat the sin of David, that I should number my goods and my powers, that I should vaunt myself great and flourish myself before Thee! Lead me to know the beauty of lowliness. Humble me, O God, and teach me to humble myself.

**Saturday** *Read 1 Chron. 22* **My Preparation**

The work that I cannot do, let me make it easier for others to do. What I cannot complete or even begin, let me store up the materials for it. Let me do what I can, however little; for in doing that I shall have done a great thing.

# WEEK 51

**Sunday**  *Read 1 Chronicles 23*  **My Charge**

In the great division of work in God's kingdom I have a part. I am assigned to some company of laborers; have I joined the company? Some particular phase of the work has been laid aside for me; are my hands empty of it? A time is coming when I shall see that all my happiness, for all eternity, depends on my being where God wants me, doing the thing God wants me to do.

**Monday**  *Read 1 Chronicles 24*  **My Lot**

They cast lots, in the tabernacle work, to determine the companies of workers. Much in my work in the world seems likewise to be an affair of chance. But nothing essential is an affair of chance, or was in David's time. God's ordering of my life is not haphazard, though my own ordering is, when I take my life out of God's hands.

**Tuesday**  *Read 1 Chronicles 25*  **My Songs**

There are skilled singers and skilled players on instruments, but I must not allow even these to make all the music in God's world. Though my voice is harsh, God listens for it also. Though my fingers are clumsy, God has a harp for them also. Let everything that hath breath praise the Lord!

**Wed**  *Read 1 Chron. 26*  **My Door-Keeping**

No work is menial, done for Jehovah! I am unworthy of the least task, unfit to perform the smallest service. It is of God's high grace that I am admitted at all to the number of His servants, and surely I shall not quarrel with the assignment He gives me.

*WEEK 51*

### Thursday  Read 1 Chron. 27  **My Commission**

Over what am I set, in the Lord's work? Over the treasuries, or the vineyards? Over the olive-trees, or the oil-cellars? Over the sheep, or the camels? Whatever it is, I should know it. And whatever it is, let me so manage my stewardship that my Lord's face will light up, when he comes to review my work.

### Friday  Read 1 Chronicles 28  **My Pattern**

Great and wise men, going before me, have not been able to complete their designs; sometimes they have not even been able to begin upon them. To me, as to Solomon, some of these designs are entrusted. It is a splendid trust, and I am unequal to it, but Thou, O my Helper, art equal to it all.

### Sat  Read 1 Chron. 29  **My Willingness**

How ashamed I am when I think of my reluctant gifts, my unwilling service! That I should accept with grudging this high privilege, and give with frowns what I should lavish with exultation! Henceforth my giving and my working shall be with a song and a shout, and I shall begin to live.

# WEEK 52

### Sunday   Read 2 Chronicles 1   My Wealth

Though I come to have the riches of a Solomon, and all of Solomon's magnificence, I must reckon, as he reckoned, that the chief riches is wisdom. And if I continue without riches, yet the wisdom of God may dwell in my heart. I must be happy and contented, knowing that within my reach is the greatest of all possessions. Help me to this wisdom, O Thou God of Solomon!

### Monday   Read 2 Chronicles 2   My Helpers

Not even Solomon could do without Hiram; how then can I hope, alone, to rear any temple for the Lord? I shall call my assistants from far and near. I shall levy upon all that will contribute. Let me have no pride of originality. Let me never think to be the sole builder. It is that the temple may be built, not that I may be praised!

### Tuesday   Read 2 Chron. 3   My Lavishing

Where is my gold? Where are my rich cloths, my gems, the valuable goods of my life? If not in precious metal or other material, then the jewels of the mind, the gold of character, where are they? Am I building them into Thy house, O my God?

### Wed   Read 2 Chron. 4   My Lesser Tasks

The great purpose of my life, my temple, involves many lesser purposes, the altar, the lavers, the tables, the brass upon the doors. Am I forgetting the littles that make up the large? Am I rearing the walls and neglecting what is to give them significance when they are reared? Forbid this, O Lord!

*WEEK 52*

### Thursday  Read 2 Chronicles 5  **My Ark**

Somewhere in my life, if it is to be a life worth living, there must be a Most Holy Place, a place of the Shekinah, a place where Jehovah dwells continually. Thither I shall bend my soul, from the midst of whatever cares or toil or sorrow. And there, whenever my longing spirit finds opportunity, I shall meet my Father.

### Friday  Read 2 Chron. 6  **My Dedication**

Here is my life, with all its contents. Have I ever knelt down, my hands outspread toward heaven, and truly given it all to the God of heaven and earth? If not, let me not delay an instant longer. For it is His, all His, and I am His, and He shall be mine, forever.

### Saturday  Read 2 Chron. 7  **My Alternative**

My alternative is the same as Solomon's, the same as the Jews'. I may honor God,—and be at peace; I may honor other gods,— and be an outcast. I cheat myself so often by fancying a midway course; but there is no intermediary, there is no third possibility. And which am I really choosing for my life?

# WEEK 53

**Sunday**  *Read 2 Chronicles 8*  **My Sway**

Solomon's was a lordly rule over a lordly kingdom; but have I not a kingdom as fine, and may I not rule it more nobly? For, after all, the only kingdom where a man may really rule is his own spirit.

**Monday**  *Read 2 Chron. 9*  **My Admirations**

Which is more to be applauded, the Queen of Sheba, who made the long journey seeking wisdom, or Solomon, who had it as a gift from God? Certainly the queen at least no less than the king. Let me not forget that, though great ability may not be mine, to admire the noble acquirements of others, and to seek the company of the wise in books, may be mine, and will be as honorable.

**Tuesday**  *Read 2 Chron. 10*  **My Arrogance**

I can have no richer wealth than humility. My enemies can lay no snare for me more dangerous than my pride. Who am I, that I should vaunt myself? What shall I become, if I do vaunt myself? A second Rehoboam, the mockery of men!

**Wednesday**  *Read 2 Chron. 11*  **My Strength**

As the priests flocked to Judah and strengthened the nation, so let my life become a rendezvous for all holy thoughts and purposes. As they are driven from other places, let them find in my heart a ready haven. In those let me see my strength, and not in men, or might, or money.

**Thursday**  *Read 2 Chron. 12*  **My Service**

How shall I know the blessedness of serving God? By serving God! Not by forgetting God, and falling into the hands of the enemy, and learning the hardnesses of his service, and then coming back, with late and repentant rejoicings,

*WEEK 53*

to the happy service of God. But by serving God—now!

**Friday** *Read 2 Chronicles 13* **My Reliance**

How prone I am to trust in my own hands and my own brain! And then I find myself in ambush, the enemy behind me and in front, and there is no deliverance in man. Then I cry to the Lord in my trouble, and He delivers me out of all my distresses. Praise the Lord forever. Trust the Lord forever and aye.

**Saturday** *Read 2 Chron. 14* **My Rescue**

They are many, O Lord, that rise up against me; but Thou, though One, art more than they. Their hosts are strong, but Thou canst wither them with a breath. They flame with hatred, but Thou dost glow with love. I will trust, and not be afraid. I will trust Thee, and not be afraid.

# WEEK 54

**Sun** *Read 2 Chron. 15* **My Encouragement**

Where is my Azariah, to meet me with exhortations, to bid me seek the Lord and He will be found of me? Rather, where is not my Azariah? Where do I not hear myself thus urged? By the memories of the past and the experiences of the present. By the gracious influences of nature without and the sacred voice within. By the Book. By the Church. By friends. By the volumes of the sages. Ah, my Azariahs abound!

**Monday** *Read 2 Chron. 16* **My Alliances**

Upon whom or what do I rely? Where is my arm of strength? Is it in men? in philosophy? in money? or is it the arm of the Lord? In the answer—the honest answer—to that question lies my sure horoscope.

**Tuesday** *Read 2 Chron. 17* **My Prosperity**

As Jehoshaphat found it, as all the Jehoshaphats have found it in all ages, so do I find it today: there is no prosperity without the Lord. There is sham prosperity enough, but there is no prosperity. And yet how much of my time and strength I waste in seeking prosperity rather than the Lord!

**Wednesday** *Read 2 Chron. 18* **My Advisers**

Do I seek smooth counsel, or true counsel? Will I be pleased, as with honey or fair fruit, when I ask for guidance? Is it to amuse me, or is it to direct me? I must forsake such folly. I must value above all other blessings the true friend, whose words are frank, and for my good; who speaks the thing as it is.

**Thursday** *Read 2 Chron. 19* **My Errors**

I shall make mistakes; only let me seek ever to avoid them. I shall sin; only let me strive

*WEEK 54*

against sin with all my might. I shall fall under temptation; only let me never set my heart upon it, but let me set my heart to seek my God. Then will He—not I—conquer temptation and sin, and keep me upright forever.

**Friday**  *Read 2 Chron. 20*  **My Fighting**

I need not fight my battles. I have only to stand still, and see the salvation of the Lord. I have only to give thanks for the victory in my valley of Beracah. For the Lord God Omnipotent is on my side.

**Saturday**  *Read 2 Chron. 21*  **My Warning**

To me also comes a writing from Elijah the prophet; yea, from many Elijahs, many prophets. And the words of all the writings are the same, and the voice of the past is one word, and that great word is "Obey!"

# WEEK 55

### Sunday  Read 2 Chronicles 22  My Hiding

When I am powerless, God is my power. When I am defenceless, He is my hiding-place. Happy is such weakness, thus to be guarded! When I am weak, then indeed am I strong.

### Monday  Read 2 Chron. 23  My Coronation

There comes a time when action must take the place of rest, and openness of concealment, and boldness of trembling. At the call of the Lord, I must take up my crown, and wear it courageously. Though dangers attend it, I must wear it the more proudly, and gladly.

### Tues  Read 2 Chron. 24  My Restorations

If the Lord's house is in ruins, it is as if my own were. If the church is not prosperous, my affairs are not prosperous. If the kingdom of God is endangered, my own throne totters. I will identify myself with the interests of Jehovah. I will not count anything a blessing apart from Him and His.

### Wednesday  Read 2 Chron. 25  My Fidelity

How many times has Jehovah saved me, as wonderfully as He saved Amaziah; and fought my battles, as He fought his! Yet I have turned to the gods that could not save their own followers, the gods of the world, the betrayers of worldlings. Let me seek them no longer—money, fame, power, ease; let me seek only the God that has blessed me.

### Thursday  Read 2 Chronicles 26  My Pride

It is indeed a leprosy, this pride and self-will of mine. It eats into my life. It turns my greatest joys to rottenness. And no touch can heal it save the touch of the Lowly One.

*WEEK 55*

### Friday  Read 2 Chronicles 27  My Might

So shall I become mighty—O just and wise saying!—if I also, like Jotham, "order my ways before the Lord my God." In that ordering there is peace. Along those ways are ranged all blessedness. And as I walk therein, every foe falls back before me.

### Saturday  Read 2 Chronicles 28  My Help

Frantic, I turn here and there. I seek many allies. I beseech many altars. I know not where to find assistance. My enemies are many, and strong. Ah, have I not known One who is stronger than they? Why do I so easily forget?

# WEEK 56

**Sunday**  *Read 2 Chron. 29*  **My Cleansing**

Is not my heart a temple of the Lord? By whom shall He be worshipped, if not by me, and others like me? And shall I allow this His temple to be defiled? Let me become to-day a Hezekiah. Sweep it out! Sweep it out! Whatever defiles my inner purity, sweep it out!

**Monday**  *Read 2 Chron. 30*  **My Passover**

If by reason of carelessness or any other sin I have failed in any duty or fallen short of any privilege, if the set time of my Passover has gone by irretrievably, yet I will not abandon the duty or forego the privilege. Let it be a month late, if it must be; but it shall be observed, nevertheless!

**Tuesday**  *Read 2 Chron. 31*  **My Oblations**

What of all my possessions do I possess? What have I that is not the Lord's? His because He made it. His because He gave it to me. His because He gives me moment by moment the power to use it and enjoy it. And to think that I should hesitate to render back a portion for His work!

**Wed**  *Read 2 Chron. 32*  **My Deliverance**

My trust shall be in the Lord; but I will prepare myself against my adversaries. My deliverance is to come from the Lord; but I will stop up the springs and strengthen the walls against them. The Lord will send His angel, to save me; but He will send him only to a prepared city.

**Thurs**  *Read 2 Chron. 33*  **My Repentance**

I have been in chains and fetters. I have been carried into exile. My crown has been taken from me. All this has been done, not by the Lord, but by myself, by my sins. And at my

*WEEK 56*

side, all the time, the Lord has stood, sorrowful and pitying! Oh, I will arise and go to my Father!

**Friday** *Read 2 Chronicles 34* **My Bible**

Sometimes, when I read the holy words, they come upon me with so full and overpowering majesty that I rend the garments of my soul, and bow myself in the dust before Jehovah. So let me read the Word at all times, with my heart attentive and expectant, and with my spirit wrapped in reverence.

**Saturday** *Read 2 Chron. 35* **My Meddling**

It is hard to keep my fingers from the loom of divine destiny! They will be changing the pattern. They will be rearranging the threads. They will be correcting the machinery. And all my intermeddling only serves to put some flaw into the fabric or smash my fingers.

# WEEK 57

**Sunday**   *Read 2 Chron. 36*   **My Captivity**

It is true of me, as of the ancient Hebrews, that my warnings have been ample. When I am punished, I have no reasonable complaint. It has all been foretold to me, so plainly, and so many times!

**Monday**   *Read Ezra 1*   **My Return**

My punishment—ever let me be sure of that—is not a day longer than it need be. It is never in wrath, but always in mercy. It is never revengeful, but always reformatory. My return from exile, my going back to my Father's house, depends always upon me, and never upon my Father. His arms are always open for me.

**Tuesday**   *Read Ezra 2*   **My Genealogy**

Some of Ezra's list could not reckon their families backward, and the Jews held it to be a great disgrace. Many of us moderns cannot go far back in our family histories. But what of that? I know whence my spiritual life, the only important part of me, has had its source, and has its continuance. What are the genealogies of earth, to that of heaven?

**Wednesday**   *Read Ezra 3*   **My Praises**

I do not rejoice as I should. My praises are feeble, few, and often wrongly directed. Do I thank the Lord for the things in which He chiefly rejoices in my life? Or is it not for the least valuable blessings, the temporal gifts, the mere framework of the unspeakable gifts? O my God, teach me to praise Thee as I should!

**Thursday**   *Read Ezra 4*   **My Associates**

Shall I let men work with me just because they want to work with me? No; my comrades must become a part of myself, and they shall be those that may without harm to me become a part of myself. When I am yoked with unbelievers it is always an unequal yoke, and my burden is not lightened, but increased.

**Friday**  *Read Ezra 5*  **My Encouragement**

How these Jewish records embody human history! For I also have enemies, as they had; and I also have a great task; and I also have many hindrances and fears in my task; and I also have prophets of encouragement, my Haggai and Zechariah. God grant that I may listen to my prophets, and be deaf to my enemies.

**Saturday**  *Read Ezra 6*  **My Decrees**

No king has ever made a decree in my favor, and bade my foes leave me alone, and ordered his officers to prosper my work. Ah, but is that true? *Has* not just such a decree been issued concerning me, and by the King of kings? Let my enemies hear it, let His officers heed it, and let me in the strength of it be bold about my work!

# WEEK 58

**Sunday**     *Read Ezra 7*     **My Purpose**

It will be a happy day for me when I also can say, as Ezra said, that my life-purpose is "to seek the law of the Lord, and to do it, and to teach statutes and judgments." Seek, do, teach! Seek the highest, do the noblest, teach the wisest!

**Monday**     *Read Ezra 8*     **My Confidence**

When the Lord has promised to be my Helper, let me not affront Him by seeking the help of the world! Let me not rely upon money, or the aid of men, or human learning, or my own ability. One only is Captain over me, and He will not share His authority with another.

**Tuesday**     *Read Ezra 9*     **My Humiliation**

I should grieve more over sin, my own sin and the sin of others. I should rend my heart, and sit in sorrow of soul. Do I not go lightly, as if it were a little thing? This thing which causes anguish in heaven! This thing which tore the Son from the bosom of the Father, and sent Him to the horrors of Calvary!

**Wednesday**     *Read Ezra 10*     **My Separation**

There is but one thing to do with sin, and that is to leave it! Yes, with whatever tears and groanings, with whatever pitiful woe, to leave it, and leave it altogether. There are other ways than the knife, but the disease returns. There are other ways than the fire, but the plague spreads.

**Thursday**     *Read Nehemiah 1*     **My Prayers**

How selfish are my prayers! How seldom do they melt in sorrow over the sins or misfortunes of others! How engrossed are they with my own hopes and fears, or with my own sins and repentance! Let me grieve, as Nehemiah grieved, over the iniquities of my people. Let the sorrows of my friends send me in an agony of supplication to my God. Yes, let me bear upon my heart the woes of the ends of the earth.

**Friday**   *Read Nehemiah 2*   **My Survey**

My work often fails because I go about it too hastily. I do not know the outlines of it. I have not counted the cost. I have not provided the tools. I have not made out my programme. No wonder I fail. Let me henceforth move wisely through life, with the leisureliness of one that is to inherit eternity.

**Saturday**   *Read Nehemiah 3*   **My Portion**

Just the particular bit of work entrusted to me, the portion over against my own house, that, O Lord, let me do, and do it well. Is the portion opposite another man's house poorly built? What is that to me? Is my portion larger or harder than any other's? So much the greater glory!

# WEEK 59

**Sunday**  *Read Nehemiah 4*  **My Adversaries**

Fie! How should ridicule disturb me, or threats, or camps of hostile men? Am I not about the Lord's work? Am I not building the wall of the Holy City? I shall look to the Lord to defend His own. I shall keep my weapon in one hand, my tool in the other hand, and my heart lifted up to God.

**Monday**  *Read Nehemiah 5*  **My Brethren**

What am I, to make gain of other men? What do I deserve of the Lord more than they? Are we not all children of the same Father, gathered around the same table? And shall I, because my arms are longer, reach out and grasp more of the food? For shame, for shame, O greedy soul!

**Tuesday**  *Read Nehemiah 6*  **My Tobiahs**

Humble as I am in myself, when I am about the Lord's work, no man on earth is before me. Let them send crafty messengers. Should I go down to them? Let the false prophets beseech me to hide myself. Should such a man as I flee? It is not my power, but the Lord's; and it is not my dignity, but His.

**Wednesday**  *Read Nehemiah 7*  **My Charge**

O that this might be my epitaph: "He was a faithful man, and feared God above many"! Happy Hananiah! Happy any man, above the possessors of gold or laurel wreaths, who fears God and does His holy will! In that is the sun of human blessedness.

**Thursday**  *Read Nehemiah 8*  **My Bible**

If I would have a Bible, I must work for it. I must spend much time reading it and studying it. I must understand the meaning. I must hold my heart open to its rebukes. When I comprehend one of its commands, I must go straightway and do it. And this, for me as for the returned exiles, will prove the way of gladness.

### Friday  *Read Nehemiah 9*  **My Past**

It has been a sad and sinful past. I have often turned aside from Thy way. I have forgotten Thy commandments. I have mocked Thy word. I have disregarded Thy warnings, and the punishments Thou hast sent have not touched my heart. But still Thou keepest hold of me, and still I will keep hold of Thee, O my God!

### Saturday  *Read Neh. 10*  **My Agreement**

The things that I know I should do for my God, God give me grace to promise to do them, and grace also to keep my promise! Seriously to consider the conditions of my life, boldly to enter upon my full duty, frankly to assent to it before men,—these are marks of a heroic soul. O that they may be true of me!

# WEEK 60

**Sunday**  *Read Nehemiah 11*  **My Jerusalem**

Let me dwell in the holy places! It is a great temptation to live elsewhere, amid the noisy throngs, beside the marts, along the caravan routes, in Tyre, in Alexandria, in Babylon! But I will shut my eyes to all that, and Jerusalem shall be my home. "And the people blessed all the men that willingly offered themselves to dwell in Jerusalem."

**Monday**  *Read Neh. 12*  **My Thanksgiving**

I will mount my wall. I will look over the goodly lot in which my God has placed me. I will fill my heart with the memory of all my Father's goodness to me. And there I will lift up my voice in praise, "so that the joy may be heard even afar off."

**Tuesday**  *Read Nehemiah 13*  **My Sabbaths**

Grant me, O God, a Sabbath of the heart! If my soul goes not to church, it matters little whether my body goes or not. If my hands itch for the ledger and my mind is casting up figures, the choir may be singing and the minister preaching, or the carts may be rumbling in the streets, it is all one to me. Grant me, O God, Thy Sabbath in my soul!

**Wednesday**  *Read Esther 1*  **My Compliance**

What another commands is not therefore mine to obey, but only when God commands as well. If I am sure that God commands a refusal, then the glory of obedience is mine in refusing. Among all the conflicting orders of earth no confusion of duty is possible for me. One alone has a right to give me orders, and His commands are always consistent.

*WEEK 60*

### Thursday  *Read Esther 2*  **My Advancement**

The pious soul, like Esther, will always consider favor among men to be of the Lord. To be sure, the decision of the fickle Ahasuerus may have depended upon any one of a thousand chances; but God controls chances. In any event, His children will always regard popularity as a gift from Him, to be used in His service.

### Friday  *Read Esther 3*  **My Foes**

If Esther is advanced, so also is Haman. On this earth the evil flourish as well as the good; but it is only on this earth, and often only for a short time on this earth. Over the head of every Haman hangs an invisible noose, which the Mordecais may see, if Haman does not.

### Saturday  *Read Esther 4*  **My Destiny**

I am "come to the kingdom" for a purpose. I was born at just the right time, my life's circumstances were precisely what they should have been, my abilities, my friends, my possessions, all are exactly in accord with the task God has marked out for me. It has all been planned so carefully! And what disappointment there will be in heaven if I fail in my part of the enterprise!

# WEEK 61

**Sunday**　　*Read Esther 5*　　**My Daring**

If I have the spirit of Christ, all doors will be opened to me, and all sceptres held out to me. If any doors are closed, they will be the doors that my Lord does not wish me to enter, and those doors I must not wish to enter. And if any sceptre is held up against me, threatening trial or death, such trial shall be joy, and such death shall be glorious!

**Mon**　*Read Esther 6*　**My Enemy's Triumph**

Sooner or later, my enemy shall triumph, and I shall assist at his triumph. If not to the eyes of men, at least in my own jealous imagination, he will don his rich garments and mount his royal steed, and I shall fancy I hear his praises shouted on every breeze. How much happier it will be for me not to have any enemy!

**Tuesday**　　*Read Esther 7*　　**My Gallows**

Whatever gallows I erect for another, upon it I shall surely hang myself! I desire poverty for him, and how poor do I become in spirit! I wish him to be friendless; and, behold! I go lonely through the world. I pray for his death, and at the very thought my better nature expires.

**Wednesday**　*Read Esther 8*　**My Reversals**

It is happy for the man that is permitted to reverse the evil decrees he has promulgated, repay his thefts, obtain pardon for his faults, make reparation for the injuries he has committed. Happy is the man whose ledger is balanced! And let me never forget that only One can balance the blurred ledger of my sinful years!

**Thursday**　　*Read Esther 9*　　**My Memorial**

If I should keep days sacred to the memory of God's special kindnesses to me, every day of all

*WEEK 61*

the year would be a festival! My mercies are more than I can number or recall. None the less, let me hold in memory those I can, and let me brighten all my years with those memorials.

**Friday**   *Read Esther 10*   **My Exaltation**

From a seat in sackcloth at the gate, to a seat next the king on his throne! That seemed impossible for Mordecai. It seems impossible for us. And yet that is just the thing that is promised us, that we shall be seated upon thrones, and that we shall reign with the King of kings and Lord of lords. What sackcloth shall be insupportable to us?

**Saturday**   *Read Job 1*   **My Testing Time**

How shall it be known that I really love God? that I serve Him because I love Him, and not for what I get from Him? How, unless I cease to get anything from Him? How, except He try me with bitter trials? And if I truly love Him, how welcome those opportunities of proof will be to me!

# WEEK 62

**Sunday**     *Read Job 2*     **My Stedfastness**

That was a great answer of Job's, "Shall we receive good at the hand of God, and shall we not receive evil?" I trust God in times of brightness; shall I not trust Him when the darkness comes? Is my guide only for the levels, my pilot only for the calms?

**Monday**     *Read Job 3*     **My Despair**

When, like Job, I would curse the day of my birth, and wish that I had never come to see the light, let me consider how very willingly, in spite of all my troubles, I continue to see the light. By my very continuance in life I prove the value of the gift; and the existence that I affect to despise I would be the last to render up to the Giver.

**Tuesday**     *Read Job 4*     **My Temerity**

Whenever I find fault with the ordering of the universe, let me bethink myself with Whom I am finding fault. Shall I be wiser than my Creator? Shall I be more just than the Founder of Justice?

**Wednesday**     *Read Job 5*     **My Correction**

Why can I not train myself to see things as they are? Why is it so hard for me to rejoice in the chastenings that the Lord sends upon me? And yet I am well assured that no number of what the world would call blessings, though they crowded a hundred palaces, would afford me the joy in eternity that will spring from the least of God's correctings.

**Thursday**     *Read Job 6*     **My Friendships**

There are many disappointments upon earth, but none more severe than to be disappointed in one's friends. Yet one must be prepared even

*WEEK 62*

for that. We are to put no trust in friends, save the Friend that sticketh closer than a brother.

**Friday** *Read Job 7* **My Weariness**

It is well that the sorrows of life should come heavily upon us, so that we cry out in sharp anguish, "I would not live alway!" This is our weaning from earth. This is our separation to heaven. This is our assurance that the next world is endlessly fairer than this, since a loving God is at such stern pains to tear us from this world.

**Saturday** *Read Job 8* **My Hope**

Yes, though my mouth as yet is filled with moans, it shall be filled with laughter. Yes, though my lips are still trembling with the burden of my grief, they are to open wide and strong with hallelujahs. A blessed time is coming, and not even my tears shall be allowed to wash away the thought of it.

# WEEK 63

**Sunday**     *Read Job 9*     **My Righteousness**

How can a man be just with God? However righteous I may seem, my own mouth shall condemn me, and my every act shall rise up against me. I cannot plead my own cause, so ashamed am I. O Christ, my Daysman, Thou wilt stand between me and my Judge, whom I have so deeply offended!

**Monday**     *Read Job 10*     **My Judge**

Why indeed should God be so strict to mark iniquity? Is it by way of persecution? Ah, no! but by way of reformation. A wise father will not neglect the smallest fault of his child. It is not because he dislikes the child, but because he loves him so deeply.

**Tuesday**     *Read Job 11*     **My Debate**

Do I dare to parley with the Almighty? Am I so presumptuous as to pass judgment upon my Judge? How can I know Him who sits at the centre of the universe, and His hands reach to its circumference? What debate can I have with Him whose intelligence holds all things of space and time?

**Wednesday**     *Read Job 12*     **My Ruler**

What man can be blind to God? What life is so bold as to disregard Him? Where shall one hide from His eyes, and the outreach of His hands? Oh, the unutterable folly of those that forget God, or scorn Him! They are like mariners that mock at the ocean, or birds that will deny the air.

**Thursday**     *Read Job 13*     **My Defiance**

Sometimes I dare to challenge God. I venture to deny His righteousness, and complain of what I call His injustice. I do not deserve this sorrow,

*WEEK 63*

I say. "Prove that I deserve it!" I bid the All-wise. And God in mercy does not strike me down, but He leaves me to myself. And I am not left long with myself before I own His justice. Ah, when I know myself, I begin to know my God!

**Friday**      *Read Job 14*      **My Immortality**

"If a man die, shall he live again?" Ah, Job! hadst thou the flood of happy light upon that question which I see, springing from the tomb of the risen Christ! Am I half as grateful for it as I should be? Do I begin to realize the darkness of those Easterless days?

**Saturday**      *Read Job 15*      **My Meditation**

Let me study to know myself. Let me not trust in vanity, deceiving myself. Let me not "diminish meditation before God." A hasty man is confident of his own uprightness, but a thoughtful man knows his sin.

# WEEK 64

**Sunday**　　*Read Job 16*　　**My Comforter**

Truly, there is poor comfort in man! How little do even my best friends know of my inward griefs, the battles of my soul! How poorly do they understand me, who so poorly understand themselves! But I have another one, a Comforter indeed. He knows me utterly, He sympathizes with me perfectly, He is nearer to me than I am to myself!

**Monday**　　*Read Job 17*　　**My Purity**

Surely, "He that hath clean hands shall wax stronger and stronger." I have seen that proved in the lives of many; God grant me the proof of it in my own soul! God help me to the victorious purity that is as the strength of ten!

**Tuesday**　　*Read Job 18*　　**My Wickedness**

I have seen it in the world, I have seen it also in myself, that sin has no rest, no safety, no peace. There is no cover that can hide it, no fire that can warm it, no hand that can comfort it. Before it the earth is a desert. Above it the heavens are iron. Oh, the endless folly of the man that seeks after sin!

**Wednesday**　　*Read Job 19*　　**My Consolation**

Let the root of the matter be in me also, as in Job. Let me also be sure that my Redeemer liveth. Let me also be certain of His coming, at the last. After whatever sorrows and pains, after whatever disappointments and postponements, after failures and shames, and the darkness of death, my Redeemer, my Redeemer, oh, my Redeemer!

**Thursday**　　*Read Job 20*　　**My Failures**

No failure of mine is decreed by Jehovah; nothing but the most entire success. But how I

*WEEK 64*

thwart the good purposes of my God! How when He plans fulness I devise emptiness, when He would execute triumphs I contrive defeats! Let me never accuse my God; let me see in my own heart the fountain of all my woes.

**Friday**     *Read Job 21*     **My Perplexity**

What if Jehovah does allow the wicked to flourish? Shall I therefore doubt His wisdom? Is it for more than a few years? Is the life of a man more than the passing of a cloud? The thoughts of God are long thoughts. Let me not judge the Most High along the line of human years.

**Saturday**     *Read Job 22*     **My Friend**

Among all my acquaintances, my familiars, the persons and things of my closest thought, is there room for the Maker of all things and persons? Am I truly acquainted with God? Or is my worship words, and my prayer a pretence, and my Bible a pile of printed sheets? Oh, let my religion be real!

# WEEK 65

**Sunday**   *Read Job 23*   **My Consolation**

When men, even my friends, misjudge me, I have one sure comfort, that God does not misjudge me. When my way seems dark, I have one unfailing cheer, that "He knoweth the way that I take." When trials are heavy upon me, this thought always lightens them: "When He hath tried me, I shall come forth as gold."

**Monday**   *Read Job 24*   **My Security**

Not for a moment am I secure in evil. Though I seem walled around with all protection, God's least breath will blow down that wall. There is no safety but in God, to me or any man.

**Tuesday**   *Read Job 25*   **My Righteousness**

Shall I be just before God? Why, in the presence of His purity my whiteness is as midnight. In front of His light my lamp is as coal. By the side of His goodness my best deeds are as a shame and a disgrace. Shall I vaunt myself, and not rather hide my head in fear and dishonor?

**Wed**   *Read Job 26*   **My Glimpses of God**

Lo, I see but the outskirts of His ways. With every advance in the knowledge of God I perceive how little I knew of Him before. So will it be forever. Lord, I thank Thee that I can see Thee. Lord, I thank Thee that I can see so little of Thee! I would not have a God whom I could know altogether.

**Thursday**   *Read Job 27*   **My Insistence**

How I persist in justifying myself, like Job! How I insist that, though God's ways may be right, at any rate I know that mine are! How little I know of that humility which sees in every affliction only my just desert, and in every blessing an unmerited benefaction! How poorly, even after all these years, do I know myself!

### Friday      Read Job 28      My Wisdom

I find myself seeking wisdom in all ways but the right way, and from all sources but the right source. It is not in nature. It is not in books. It is not in teachers. It is not in myself. It is not in history or experience. God, who made all these, is the only fountain of the wisdom of them all. When I seek wisdom elsewhere, I do not wisely.

### Saturday      Read Job 29      My Past

Alas for me, if my eyes turn longingly to the months of old, if any days seem better to me than these days in which I am living now! God has not grown worse. The world has not grown worse. If my fortune is worse, whatever the outward husk of things may appear, it is because I am worse. There is no other way of worseening my fortune.

# WEEK 66

**Sunday**  *Read Job 30*  **My Despair**

When it seems as if all the world was against me, let me not for an instant forget that Thou art not against me, that Thou canst never be against me. Over the howling of the wolves let me hear Thy whisper of love, and even in the mocking of my adversaries let me listen for the word of Thy comfort, O my God!

**Monday**  *Read Job 31*  **My Morsel**

Though it be only a morsel of comfort and happiness that I have, let me not eat my morsel alone! What is want to me would be abundance to many. When sorrow comes upon me, grant me the consolation of others' joy which I have brought about. So shall I find an alleviation of my woes.

**Tuesday**  *Read Job 32*  **My Confidence**

To me also God has given a message. It may not be a great message, but it is mine. It may be far inferior to what others have said, but they have not said it. And since God has given it to me to say, it is as important for me to say it as for Paul to utter his resplendent discourses, or Dante to write his Inferno.

**Wednesday**  *Read Job 33*  **My Redemption**

What cannot be wrought in me by reproaches, may instantly be wrought by love. What the thunders of Sinai cannot do, is done in my hard heart by a whisper from the cross of my Redeemer. He has redeemed my soul from the pit. And now I know that my soul was in the pit.

**Thursday**  *Read Job 34*  **My Rebellion**

I must not condemn in Job what I may find in myself. Do not I also boast my own righteous-

*WEEK 66*

ness? Do not I also rebel against God's decrees? Do not I also set up my judgment against His?

**Friday** *Read Job 35* **My Words**

Let me not "multiply words without knowledge." Let me think before I speak. Especially, let me think before I speak about God. If for every idle word I shall give account in the last day, how much more when the idle words are directed against my Maker!

**Saturday** *Read Job 36* **My Affliction**

It is not only that God will deliver me in my affliction. He will also, as was said to Job, "deliver the afflicted by his affliction." My sins and sorrows shall become stepping-stones to higher things. I shall be cured by the poison that brought me low. God will make my wrath to praise Him.

# WEEK 67

**Sunday**     *Read Job 37*     **My Tempest**

There is no tempest, however terrible, in which I may not see the hand of my Father. Though the storm uproot trees and overturn houses, yet it is His hand. Though the lightning destroy life, yet every bolt proceeds from the hand of my Father. And if I hold His hand, I shall be safe in any storm.

**Monday**     *Read Job 38*     **My Provision**

There is much in the natural world that I do not understand, but enough that I do understand to convince me of the goodness of God. There is the thunder-cloud, but there is also the sunshine. There is the howling wolf, but there is also the raven provided with food, "when his young ones cry unto God."

**Tuesday**     *Read Job 39*     **My Outlook**

The beautiful world is a university, ever open to open eyes. How many lessons are daily presented to me, lessons that I do not learn! Every field is full of parables, and every hill is a Sermon on the Mount! Enlighten my eyes, that I may see, O Thou God of nature.

**Wednesday**     *Read Job 40*     **My Silence**

Have I spoken, when God was speaking? Or have I laid my hand upon my mouth, and proved myself listening-wise? With what loud and preposterous words have I clamored up to heaven, and how seldom have I harkened to the great orations of the sky!

**Thursday**     *Read Job 41*     **My Leviathans**

Has the progress of my science made leviathan seem a small thing? Has the familiar universe grown commonplace? Are the primal curiosity and freshness worn off from my soul? Alas for me, when God's leviathans are only flies on my horizon!

### Friday   Read Job 42   My Repentance

When I bow the head of my pride, when I know the sin of my heart, when I am willing that all men should know it, when I see how little I know, how little I can do, and see also how much God knows, how much God can do, and when I escape from the captivity of my pride and passion into love for my friends,—then, ah! then God can bless me.

### Saturday   Read Psalm 1   My Delight

I am not safe when I obey the law, but when I love it. I am not safe when I can explain the law, but when I meditate upon it with pleasure. The river of all blessings may flow at my feet, but thirst alone can lift its waters along the channels of my life, and out into leaf and flower.

# WEEK 68

### Sunday     *Read Psalm 2*     My Victory

I am on the winning side, when I side with God! Let the heathen rage; God will laugh. Let the worldlings vaunt themselves; God will turn their triumphs into dust. The earth is the inheritance of my Christ; therefore the earth is my inheritance also.

### Monday     *Read Psalm 3*     My Shield

In the presence of my enemies,—I shall go to sleep! It shall not be the sleep of carelessness, but the sleep of confidence. And I shall awake in safety, refreshed, for the Lord will sustain me; His shield will ever be over my head.

### Tuesday     *Read Psalm 4*     My Safety

Upon my bed, in the awed night watches, I will think of God, and be still. Upon my bed I will lay me down in peace, and sleep. The awe and the peace both speak of Thee, O my Protector. The fear of Thee casts me at Thy feet, and there the love of Thee casts out the fear.

### Wednesday     *Read Psalm 5*     My Worship

In the morning shalt Thou hear my voice, O God; in the morning, in the privacy of my own familiar place. And also Thy house shall hear me, and Thy holy temple shall know me. My worship before men shall be built upon my secret prayers; and my secret prayers shall be quickened and enlarged by my worship in the open. Thus shall my whole life be made a communion with God.

### Thursday     *Read Psalm 6*     My Fear

Surely many are they that seek after my soul. My enemies are without, hostilities of evil men. sneers of unbelieving men, temptations from crafty men, hindrances thrust in my way by careless men. Far more are my enemies within, the sins that so easily beset me. But Thou, O Lord, wilt deliver my soul, and all my enemies shall turn back. I shall pray to Thee, and they will be ashamed.

### Friday     Read Psalm 7     My Foes

What trouble is greater than an undeserved enemy? When my motives are misconstrued, and my words wrested from their meaning, my honey turned to gall, and my outstretched hands interpreted as a threat, life is indeed awry, and bitterness enters my soul. But God does not misinterpret, and God shall interpret me to the world. Indeed, what care I for the world, while God interprets me to Himself?

### Saturday     Read Psalm 8     My Humility

Surely the heavens, so lordly high, shall abase my pride. Surely in all space, reaching out endlessly, there is room for all things save one,—the self-conceit of man! Thy name, Thy glory, O Lord, my God; and let me have done with even the thought of my name and my glory!

# WEEK 69

**Sunday**     *Read Psalm 9*     **My Judge**

He that judges the nations will judge me. And as I see Him judging the nations, I know that His judgment of me will be kind and right. He is patient with the nations, long-suffering and merciful. When He punishes, there is no escape from the sentence; but He does not willingly afflict the children of men. And I need all of His mercy.

**Monday**     *Read Psalm 10*     **My Folly**

Am I of those that say in their hearts, "There is no God"? Do I cheat myself with the thought, "He will not require it"? Let me examine my soul, that it be not guilty of such final folly. One thing let me never forget, that God knows, that God remembers.

**Tuesday**     *Read Psalm 11*     **My Temple**

The Lord is in His holy temple. And where is His holy temple? Is it in the heavens? Yes. Is it on earth? Yes. It is where God is. God never leaves His holy temple. And what if I obtain God for my heart?

**Wednesday**     *Read Psalm 12*     **My Tongue**

My lips are not my own. It would be a dreadful thing if my words were my own. I who cannot keep my heart, how could I keep my lips? I whose deeds go so sadly awry, how could I control the wings of words? Do Thou, O Lord, govern my mouth, for by my words I am justified, or condemned.

**Thursday**     *Read Psalm 13*     **My Impatience**

"How long?" I often cry. "How long this sorrow?" "How long this delay?" "How long this temptation and this failure?" "How long, O Lord, how long?" But that is when I look upon my lot, and do not look upon Thee, who orderest my lot. When I look upon Thee, my heart begins to sing.

**Friday** *Read Psalm 14* **My Ransom**

I am a captive now. Captive to dread. Captive to doubt. Captive to sin. Captive to misery and weakness. But the Lord will bring back my captivity. Its end is certain, however the chains may press upon me; for I trust in God. And in that thought the chains almost become garlands.

**Saturday** *Read Psalm 15* **My Foundation**

Uprightness, innocence, heart truth, love to neighbors, a governed tongue, honorable and merciful dealings with all men,—" He that doeth these things shall never be moved." But who can do them? On what sliding foundation do we all stand! Ah, let mine be the righteousness of the One Only Good! Ah, let me be founded upon the Rock!

# WEEK 70

**Sunday**     *Read Psalm 16*     **My God**

What words can I find to praise Thee, O my God! I have no good beyond Thee, no safety, no joy, no hope. The thought of Thee is ever before me; and if at any time it is not before me, that is a time of darkness and sorrow. Ever be Thou mine, O my God!

**Monday**     *Read Psalm 17*     **My Protection**

I do not pray to be saved from the world, but from worldliness; nor from proud men, but from pride; nor from others at all, but from myself. Save me from myself, O God; save me to Thyself! Let me behold Thy face day by day, and ever more and more clearly, until I awake in Thy kingdom, and am satisfied with the perfect vision.

**Tuesday**     *Read Psalm 18*     **My Red Sea**

Pharaoh is in pursuit of me, with all his host. His chariots shine in the sun; I hear the shouts of his horsemen. All the troops of ungodliness haste after my soul. But Thou hast made a way for me through the sea. Thou dost cause a storm to break over their heads. None that trust in Thee are ever confounded.

**Wednesday** *Read Psalm 19* **My Firmament**

As the stars gleam above me in the heavens, so brightly shine the words of the Book. As the sun is king of the sky, so the Lord Jesus is King of Light in the Book. Oh, may I learn the astronomy of the Bible!

**Thursday**     *Read Psalm 20*     **My Banner**

What banner do I really follow? Not the fluttering cloth that men see, but the true ensign that God sees, and that really leads me on? Oh, if it bears the token of the world, a golden coin, a

*WEEK 70*

crown, a bunch of grapes, let me tear it from the staff, and let me raise in its stead over my life the white-red banner of the cross!

**Friday** *Read Psalm 21* **My Power**

I am mighty, for my God is mighty! I am more powerful than all my enemies, for my God is more powerful than all my enemies. I am blessed in all ways, for my God has all blessing in His keeping.

**Saturday** *Read Psalm 22* **My Despair**

"My God, my God, why hast Thou forsaken me?" If even Christ cried out thus, why not I? Because Christ thus cried out, and received an answer, for Himself, and me, and all men. Because His despair received the eternal assurance of union with the Father, and with all Goodness and Love and Joy!

# WEEK 71

**Sunday**   *Read Psalm 23.*   **My Shepherd.**

The Lord is my Shepherd. He is my Shepherd if I will let Him lead me. He is my Shepherd if I choose His still waters and green pastures. He is not my Shepherd if I choose the barren rocks and the desert sands. Lord, wilt Thou be my Shepherd indeed!

**Monday**   *Read Psalm 24*   **My King**

The Lord is my King of glory. The earth is His, and therefore mine. The battle is His, and therefore mine. The glory is His, and therefore mine. And clean hands and a pure heart shall make me His.

**Tuesday**   *Read Psalm 25*   **My Guide**

The Lord will show me His ways. He will teach me His paths. He will guide me in His truth. He will guide me in His judgment. He will instruct me in the way of His choosing. It must be the way of His choosing. He will not guide me in my way.

**Wednesday**   *Read Psalm 26*   **My Judge**

I have walked in my integrity; judge me, O God! for I have trusted in Thy integrity. I have washed my hands in innocency; judge me, O God! for I have washed them in the blood from Thy altar. I will walk in my integrity; judge me, O God! for I have been redeemed from my unrighteousness.

**Thursday**   *Read Psalm 27*   **My Stronghold**

Though a host is encamped against me, God is the stronghold round about me. Though persistent enemies seek me out, God will hide me in His tent. Though an ocean of trouble rage around me, God will lift me up on a rock. I will

*WEEK 71*

not be proud, for I am very weak; but I will not fear, for God is very strong.

**Friday** *Read Psalm 28* **My Answer**

Men may close their ears against me, but God is obliged by His very nature to hear me. If it were possible for God not to hear my supplications, or, hearing, not to answer in the way that is best, God would not be God. How is it, then, that my prayers have so little confidence?

**Saturday** *Read Psalm 29* **My Listening**

Do I not hear all other voices more than the voice of God? that voice which is so much better worth hearing than all other voices! It is everywhere to be heard, yet I hear it in so few places. Is it not because I fill my soul with the foolish clamor of the world?

# WEEK 72

**Sunday**     *Read Psalm 30*     **My Recovery**

My weeping was only for a night; joy has come in the morning. Joy comes always in the morning, when one has spent the night with Thee, O my God! Every hour of darkness, however black with distress, is preparing it. Beneath the darkness Thy sun is steadily moving, bringing it. And nothing is surer than the sunrise.

**Monday**     *Read Psalm 31*     **My Trust**

Whatever terrible thing assails me shall have no terror for me. Every foe shall bring a present in his hand. All slanders shall be cryptograms of praise. This is because Thou, my Father, art in all things, and because I trust in Thee.

**Tuesday**     *Read Psalm 32*     **My Confession**

God be praised for the human conscience! God be praised for the agonies of remorse! God be praised that He does not leave the sinner at rest! It was my distress led to confession, and confession led to pardon, and pardon led to peace. Blessed the road, however rough, that leads to such a home!

**Wednesday**     *Read Psalm 33*     **My Praise**

It is good to rejoice in the world, but it is better to rejoice in the world's Creator. It is good to value beauty, but it is better to value the Beautiful One. Praise is comely, but the nobler its object, the more ennobling it is.

**Thursday**     *Read Psalm 34*     **My Boast**

If I am proud, let me be proud of my God! My soul shall make her boast in Him. If I am proud of father and mother, sister and brother, wife and children, how much more of Him who gave me all these! If I am glad of my own abilities,

## WEEK 72

how much more shall I rejoice in Him who fashioned them and sustains them from day to day!

### Friday  *Read Psalm 35*  **My Imprecations**

The Lord has pleasure in the prosperity of His servant. My enemies are the enemies of the Lord, so long as I am the Lord's. That the Lord's cause may triumph, let them be confounded! That their own true cause may triumph, let them be confounded!

### Saturday  *Read Psalm 36*  **My Refuge**

Under the shadow of Thy wings! Peace is there, and safety. Loving-kindness is there, and all satisfying pleasures. Light is there, in that shadow; light more illuminating than the brightest sunshine. And life is there, the life that never dies, under the shadow of Thy wings.

# WEEK 73

**Sunday**   *Read Psalm 37*   **My Fretting**

I am guilty of many sins, but worrying is so incessant that perhaps in its aggregate it exceeds them all. I fret over the wrong-doing of others, over my own misfortunes, over the failures of yesterday and the fears of to-day. And all the time God is in His heaven! Yea, all the time God is on His earth!

**Monday**   *Read Psalm 38*   **My Wounds**

I cut myself, I bruise myself, I weaken myself, I poison myself, and when my wounds rankle and my strength fails, I make bold to cry out against the Lord! It would be just if the heavens should open with a thunderbolt for my head, if the earth should open and swallow me up!

**Tuesday**   *Read Psalm 39*   **My Chance**

Few are the days in which I may yet do well. Each nightfall brings me nearer my final accounting, each dawn may be the dawn of the judgment day. O that I may make haste to serve the Lord! To-day, while each minute grasps the skirts of an eternity, to-day, ere it is too late, let me make haste to be wise!

**Wednesday**   *Read Psalm 40*   **My Offerings**

Such offerings as can be laid upon an altar and burned with fire, or placed in a contribution-box and put in a bank, are little pleasing to my God, without my heart. One thing He desires, and that one thing must be the sum of my desires,— that I should give Him myself. How strange that He, the Lord of the universe, should be kept out of this one desire!—how strange, and how sad!

**Thursday**   *Read Psalm 41*   **My Poor**

Not merely the poor in purse, but the poor in strength, the poor in friends, the poor in hope

## WEEK 73

and cheer,—these are my poor, because they are my God's. They are mine to know. They are mine to help and comfort. They are mine, yea, I see sometimes that they are the very best of my possessions.

**Friday**   *Read Psalm 42*   **My Thirst**

Mine is a thirsty soul, in a thirsty land. I pant after something, I seldom know what. Ever it is Thee, O God, for which I pant, even when I do not know it. Ever, though I drink from many fountains, my soul is thirsty till it drinks of Thee.

**Saturday**   *Read Psalm 43*   **My Leading**

I follow the mirages of the world. Fair over the desert they falsely shine, and tantalize my soul with promise of shelter and refreshment. Over and over they cheat me, but I follow them just the same. O send out Thy light, which is Thy truth, and let it lead me to Thy holy hill!

# WEEK 74

**Sunday**  *Read Psalm 44*  **My Complaint**

How strange it sometimes sounds, to call upon God to awake! He sleep, who made sleep? And yet I often raise that impious cry. I often charge the Lord with forgetfulness, with carelessness. Why, if God could forget, if God could cease to care, in that instant the foundations of the world would return to chaos, and the universe would cease to be.

**Monday**  *Read Psalm 45*  **My Gladness**

Let me not, because it is mine, fail to sing the praise of the goodness of God! These gifts He has given me, are they to my credit? Nay, rather to my great discredit, because I have made so little of them! It is false modesty that keeps me from singing their praises, for they are all of God.

**Tuesday**  *Read Psalm 46*  **My Refuge**

How instinctive is my recourse to God? Do I turn to Him at the first hint of misfortune, or do I seek rather to exhaust my other supports, and go to Him as the last resource? Not thus does a father like his son to depend upon him, or a mother her daughter.

**Wed**  *Read Psalm 47*  **My Inheritance**

God shall choose my inheritance for me. I shall not choose it myself. Sometimes I wish to choose it for myself. Sometimes God gives me my choice. And then what folly is in my choice! And how unwise it is to choose, when perfect Wisdom is ready to make the selection for me!

**Thursday**  *Read Psalm 48*  **My Permanence**

My God is God for ever and ever. The city He establishes is forever established. To death and beyond, for generation after generation, unmoved, unchanged, the one Permanence of the

*WEEK 74*

universe! And shall I build except upon His laws?

**Friday**  *Read Psalm 49*  **My Honor**

What wealth I have, whether much or little, what reputation I have, whether much or little, what ability I have, whether much or little, let it all be one. My wealth I must leave to others, my worldly lore will perish with the world, and in heaven there's many a child will be honored before Alexander!

**Saturday**  *Read Psalm 50*  **My Sacrifices**

If I have set up God's altar in my heart, if I burn there the fire of sincere devotion, what cares my God for other temple, or other sacrifices? Other altars are good, but as the symbols of this altar. Other temples are to be raised and honored, but only that this temple may be raised and filled with song.

# WEEK 75

### Sunday   *Read Psalm 51*   **My Purification**

There is no delight like the delight of cleanness. There is no strength like the strength of purity. There is no beauty like the beauty of whiteness. And this cleanness, purity, and beauty come from no spring of earth. Wash *Thou* me, and I shall be whiter than snow.

### Monday   *Read Psalm 52*   **My Boasting**

Am I among those that make not God their strength, but trust in the very abundance that God has given them? Do I boast of my goods rather than give praise for my God? Let me take warning from other fools in their folly. Let me behold and see that there is no strength save in the Almighty.

### Tuesday   *Read Psalm 53*   **My Atheism**

If I live as if there were no God, no God to protect, no God to console, no God to punish, what am I but the fool that said in his heart, "There is no God"? What is the atheism of the lips, compared with the atheism of the life?

### Wednesday   *Read Psalm 54*   **My Helper**

There is no human help but may fail me. Human wisdom is weak, human strength falters, even human love may lapse; but when these all give way, then most of all the arms of the Lord sustain me. It is worth the failure of all else to know that the Lord never fails!

### Thursday   *Read Psalm 55*   **My Flight**

How often have I also, like David, longed for wings to fly from all my trouble, to some wilderness lodge, where I might be at rest! But the Lord has not given me wings, but a burden instead. And He bids me remain where I am, and carry it. Ah, but He is ready to carry it with me!

**Friday** *Read Psalm 56* **My Tears**

If God numbers every hair of my head, surely He has regard to every tear of my eyes! He records them in His book, He treasures them in His bottle,—tears of sympathy, tears of repentance, tears of excess of grateful joy!

**Saturday** *Read Psalm 57* **My Snares**

They are all about me,—the liers in wait, the traps set, the pits dug, the net cunningly spread. I cannot move without peril. How dare I move without Thee, my God! But with Thee, the ambush is discovered, the traps are sprung empty, the net is blown away, and my enemies fall into their own pits!

# WEEK 76

**Sunday**     *Read Psalm 58*     **My Deafness**

To what purpose are the wise wise, except as men hear? What noble thoughts are brought to naught by closed ears! How many great lives are rendered nugatory for lack of listening! If I cannot be a wise thinker, let me at least not be deaf to the words of wisdom.

**Monday**     *Read Psalm 59*     **My Tower**

When I would rise above the trials that vex me, the Lord shall be my high tower. When I seek a hight from which to overcome my adversaries, the Lord shall be my high tower. When I would be quiet and at peace, away from the turmoil of earth, the Lord shall be my high tower.

**Tuesday**     *Read Psalm 60*     **My Banner**

It is not a banner of pride, but a banner of humility, and the fear of the Lord. It *is* a banner of pride, but not the pride of man; pride in the Almighty One, who is my leader. And it is displayed, not to terrify men, even my foes, but to lead men, to draw them to God's truth.

**Wednesday**     *Read Psalm 61*     **My Rock**

It is a rock that is higher than I. If it were not, it would not be higher than the waves of my troubles, for they mount over my head. But the rock to which I cling rises majestic over all waves. It reaches down to the bottom of the sea. No storm of heaven can move it.

**Thursday**  *Read Psalm 62*  **My Expectation**

Truly hope is a mighty power. It is the spring of life. When spring is at hand, I do not mind the final storms, however bleak, for I know that the blossom time is near. And Thou, O Lord, art my expectation, my hope, my spring eternal!

*WEEK 76*

### Friday   *Read Psalm 63*   My Nights

Then, when the noises of the world are hushed, speak Thou to me. When a curtain is drawn over the sights of earth, appear Thou to me. When I have leisure from earth's toil, let me find time for Thee. May my nights be holy with the practice of the presence of God.

### Saturday   *Read Psalm 64*   My Gladness

Let my religion be an exultation! Not merely a duty, not merely a routine, not merely a task, not merely a satisfaction and a pride, but a joy, a delight, an exhilaration, a passion! If I have any desire that surpasses it, that desire shall be accounted treachery to my King.

# WEEK 77

### Sunday    Read Psalm 65    My Abundance

All Thy ways are ways of plenty, my Father. Along other paths there is poverty, along other paths men's faces are haggard and their souls faint within them; but along Thy paths the trees are heavy with fruit, and the springs sparkle with health. There is no want to them that love Thee.

### Monday    Read Psalm 66    My Testing

What though Thou makest me to go through fire and water, to test me? If it is to test me, is not Thine eye upon me, and can I be afraid? What though the furnace of affliction is my lot? It is silver, or the possibility of silver, that is cast into the furnace. Thou dost do it to my praise!

### Tuesday    Read Psalm 67    My Return

God's mercy upon me, God's blessing upon me, the shining of God's face upon me,—and why? That His way may be known upon earth, His health to all nations. Ah, what return am I making to the Lord for all His benefits?

### Wed    Read Psalm 68    My Burden-Bearer

Shall I stagger under the weight of my burdens, when the Almighty is ready to lift them up and bear them, and me with them? That would be worse pride than folly, and worse folly than pride. Nay, blessed be the Lord, who daily beareth my burden!

### Thursday    Read Psalm 69    My Zeal

All strong affection has its pains. The more I love God, the more I shall be disturbed by the hostility of God's foes, the sneers of infidels, the injuries of the church and the barriers set up in

## WEEK 77

its way. But though love has its pains, who would not love?

**Friday**  *Read Psalm 70*  **My Impatience**

Make no tarrying, O my God! My needs cry out to Thee. My poverty cries out to Thee. My sins and temptations cry out to Thee. I cannot do without Thee, not for a day or a night. Make haste, O my God, to deliver!

**Saturday**  *Read Psalm 71*  **My Posterity**

All that God has done for me is a plea that I should do much for those that are to come after me. What right have I had to these many blessings? And surely no right, if I do not pass them on to others. I stand at the gatehouse in the great aqueduct of God's blessings. Shall I shut down the gate?

# WEEK 78

**Sunday**   *Read Psalm 72*   **My Dominion**

Where my Lord is King, there am I also a king! He grants me His glory, and whatsoever is His is mine. In seeking to extend His kingdom I am seeking to extend my own. In exalting Him I am exalting myself. Oh, blessed union of disciple and Master, where neither knows what it means to withhold!

**Monday**   *Read Psalm 73*   **My Peril**

My feet had slipped, my danger was great, I had almost fallen. My peril was an invisible peril, the great danger of envy, leading to the greater danger of a distrust of God. Let me see that this is my greatest danger, and that recognition of it will be a safeguard against it.

**Tuesday**   *Read Psalm 74*   **My Impatience**

The Lord's time seems a long time! But I must remember that with the Lord a thousand years are as one day. I must seek to accustom myself to the long reaches of heaven. I must not wish to dwarf God's great providence to the petty measure of my impatience.

**Wednesday**   *Read Psalm 75*   **My Cup**

The cup of my fortune, in the hand of the Lord, shall I not drink it, and gladly? If it is bitter, it is medicinal. If it is but a swallow, more would harm me. If others have a fuller cup, they are no more blessed than I; for the blessing is to have a cup at all, in the hands of the Lord!

**Thursday** *Read Psalm 76* **My Contribution**

All the earth shall praise the Lord. But some will praise Him with joy and by lives in which His will is done. And others will praise Him in spite of themselves, and by lives upon which His will is imposed. Which is to be my contribution to the universal pæan?

### Friday  *Read Psalm 77*  **My Remembrance**

I, too, have had songs in the night. I, too, have seen Christ shining against the darkness. I, too, have had prison doors opened, and rainbows against the clouds, and a refuge in the storms. And what I have had once, let me perpetuate it, and have it daily, by the regal power of memory.

### Saturday  *Read Psalm 78*  **My History**

I am a part of the history of God's people. What they have suffered, I have suffered. Their calamities are mine, their rescues are mine, their triumphs also are mine. What God has done for His people, all through the ages, He has done no less for me. I will live upon God's goodness in the past as well as upon His goodness in the present.

## WEEK 79

**Sunday**     *Read Psalm 79*     **My Ruins**

The enemy has come, and has left my life in ruins. The enemy is Sin. The ruins are ruins of character, and of all else that ruined character brings down with it. "Help me, O God of my salvation, and purge away my sin, for Thy name's sake."

**Monday**     *Read Psalm 80*     **My Quickening**

Until I turn from death, how shall I be quickened into life? Until God turn His face upon me, how shall I turn from death? But God has turned upon me the shining of His face. Nay, He has never turned it from me. I have only turned away my eyes, and closed them.

**Tuesday**     *Read Psalm 81*     **My Feasting**

The finest of the wheat is mine, and honey out of the rock. Nothing that is sweet and strengthening, nothing that is healthful and satisfying, is left out of my larder, is lacking from my table. For it is the table that God prepares for me, even in the presence of my enemies.

**Wednesday**     *Read Psalm 82*     **My Judge**

If I were to be judged by a man, I could never stand. If I had to confess my sins to a man, my tongue and my heart would fail me. But He is to be my judge who knows me thoroughly. He knows my desires for good as well as my falls into evil. He knows my sins, but also my temptations. He knows my frame, He remembers that I am dust; for was it not from the dust that He formed me?

**Thursday**     *Read Psalm 83*     **My Foes**

Let my enemies be the enemies of my God! Let me forget who are my own foes, in remembering His. Let me bury my poor quarrels in

*WEEK 79*

waging His great war, a war whose end is peace and whose weapons are love.

**Friday** *Read Psalm 84* **My Home**

My home shall be the house of the Lord. There, where He loves to dwell, shall be my favorite abiding place. Those walls shall be my shield, that altar shall be my sun. All the paths of my business shall be high ways thither. And my longings shall fly to those courts with the instinct of a bird for her nest.

**Saturday** *Read Psalm 85* **My Mercy**

It is my mercy, and not another's. It is the mercy that God has shown to me alone. He has taken thought for me. He has singled me out from the host of sinful men. He has reached His hand to me. He has laid it upon my head, feverish with sin. He has touched me, and the fever has left me. He has shown me His mercy, and it has become mine.

# WEEK 80

**Sunday**   *Read Psalm 86*   **My Teacher**

Unless God teach me His way, I cannot learn it. Man cannot teach it to me, not even the wisest man. Books cannot teach it to me, not even the Book of books. My own heart, least of all, can teach it to me. But if God teach me, then I can learn from my own heart, and from other men, from books, and from the Book.

**Monday**   *Read Psalm 87*   **My Fountains**

The springs of my life are in Thee, O God. If at any time I turn in my folly to other fountains, I find them dry. Some of them are worse than dry: they run poison. But in Thee, O God, is a well of living water, springing up unto eternal life.

**Tuesday**   *Read Psalm 88*   **My Affliction**

Darkness is round about me, but Thou art in the darkness. I cannot see Thee, but Thou canst see me. I cannot hear Thee, but I can cry unto Thee, and Thou canst hear me. It is a comfort to know that Thou art there, and listening. It is all the comfort I have. Therefore it is all the comfort I need.

**Wednesday**   *Read Psalm 89*   **My Light**

Let me walk, O Lord, in the light of Thy countenance. It is easy to stray aside to other lights. The world's will-o'-the-wisps seek to draw me hither and yon. The torches of their triumphs would allure me, the glare of their festivities, the glitter of their rainbow beauty. But the light of Thy countenance is pure and sweet as a May morning. It is holy as a twilight in June. It is invigorating as a noon in December!

**Thursday**   *Read Ps. 90*   **My Dwelling Place**

God, the Home of my soul! Its ancient home, before the mountains were brought forth. Its

*WEEK 80*

present home, as I number my days on earth. Its future home, as the beauty of the Lord descends upon me, and the work of my hands is established forever.

**Friday** *Read Ps. 91* **My Shadow Refuge**

God is my shadow from the sun, from the scorching of life's deserts. God is my shadow from my foes, hiding me from their pursuit. God is my shadow for rest, for the sleep that means renewing of life. God is my shadow even when I enter the land of the shadow of death, and I shall fear no evil.

**Saturday** *Read Psalm 92* **My Prosperity**

I will allow myself no fear of poverty or failure. I cannot fear God, and fear these things. I cannot trust God, and not trust Him for all things. Because He is my God, I shall flourish and prosper in every way. Not because I am I, but because He is God, and my God.

# WEEK 81

**Sunday**     *Read Psalm 93*     **My Lord**

I rejoice in God. I exult in the majesty of Jehovah. Who is King, like my God? Who is Power, like my God? Who is Sublimity, like the Lord of Hosts? In the firmness of His throne my heart is established. In His glory my life is illuminated. In the splendor of His presence I walk erect.

**Monday**     *Read Psalm 94*     **My Doubts**

When my words seemed to return to me fruitless how did I forget God! When I fancied that my Father in heaven did not see my need, what injustice I did Him! He that planted the ear, shall He not hear? He that formed the eye, shall He not see?

**Tuesday**     *Read Psalm 95*     **My Heeding**

God's voice is to be heard to-day, and no other day. My heart must be attentive to-day, and at no other time. I have no other time. There is no other day. In all the measureless reaches of eternity, there is no time that is mine except to-day. Oh, let me hear, and let me heed!

**Wed.**     *Read Psalm 96*     **My Expectation**

He is to come! He is to judge! His Kingdom is to rule! His will is to be done! His joy is to flood the earth! His praise is to fill the heavens! Before Him the wicked are to tremble! Before Him the righteous are to bow adoringly! And to-morrow, yea, this very day, may be that time!

**Thursday**     *Read Psalm 97*     **My Hatred**

If my love of the Lord is to be measured by my hatred of evil, how much do I love the Lord? Do I hate it with a perfect hatred? The evil that is in other men, do I loathe it, or condone it? The

*WEEK 81*

evil that is in me, do I strive against it to the death? How much do I really love the Lord?

**Friday**   *Read Psalm 98*   **My New Song**

What is in the new song that was not in the old songs? The other psalms have said all this, over and over. Ah, yes; but that is the joy of true religion, that it is ever new. New as God's morning mercies. Fresh as His evening faithfulness. God's never-old love shall be praised in ever-new songs.

**Saturday**   *Read Psalm 99*   **My Pardon**

When I ask for forgiveness, is it not often merely for escape from penalty? I do not like the consequences of my sin. I do not so much dislike sin itself. But what I need is to get rid of the love of sin, not of sin's consequences. The last is only pleasant, but the first is necessary. Take vengeance, then, of my doings, O God, but forgive me.

# WEEK 82

**Sunday**     *Read Psalm 100*     **My Owner**

I am not my own. I am bought with a price. It is a price that a Creator alone could pay. I am His because He made me. First He created me, and then He created me anew in Christ Jesus. Surely I will enter His gates with thanksgiving, and His courts with praise.

**Monday**     *Read Psalm 101*     **My Resolve**

Since I am the Lord's, since He actually cares that I should be His, I will try to walk worthily of my Lord. His enemies shall be mine. His friends shall be mine. His desires shall be mine. His tasks shall be mine. And his presence shall be with me, forever.

**Tuesday**     *Read Psalm 102*     **My Sighing**

How pitiful are my complaints, O Thou the Joy of the whole earth! How childish are my fears, O Thou who hast never failed! How shortsighted is my vision, O Thou the Creator of the ends of the earth! Turn Thou my groanings into rejoicings, and teach me the wisdom of happiness.

**Wednesday**     *Read Psalm 103*     **My Father**

I know how earthly fathers love; and God made earthly fathers and their love. I know how long-suffering are the earthly fathers whom God has made. I know their joy in their children when they do well, and their great sorrow in their children when they do ill. And yet from all this how little do I learn, in my stupid heart, about the perfect Father who made fathers!

**Thursday**     *Read Psalm 104*     **My Universe**

In what a large and wonderful place God has set my feet! It has no bounds of space or time. It is endless in variety, exquisite in loveliness.

It is warm throughout with the Father's love. It thrills throughout with the Creator's power. It is firm everywhere with Jehovah's wisdom. O God, help me to be more worthy of Thy universe —and mine.

**Friday** *Read Psalm 105* **My Predecessors**

I praise Thee, O God, for the way in which Thou hast led the world hitherto. I praise Thee for noble women and strong men. I praise Thee for great thoughts, sweeping down through the ages. I praise Thee for the marvels of Thy providence. I praise Thee for Thyself!

**Saturday** *Read Psalm 106* **My Inborn Sins**

Yes, I also have sinned with my fathers. Their iniquity has descended upon my generation, and I have taken it unto myself. They were disobedient, and I am repeating their rebellion. They forgot Thee, and I constantly forget Thee. O that I might become wiser than my fathers, instead of more foolish than they!

# WEEK 83

**Sunday**   *Read Psalm 107*   **My Mercies**

How long would be the catalogue of God's goodnesses to me! Not all earth's libraries could contain the books that would need to be written. Yet how short is the list that I have ever written, either upon paper, or upon the fleshly tablets of my heart!

**Monday**   *Read Psalm 108*   **My Decision**

No more will I waver, with half a mind for God and half a mind for mammon. My heart is fixed for Thee, O God! Thy heart has always been fixed for me. How ashamed I am that not until now has my heart been wholly yielded to Thy great heart!

**Tuesday**   *Read Psalm 109*   **My Need**

Men do not know how poor I am, and needy. Men cannot know me, or my poverty and need. To know that, they must know my soul. But Thou dost know, for Thou canst see me within and without. While others help me wherein I do not need help, Thou canst reach to my ultimate need. And Thou canst meet it with perfectness.

**Wednesday**   *Read Psalm 110*   **My Youth**

Though I grow old with the swift passing of the years, I live with the Ever-young, and His youth shall be mine. Thou who didst fashion time, and dost hold it as Thy instrument, wilt place me also superior to time, so that the dew of youth shall be upon me, however the hairs may whiten on my head.

**Thursday**   *Read Psalm 111*   **My Covenant**

The promises are the Lord's. The promises are mine. Great and precious promises are they. They extend to all blessedness and wealth. And

## WEEK 83

they are His and mine. We hold these possessions together!

**Friday**     *Read Psalm 112*     **My Light**

Is it dark round about me? The darkness is God's promise of light! If I am of His upright ones, my darkness is more fortunate than the noonday of other men; for that noonday has no such promise in it as my midnight happily contains.

**Saturday**     *Read Psalm 113*     **My Day**

It is the sun-rising. The Lord's name be praised! I will go forth into the day with Him, for it is His day, and I am His man. It is the sun-setting. The Lord's name be praised! I will go forth into the night with Him, for it is His night, and I am His man. Day unto day uttereth this speech, and night unto night showeth this knowledge.

# WEEK 84

### Sunday   Read Psalm 114   My Model

Among the many models that God has given me in this world is the great world itself. How it obeys its Maker! How it worships Him! How the hills rejoice in Him, and the seasons sing His praise! Man alone, with reason, with an immortal soul, turns from the Lord, and abuses His benefits. Let me not fall behind the sticks and the stones in honoring my God.

### Monday   Read Psalm 115   My Trust

It is so easy to worship idols. It is so easy to make some shape with my own hands, and trust to what I can see and handle, and fail to trust in the great Reality whom I cannot see and handle. But that folly shall be far from me. Have I not learned that the real things are the invisible things of God?

### Tuesday   Read Psalm 116   My Return

The Lord does not need any return of His kindness that I might make. He does not need it, but He desires it. He does not need it, but He entreats it. And what return can I make except the return He wants me to make, that I should tell all men what He has done for me? And why does He want this? In order that He may have still more men to bless!

### Wednesday   Read Psalm 117   My Praise

There are so many things for which to praise the Lord! I may praise Him for His beauty, for His wisdom, for His power. I may praise Him for the abounding excellency of His universe. But the praise He most wants from my lips is praise of what I have experienced, His mercy, which is great toward me, and His truth, which has been shown to me. For this I will praise Him forever.

*WEEK 84*

**Thursday**   *Read Psalm 118*   **My Day**

Every day is a day the Lord has made. Let me therefore rejoice and be glad in every day. This day is a new gift from God's right hand. For me it has been fashioned, fresh in the divine laboratory. And shall I take it as a matter of course, or with no word of thanksgiving?

**Friday**   *Read Psalm 119*   **My Law**

I have many possessions, but Thy law shall be my chief possession. It is the goodness of all my goods, the beauty of all lovely things, the power at the base of all my strength. As I am true to it, I am true to others, and to myself, and to Thee.

**Saturday**   *Read Psalm 120*   **My Neighbors**

What shall I do, if I who love quietness am surrounded by lovers of turmoil? Or if my pursuit of wisdom is thwarted by their folly? If the contagion of their diseases is upon me, and if their clouds overshadow my tent? Ah, then let me know the Lord for a neighbor, and let me ever dwell in His house!

# WEEK 85

### Sunday     Read Psalm 121     My Helper
I lift up my eyes to the mountains, to the lordliest thing that God has made; but my help comes not from them. My help comes from no lordly thing, but from the Lord Himself, the Maker of all lordly things. He that upholdeth them will ever uphold me.

### Monday     Read Psalm 122     My Goal
Many are the ends of the journeys of men, and many are the goals they have set up for themselves. Be the goal of my desires, the end of my journeys, but one, O my God! In all my seeking let me seek Thee, and in all my finding let me find nothing else.

### Tuesday     Read Psalm 123     My Master
Not always does the servant look to his master's hand; but where else shall I look, O God, for the direction of my life? Thou canst see the way, however far before me. Thou canst protect the journey, however beset with foes. If I travel in Thy service, I shall know no fear; and if I travel in Thy service I must go Thy way.

### Wednesday     Read Psalm 124     My Ally
Not so much that I am on the side of God as that God is on my side! Oh, glorious condescension, that the Lord of heaven and earth will be on the side of His creatures! And yet, being what He is, where else should He be? Where else could He be?

### Thursday     Read Psalm 125     My Abiding
The mountains can be moved, but the Lord who made the mountains cannot be moved. He touches the earth and it trembles; the hills, and they quake. But He Himself never trembles,

*WEEK 85*

and they that rest in Him shall always be unmoved.

**Friday** *Read Psalm 126* **My Reaping**

What matter how it was sown, whether in tears or with laughter, now that the harvest has come? What matter the winter's snow and ice, and the delay of the spring, now that the sheaves fill my arms? It was mine to sow, and it was mine to wait. It is God's to furnish the harvest, and His work is better than mine!

**Saturday** *Read Psalm 127* **My Building**

I have tried to build without the Lord, and lo! a tumbled pile of bricks upon the ground! I turned, and built with the Lord, and lo! the walls rise fair and firm, and the sky is their roof, and eternity is their foundation.

# WEEK 86

**Sunday**   *Read Psalm 128*   **My Fear**

There is a boldness that befits a coward, and that is boldness in the presence of the Lord! There is a fear of which a hero may be proud, and that is the fear of the Lord! For that fear is the beginning of wisdom. Only a wise man will know that fear.

**Monday**   *Read Psalm 129*   **My Stripes**

My back is furrowed with the blows of affliction. Long and bleeding furrows are they, and the Lord has sowed in them the most fruitful seed! Out of my sorrows has sprung gladness of heart. My tears have brought me a harvest of joy!

**Tuesday**   *Read Psalm 130*   **My Watch**

Ever, through what I see, I am looking forth, as through a door, waiting to see something more. For what am I looking? Why am I not satisfied with what I see? Why is my soul ever on the watch? Because Thou hast not yet come, Thou who art the rest and joy of my soul. When Thou dost come, it will be as the morning to the watchman who has been watching all the night.

**Wednesday**   *Read Psalm 131*   **My Humility**

It is well for me to know what affairs are too great for me. It is well for me not to attempt a man's part in matters where I am but a child. They only become men who are willing to be children. And the noblest men never lose the heart of a child.

**Thurs**   *Read Psalm 132*   **My Resting-Place**

Where God rests, there let me rest. In His abiding-place I also will abide; for He has invited me, and my soul has answered Yes. Indeed,

## WEEK 86

where else can I find rest except where He finds rest?

**Friday** *Read Psalm 133* **My Comradeship**

Hardly am I one man till I am united with some other man! Hardly is my mind my own till it is exercised in another's behalf, or my body till it is worn out for another. And hardly can I know the supreme companionship with the Most High till I know the lower comradeship with His creatures.

**Saturday** *Read Psalm 134* **My Blessings**

As Abraham was blessed in order that he might be a blessing, so let me bless the Lord, and receive blessings from His hand! There can be no blessing without reflection. Seeds may grow or die, but blessing must always bear fruit.

# WEEK 87

**Sunday**     *Read Psalm 135*     **My Idols**

Am I worshipping silver and gold? Am I listening to things that cannot speak, and praying to things that cannot hear? Am I living for things at all, and not rather for the Creator of things, in whose power they all lie, to give or to withhold?

**Monday**     *Read Psalm 136*     **My Mercies**

The mercies that I have from the Lord endure forever. How I need to have the truth repeated, and reiterated, and pressed upon my heedless mind! The mercy of the Lord endureth forever! Though things decay, though friends pass away, though fortune fades and beauty vanishes, and health and even life are gone, yet the mercy of the Lord endureth—forever!

**Tuesday**     *Read Psalm 137*     **My Exile**

Am I in Babylon? Yes, often and often! When I forget Zion, I am in Babylon, but not when I remember Zion. When I weep over the fate of Jerusalem, I am not in Babylon; but I am in Babylon when the fate of Christ's Kingdom brings no tears nor awakens any fears.

**Wednesday**     *Read Psalm 138*     **My Answers**

In the day that I call, God answers me. Not the next day or the next week, but in that same day. Not always does the answer come such as I had expected or at the moment wish, but it always comes. For God loves to be petitioned, and He loves to answer petitions. Shall He not do what He loves to do?

**Thursday**     *Read Psalm 139*     **My Overseer**

Does the thought of God as my Overseer trouble me? Do I seek to hide from Him, to run away from Him? Do I resent His absolute knowledge

*WEEK 87*

of me? Let me commit no longer such useless folly. Let me know that there is no safety for me anywhere except in the knowledge of God; and let me be sure that within the refuge of that knowledge it is perfect love.

**Friday** *Read Psalm 140* **My Preservation**

I must not be blind to my foes. I must not fall into the dangers that surround me. They rear their heads against me. I make light of them, but they are not light. I build a wall against them, but they overtop any wall. God is the only wall they cannot pass.

**Saturday** *Read Psalm 141* **My Reproofs**

Perhaps my greatest folly is to be angry when I am reproved by wise men. No better blessing could come into my life, except the driving away of the faults that call for their reproof. It is not easy for them to reprove me. They would far rather not do it, and keep my pleasure in them. Ah, let them still have my love, and let it be doubled toward them!

## WEEK 88

**Sunday**  *Read Psalm 142*  **My Prison**

Verily my soul is in prison. Bring Thou me out of it, O Redeemer! My prisoner is myself. Rout him, O Thou Conqueror! My prison walls are my selfish desires and passions. Break them down, O Thou Captain of my salvation, and let in Thy light!

**Monday**  *Read Psalm 143*  **My Dark Places**

I dwell in dark places, I who am the child of the Light. As those that have been long dead, I live in my tomb. It is a tomb I have made for myself, and no man could make it for me. Yes, and no man can release me from it. Stand by the door of my tomb, O Christ, and bid me come forth!

**Tuesday**  *Read Psalm 144*  **My New Song**

I have sung the old song so long, the heavens must be tired of it! I will learn a new song. I will discover new mercies, there are so many of them to discover! I will see new beauties in my Lord. I will anticipate new joys in heaven. I will find new delights upon earth. I will have new communion with God. And from it all a new song must burst forth.

**Wednesday**  *Read Psalm 145*  **My Desires**

The Lord made me with desires. It is by my wants that I grow. It is by my wants that I have enjoyment. Without desire I should be a stick or a stone. The Lord is on the side of all just desires. He opens His hand and grants them freely, because He has opened His hand and inspired them. Why should I fear to present my desires to Him?

**Thursday**  *Read Psalm 146*  **My Hope**

I have but one hope. I do not hope in the

*WEEK 88*

world or the ordering of it. I do not hope in myself or my powers. I do not hope in my friends, however loving. I do not hope in heaven, however alluring. I do not hope in justice, or in truth, or in any other abstraction. My hope is in the Lord my God, the Creator of the world, the Ruler of heaven, the Arbiter of justice, and the Fount of truth!

**Friday** *Read Psalm 147* **My Upholding**

Am I among those whom the Lord upholds, or those whom He casts down to the ground? Am I downcast or exultant? Is my head held high in happiness, or bent in gloom? Does darkness or light fill my eyeballs? By its fruits I shall know it, this upholding from the Lord!

**Saturday** *Read Psalm 148* **My Concert**

How am I joining the universal praise of nature? The morning stars sing together. The grass smiles it to the trees, and the trees to the sky. The birds carol it, and the wind trumpets it, and the sea murmurs its undertone. Am I alone silent amid this singing host?

# WEEK 89

**Sunday**  *Read Psalm 149*  **My Sword**

How shall the praise of the Lord be a sword in my hand? It shall drive out, as an armed warrior, my doubts and gloom, and the doubts and gloom of those that hear me. It shall smite fear to the earth, and all worries. It shall slay despair. It shall cleave a way through the foes that most persistently oppose my progress, the spiritual wickedness in high places!

**Monday**  *Read Psalm 150*  **My Praise**

How can I ever praise the Lord according to His excellent greatness? My praise is so feeble, and His greatness is so majestic! Ah, for this, as for all duties and delights, His is the power at my command. He will give me words, even for the praise of Himself.

**Tuesday**  *Read Proverbs 1*  **My Fear**

Have I the fear of the Lord, which is the beginning of the knowledge of the Lord? There is a time when wisdom may be found, and there is a time when it is too late to find her. Have I fear of that time? It is well to love the Lord for Himself, but have I even begun to fear the fate of those that do not love the Lord?

**Wednesday**  *Read Proverbs 2*  **My Search**

There are so many things for which I search more eagerly than for wisdom! For the appearance of wisdom, perhaps, or the rewards of wisdom, the friends and peace and power that wisdom will give, rather than wisdom herself. But wisdom will be sought for herself, and no otherwise will she be found.

**Thursday**  *Read Proverbs 3*  **My Necklace**

The law of the Lord is not my law except as I carry it with me. If it is only a book at home, or

*WEEK 89*

a sermon on Sunday, it is not my law. Only what I myself have written of the book, inscribing it upon the tablet of the heart, binding it about my neck, is my book, and my law.

**Friday**  *Read Proverbs 4*  **My Exaltation**

I am exalted by that which I exalt. If I exalt wisdom, she will exalt me. If I exalt unwisdom, she will lift me beside her upon her shameful throne. My own crown is a duplicate of the crown I place upon the head of my ideal.

**Saturday**  *Read Proverbs 5*  **My Home**

That I may find the Lord in my home, let me not depart from Him outside my home. Where my love is, there is my home; let it be in such places as I can own before God and man. Be Thou, O Lord of love, the Lord of my love and of my home!

# WEEK 90

**Sunday**     *Read Proverbs 6*     **My Sloth**

How is my sluggishness rebuked by the prodigious industry of nature! For am not I a part of nature? How continually do all things work, —all but man! How peacefully do all things work—all but man! God of the ant, teach me Thy ways, and give me of Thy strength!

**Monday**     *Read Proverbs 7*     **My Kindred**

Can I call Wisdom my sister, and Understanding my kinswoman? Am I well acquainted with them? Do they live in the home of my soul? Do they own me of their family? Better that than to be of the family of any king. Better that than to sit at the table of any great man.

**Tuesday**     *Read Proverbs 8*     **My Rubies**

A great ruby is the king of gems, but wisdom is more precious than all rubies. To know a matter is a diamond, but so to know it as to act upon it is a ruby. No wealth is more portable than rubies, except wisdom; but that needs not even a bag. Oh, with all my getting let me get understanding!

**Wednesday**  *Read Proverbs 9*  **My Reproofs**

A fool will slap the mouth that reproves him, but a wise man will kiss it, and bless it. What do I say inwardly, when I am wisely reproved? It is not what I say outwardly, but the words of my heart. Who knows the sacrifice my reprover is making? And shall I receive him with a sneer?

**Thursday**   *Read Proverbs 10*   **My Tongue**

Into how many pits hast thou led me, O thou foolish tongue! What losses hast thou caused me, what shame hast thou brought me, how hast thou been my foe! All that thou hast given me is less than what thou hast taken from me, O foolish tongue!

*WEEK 90*

**Friday**   *Read Proverbs 11*   **My Liberality**

Far from me be the folly of a wasteful hoarding! Let me learn the thrift of spending wisely, the prudence of liberality! And yet I shall not give because it is prudent, because it is to be given to me again, for there is no giving in that.

**Saturday**   *Read Proverbs 12*   **My Way**

Surely my way is wise in my own eyes, or I would not take it; and must I not take the way that seems wise? Yes, but I can correct my seeing by the seeing of others. I can ask those that have traversed my way and can report upon it. I must go my way, but I can make my way the way of the wise.

# WEEK 91

### Sunday  Read Proverbs 13  My Poverty

Every dollar I gain is a loss to me, if it is gained by injustice, or by the neglect of something higher than dollars. Every dollar I lose is a gain to me, if it is lost for the sake of something higher than dollars. Lord of all wealth, teach my inmost soul what is true riches!

### Monday  Read Proverbs 14  My Judgment

Let me not forget that the ways that men take seem right to them, yet many of them are the ways of death. Let me beware lest that be true of me. It is no commendation of a way that it seem right to me, but that it seems right to Him who is the Way.

### Tuesday  Read Proverbs 15  My Feast

If a cheerful heart is a continual feast, how should the Christian be fed! I have the Bread of life. I have the Water of life. I have the Joy of life. I have the Life Himself! To be morose would be a sin against all the past and all the present and all the future.

### Wed  Read Proverbs 16  My Pride

Not only does a haughty spirit go before a fall; a haughty spirit is a fall. Pride is ruin. It prevents increase of wisdom, and is in itself a folly. For what have I that has not been given me?

### Thurs  Read Proverbs 17  My Friendship

Am I a fair-weather friend? Or am I a friend for all times? Am I a friend when I can be helped, but not when I should give help? Is my friendship a matter of advantage and not of sacrifice? Ah, then it is not a matter of advantage! Ah, then it misses the chief delights and main benefits of friendship!

*WEEK 91*

**Friday**   *Read Proverbs 18*   **My Tongue**

Death and life are in the power of my tongue. With it I can slay my soul. With it I can slay the souls of others. And with it I can save my soul, when I call upon the Lord; or save the souls of others, when I persuade them to do the same. Oh, to become skilled in the use of this great instrument!

**Saturday**   *Read Proverbs 19*   **My Lies**

Sure as the reward of truth, that never fails, is the punishment of falsehood. Sure as the disclosure of truth, that is inevitable, is the discovery of a lie. And the lie may be spoken or unspoken, thought or acted, worked out in deed or by the absence of deed or word; yet in all its forms a lie is a lie.

# WEEK 92

### Sunday     Read Proverbs 20     My Sleep

There is a sleep of the body, that tends to poverty of the body; and there is a sleep of the soul, that tends to poverty of the soul. There are open eyes, that satisfy with bread, and the soul has open eyes, that also satisfy the soul. Lord God, grant me this vision!

### Monday     Read Proverbs 21     My Way

Oh, the fatal egotism of my heart! When shall I learn that not every way of mine is right, not every thought of mine is wise? that my ways are usually *not* right and my thoughts are unwise? that my only safety is in taking God's ways and my only wisdom in thinking God's thoughts?

### Tuesday     Read Proverbs 22     My Diligence

Let me not care to stand before kings, but let me care to be diligent in business. Let me seek the inner royalty of industry, the crown of achievement. Be grace to me and strength, O God, and advance me in Thy presence. Then shall I inevitably be advanced in the presence of men.

### Wednesday     Read Proverbs 23     My Envy

The envy that looks longingly after any fortune of a sinner is next door to his sin itself. One lot only is to be envied: it is his who is in the way of the Lord all the day long. Surely he is among the favored of the earth, as he is one day to be among the favored in heaven.

### Thursday     Read Proverbs 24     My Building

Not with wood and nails, not with stone and brick and mortar, but with wisdom and understanding and knowledge! Oh, Thou only Wise, help me to be a worthy carpenter, a mason that needeth not to be ashamed! So shall I dwell in my house happily.

*WEEK 92*

**Friday** *Read Proverbs 25* **My Fruit**

Let my tongue be a godly tree, and the fruit therefrom shall be golden! In baskets of silver shall men gather it, and do it high honor. But let my tongue be a crabbed tree, and its fruit shall rot uncared for on the ground.

**Saturday** *Read Proverbs 26* **My Lions**

When I look through the window of unwillingness, how are the hens magnified to hyenas and the gnats to lions! Through the door of sloth I hear the street full of roarings. To the slippers of idleness, ah, how sharp are the pebbles in the road!

# WEEK 93

### Sunday  Read Proverbs 27  My Wounds

When I am sore and smitten, when my flesh burns and smarts and my soul is pierced with many sorrows, let me stop and consider whence these come, whether from an enemy or a friend. And if the latter, especially if the Friend is One that never fails in wisdom or in love, let me count my wounds my noblest wealth.

### Monday  Read Proverbs 28  My Flight

Hurry-skurry, panting, weary to the death. how I press my flight from—nothing! I run from a shadow and retreat before a waving leaf. It is my cowardly heart that runs away, and not my obedient legs. O Lord, strengthen my soul!

### Tues  Read Prov. 29  My Thoughtfulness

When shall I know that words are deeds? that idle words are a wandering in the wilderness, that stinging words are weapons, that foolish words are a clown's attire? Let me not set guards everywhere else, but fail to set a guard over my tongue!

### Wednesday  Read Prov. 30  My Content

It requires strength and a firm will to get a little wealth, but greater strength and a firmer will to be satisfied with a little wealth. When one can say, "Enough," one can say any wise word, one can address any assembly!

### Thursday  Read Proverbs 31  My Speech

It is not enough to open my hands for the poor, if I do not also open my mouth. They need my championing words more than my too-ready weapons. If the righteous would all speak for the oppressed, righteousness would be done them without more ado.

*WEEK 93*

**Friday**  *Read Ecclesiastes 1*  **My Striving**

There is a wisdom that is grief; but there is also a wisdom that is joy forever. There is an increase of knowledge that increases sorrow; but there is a growth of wisdom that is a growth in blessedness. Be mine the search for the true wisdom, the striving after the genuine joy.

**Saturday**  *Read Ecclesiastes 2*  **My Pleasure**

It is of no avail that I strive to please myself. There is no pleasing of myself. That is a maw that is never satisfied, a gulf that is never filled. My pleasure is found only when I do not seek it, but seek instead the joy of others and the good pleasure of my God.

# WEEK 94

### Sunday  *Read Ecclesiastes 3*  My Seasons

I would have a well-ordered life, O Thou God of beautiful order! I would imitate the steady revolving of Thy years. I would do this hour the work of this hour, that next hour I may do that hour's work. And so I would put myself in work-harmony with Thee.

### Monday  *Read Eccl. 4*  My Quietness

Let me not strive beyond peace. If I cannot have two handfuls with quietness, let me have one handful, and be at rest. For why should I toil after discomfort? and why should I strive to be distressed?

### Tuesday  *Read Ecclesiastes 5*  My Increase

When my goods increase beyond my power to enjoy them, then further increase is a suicide of happiness, and a sinful greed. Day by day let me look to my use of what I have; and if I have it but do not use it, let me count it a gain to give it away.

### Wednesday  *Read Eccl. 6*  My Fulness

What profit if my barns burst with grain, when my soul is not filled with good? What profit all manner of knowledge, if I also know myself to be miserable? What profit the praise of men, if I pity myself? I will seek the inner fulness, the satisfaction of the soul.

### Thursday  *Read Eccl. 7*  My Sorrow

When is sorrow better than laughter? When it ends in laughter. For as granite is the best basis of a house, so the best foundation of joy is not the sand tossed up by the flashing waves, but the rock that has been fused in the volcanic furnace of affliction. Thus, O God, by whatever

*WEEK 94*

stress of life, wilt Thou found my house upon the living rock.

### Friday  Read Ecclesiastes 8  My Face

What countenance am I turning upon the world? Does wisdom make my face to shine, or does unwisdom darken it? Am I goodly to look upon, with the beauty that is deeper than color and form, and more enduring than any flesh?

### Saturday  Read Ecclesiastes 9  My Might

I know that an energetic deed has grace and glory, but a half-hearted deed is clumsy and of little worth. I know this, yet I continue with half my heart in many things. Let me withdraw myself from all into which I cannot pour myself. Let me do with my might what my hands find to do.

# WEEK 95

### Sunday   Read Eccl. 10.   My Confession

Well is it said, if I am a fool, I shall tell every one of it! Murder will out, and so will folly. There is no hiding of understanding; but also, there is no hiding of a lack of understanding. So let me live in the remembrance that character is confession.

### Monday   Read Eccl. 11   My Benefactions

What is less likely than that bread, cast on the waters, will return again? and what is more sure? For the waves of God's providence are refluent ever, and the good we scatter comes surely back to us. So let me never fear to spend myself for others.

### Tuesday   Read Ecclesiastes 12   My Duty

My duty is twofold, and only twofold. I am to fear and to keep. I am to fear that alone which should be feared, and all else I am to disregard; and I am to keep that alone which is worth keeping, all else being thrown away. What I am to fear, then, is God; and what I am to keep is God's commandments.

### Wed   Read Song of Songs 1   My Vineyard

Oh, the pity of it, to keep another man's vineyard, but not my own! to preach to others, but be a castaway! to toil for others, but leave my task undone, and sing for the wide world, but let my song go unsung! My life shall begin at home. Yes, my life shall begin at home, that thus it may truly go abroad.

### Thursday   Read Song of Songs 2   My Foxes

What though the foxes are little, if they spoil the vines? What though the fault is slight, if it is ruining my life? What is little, anyway, and what is great, when it comes to that?

*WEEK 95*

**Friday**  *Read Song of Songs 3*  **My Cushion**

Oh, may my seat be "paved with love," like the seat of King Solomon! Love be all the furnishings of my chair of ease! In what shop shall I buy it? What artificer will fashion it for me? It is made by Master Thoughtfulness, and it is sold in the shop of Pain!

**Sat**  *Read Song of Songs 4*  **My Garden**

Is my life a garden shut up, a fountain sealed? To what avail are the waters in the pipe, or the flowers behind the wall? Bid thy springs flow freely, O soul, and invite all men to the fragrance of thy blossoming.

# WEEK 96

**Sun**  *Read Song of Songs 5*  **My Wakefulness**

Though I sleep, grant me, O Lord, the wakeful heart. May I be ever ready for Thy tasks, of love, of helpfulness, of compassion. When the eyes of my body close, let me never close the eyes of my soul.

**Mon**  *Read Song of Songs 6*  **My Fealty**

I am his who loves me, and he is mine. There are no possessions in love, for love is all possession! I will give myself to him who gives himself to me. Yea, I will give myself first to him, in the bare hope that he will give himself to me!

**Tues**  *Read Song of Songs 7*  **My Fruits**

It is good to lay up fruits, but only when they are stored for love. Orchards are good, and vineyards, and gardens, but only when two eat of the apples and press the grapes and wander among the flowers. Let me till no ground for myself.

**Wed**  *Read Song of Songs 8*  **My Permanence**

If I would ally myself to deathlessness, I must ally myself to love. If I would place myself beyond the reach of the waters of oblivion, I must love, I must love greatly. Everything is fleeting but love, and love will endure forever.

**Thursday**  *Read Isaiah 1*  **My Whiteness**

My sins are as scarlet, but they are to be white as snow. My soul is ugly as blood, but it is to be beautiful as the soft garment of winter. My sins speak of wounds, but they shall be healed; and of turmoil, but over it all is to steal the quietness of the snow.

**Friday**  *Read Isaiah 2*  **My Pride**

How am I preparing for the day when the Lord

*WEEK 96*

alone shall be exalted? If I am exalting myself, though only to myself, what a fall am I preparing for my spirit! Oh, there is no safety, no comfort, no measure of any peace, but in humility!

**Saturday**　　*Read Isaiah 3*　　**My Food**

Surely I shall eat the fruit of my doings. Will it be bitter or sweet in my mouth, apples of New England or apples of Sodom? What I ate to-day, of joy or sorrow, I prepared yesterday and yester-year. I gathered the materials, I fashioned them, I cooked them. How does the food taste? And do I want more of it?

# WEEK 97

**Sunday**     *Read Isaiah 4*     **My Covert**

After the purification, the peace! After the purging, the shadow from the heat and the covert from the storm! And let me not expect anything except heat and storm till I am cleansed from my sin, and my heart is made pure within me.

**Monday**   *Read Isaiah 5*   **My Wild Grapes**

Surely God has tended me, as a fruitful vineyard should be tended. He has tilled my soil, He has watered it from the clouds, He has shone upon it with the sun. Nothing has failed, that should bring forth fruit; and what worthy fruit has come from the vineyard of my soul? Is not God, alas! a disappointed husbandman?

**Tuesday**     *Read Isaiah 6*     **My Lips**

A coal from Thy altar, O Lord of Speech! Lay it upon my lips, though it sear them. Cleanse them, though as by fire! Let them know the quiver of Thy righteousness, the stress of Thy purity; and let them henceforth know nothing that is common or unclean.

**Wednesday**   *Read Isaiah 7*   **My Confidence**

What though kings set themselves against me, strong men of the earth and powers of the air? My allies fill the firmament, my allies rise from every dust grain. I shall not fear, nor shall my heart be faint. Let them fear that oppose the Lord's will, and let their hearts justly faint within them.

**Thursday**   *Read Isaiah 8*   **My Testimony**

Against the clamor of evil men, and all the bluster of the world, I will set Thy law, O God, and Thy testimony, O my King! It is my law also; therefore it is a testimony against them.

*WEEK 97*

**Friday**  *Read Isaiah 9*  **My Light**

A great Light, for a great darkness! I had dwelt in the one, and now I walk in the other. I had known the fear, and now my joy is increased; and the yoke, but now I walk in freedom. For unto me, yea, unto all men, has been born the Wonderful Child.

**Saturday**  *Read Isaiah 10*  **My Visitation**

The day of visitation! of desolation, and searching, and dismay! What shall I do in that day? Whither shall I flee in that day? Ah, whither but to the Source of the desolation, the Sun whose burning shrivels the chaff? For back of His burning, to those who love Him, there is coolness and there is peace.

# WEEK 98

**Sunday**   *Read Isaiah 11*   **My Judge**

He shall not judge me after what He sees in me, nor after what He hears of me. His shall not be the spirit of revenge, but the spirit of understanding. He shall see what I have poorly tried to do, and shall cover with it the paltry thing I have done.

**Monday**   *Read Isaiah 12*   **My Salvation**

Not in myself is my trust. I do not trust myself even for trusting. The Lord is my strength, even to reach to Him for strength. The Lord is my song, even to the impulse for singing. And thus has the Lord become my salvation.

**Tuesday**   *Read Isaiah 13*   **My Dismay**

Let my fear be fixed upon the right things. I who fear the penalty, let me dread the sin. I who dread the dungeon, let me rather dread the dungeon's deed. Care of matches is wiser than care of fire, and the cleansing of sewers than the healing of plagues.

**Wednesday**   *Read Isaiah 14*   **My Fall**

Though I were a chief one of the earth, though my throne were on high, yea, though I were as the day star, son of the morning, yet if I contemn the Most High, a hand shall reach up and take me, and hurl me to the depths. For those that despise the Lord, there is nothing but fall.

**Thursday**   *Read Isaiah 15*   **My Sackcloth**

When shall I change my sackcloth for a wedding garment, my spirit of heaviness for garments of praise? When I clothe myself with Thee, Thou Soul of all beauty. When I do Thy will, Thou Heart of all righteousness.

**Friday**   *Read Isaiah 16*   **My Prevailing**

I am not heard for my words. Though I mount

*WEEK 98*

to the high places of petition, though I go to my sanctuary and pray with anguish; if I carry not with me an obedient soul, I shall not prevail. For as the answer to prayer is in Thy hands, so it is also in my hands; in my hands, as they seek to do Thy will.

### Saturday   *Read Isaiah 17*   My Looking

Whither is the gaze of my soul, and whence do I expect my help? Is it one thing before men, and another in my heart? Is it one thing as I fancy it, and quite another thing in reality? What is the true hope on which I lean? Is it the rock, or a reed?

# WEEK 99

**Sunday**     *Read Isaiah 18*     **My Hearing**

An ensign is lifted up on the mountains. Am I looking to it? A trumpet is blown with a great voice. Are my ears open to it? When the Lord speaks, let all men be silent. Let me clear my ears and my spirit for that hearing alone.

**Monday**     *Read Isaiah 19*     **My Perverseness**

If the Lord has mingled in my life a spirit of perverseness, it is I that have opened a way for it, and invited it in. I have trained myself in it, and have not fought against it. If I turn and fight against it, all of God will be upon my side.

**Tuesday**     *Read Isaiah 20*     **My Shame**

How do my sins tear from me every garment, the cloak of honor, the coat of respect, the inner raiment of love! I go naked before my foes and ashamed before my friends. And Thou only canst clothe me again, O Christ; and the robe of Thy righteousness alone can cover me.

**Wednesday**     *Read Isaiah 21*     **My Watch**

"What of the night?" they will cry to me. They whom God has given me to guard, they whose reliance is in me. "What of the night?" they will ask, "and what of the day?" My answer must not be mockery. True warning must I utter, peril of storm, pleading for retreat, "Turn from the ways of the storm, and find a refuge!"

**Thursday**     *Read Isaiah 22*     **My Keys**

If I am clothed with the Lord's robe, and strengthened with His strength, then His key shall be laid upon my shoulder; I shall open and shut, and none shall shut and open. My authority shall be His, for I am His, and all His authority shall be mine, for He is mine, forever.

*WEEK 99*

**Friday** *Read Isaiah 23* **My Oblivion**

Though I be exalted, if I exalt not the Lord, how shall I be laid low! Though I sing many songs, if I forget to sing of the Lord, how shall I and my songs be forgotten! How shall my merchandise be transferred to others, and my beautiful attire to others, and I myself be forgotten!

**Saturday** *Read Isaiah 24* **My Mirth**

Though I shake the clusters on high and press the grapes into goblets, though I shout with the shouters and hold the centre of the feast, yet if my heart is empty of God, it shall all be emptied out; and if my soul dishonors the Lord, it shall loathe all other joys.

# WEEK 100

**Sunday**     *Read Isaiah 25*     **My Tears**

There will come a time when my face will say good-by to tears forever, when they will be remembered only as a dream of the past, when the very memory of them will be forgotten! Not when philosophy wipes them away; not when my will power wipes them away; not when pleasure wipes them away; but when the Lord God lays His hand upon my face in love.

**Monday**     *Read Isaiah 26*     **My Stay**

There is a perfect peace. Not hereafter, but now. Not for the few, but for all men, for me. It is a perfect peace. Not a fret is left, nor a fear. Not a single smallest cloud mars its sky. It is perfect, because it is God, and my mind is stayed on Him.

**Tuesday**     *Read Isaiah 27*     **My Keeping**

I am a watered vineyard, watered every moment. I am a kept vineyard, kept night and day. No thief shall break in, no enemy shall cut and harm. I am a vineyard, and He who made all vines is my Husbandman.

**Wednesday**     *Read Isaiah 28*     **My Diadem**

If I am to have a crown of glory, it is chosen. If I am to have a diadem of beauty, it is selected. The Lord shall be my crown of glory and my diadem of beauty. He shall flash from my head, He shall shine in my eyes, and His words shall fall as diamonds from my mouth.

**Thursday**     *Read Isaiah 29*     **My Reversals**

Verily my living continually turns things upside down! I reckon God as a man and men as gods. I count the transient as permanent, and the eternal things as matters of a moment.

*WEEK 100*

When shall I see clearly? and when shall I know things as they are?

**Friday**     *Read Isaiah 30*     **My Wall**

Is my life like a breached wall, a high wall broken, that totters, ready to fall? Is it doomed to shattering, that no piece of it shall be found? There are such lives, and they do not know it, though they might know their sin. Lord, forbid that such a life should be mine!

**Saturday**     *Read Isaiah 31*     **My Trust**

It is woe to me, if I trust in man or beast or motionless thing, and not in the Creator of all these, who holds them all at the turning of a finger. If I trust in them, I lean upon bubbles; if I trust in Him, I rest upon the Rock.

# WEEK 101

### Sunday     *Read Isaiah 32*     **My Sowing**

Beside all waters! Oh, to win the Lord's blessing for such sowing! Oh, for the full seed-basket, and the ready hand! The plough is waiting, and the ox. Yes, and mouths are waiting, open and hungry. Oh, for grace to sow beside all waters!

### Monday     *Read Isaiah 33*     **My Stability**

If my times are the times of the Lord, in my times shall there be stability. No war and the famine of war, no folly and the uncertainty of folly, but wisdom and righteousness, and abundance therewith. For the Lord is good, and all good things are his who is the Lord's.

### Tuesday     *Read Isaiah 34*     **My Reading**

I will seek me out the book of the Lord, and read. I will not pass over any page or any paragraph. I will give heed to every syllable. I will begin at the first page, and continue even to the end, and there is no end! I will read as fast as the Lord turns the pages.

### Wednesday     *Read Isaiah 35*     **My Knees**

When I totter upon my way, when my strength fails under me, when fear takes hold of my knees and terror turns my feet backward, O confirm my faith, my God, in that evil hour! Let me fall upon my feeble knees, and let my prayers reach up into Thy power.

### Thursday     *Read Isaiah 36*     **My Answer**

When the boasters brag against the Lord, when worldlings mock the Most High, when His foes cry Aha and flirt their fingers in the faces of His followers, how shall I reply! By the silent of indifferent contempt. By the scorn that will not waste a word upon their emptiness.

*WEEK 101*

**Friday**   *Read Isaiah 37*   **My Defence**

I have an armor; it is prayer. I have a high tower; it is prayer. I have a thick wall; it is prayer. I have munitions of war; they are prayers. Let the enemy rush against me. Let them be as many as the leaves on the trees. My defence shall be one, a single prayer; and I shall need no more.

**Saturday**   *Read Isaiah 38*   **My Token**

God speaks to me, as to Hezekiah. No longer in the backward shadow, but in the forward dial. In the ordered courses of nature, and no longer in nature's reversals. But it is the same God, and He is the token, in whatever form.

# WEEK 102

**Sunday**  *Read Isaiah 39*  **My Selfishness**

If there is peace in my day, to be heedless of war to come,—what is that but ruin of soul? To be satisfied and sleek, so long as harm comes not nigh me,—what is that but to receive and entertain the chief of harms?

**Monday**  *Read Isaiah 40*  **My Tidings**

The Lord has given to my feet an errand and to my mouth an evangel. Woe to my feet if they run not and to my mouth if it cries not aloud! Woe to my heart if it hastes not along the highway, and to my hands if they do not prepare the highway for a way for my good tidings!

**Tues**  *Read Isaiah 41*  **My Encouragement**

For what have I good courage, but that others also may have it? Why am I strong, but that others may cease to be weak? Why have I a voice, but to say to my brother, "Be of good courage"? Yea, why am I living at all, but to help some one else to live?

**Wednesday**  *Read Isaiah 42*  **My Blindness**

I know not my way. It lies all dark before me, a place of groping, a road of stretched-out hands. But I have a Guide. While He brings me where I would go, what care I how He brings me? While He makes darkness light before me, and crooked places straight, what care I how dark or crooked they may be?

**Thursday**  *Read Isaiah 43*  **My Name**

Since God has called me by my name, it is a new name altogether. It would be a new name, for the honor and glory of it, if pronounced by any earthly king. How much more when pronounced by the King of kings! Surely I cannot be less than His, with my fair new name, forever!

*WEEK 102*

**Friday**  *Read Isaiah 44*  **My Confirmation**

The same Lord that frustrates the designs of the proud, will confirm the word of His servants. If I speak the emptiness of human wisdom, God will bring to naught both it and me. If I speak the words that God's wisdom teaches, they shall stand when all the hills are vapor.

**Saturday**  *Read Isaiah 45*  **My Striving**

Do I set myself against the Almighty? Do I give His promises the lie and by my life proclaim His futility? Shall the creature set at naught the Creator, the potsherd mock the potter? What is all this but the very crown of folly?

## WEEK 103

**Sunday**   *Read Isaiah 46*   **My Counsel**

If God be my counsellor, my counsel shall stand. If God conduct my affairs, they shall not wander into failure. If God be the Man of my counsel, all men shall enter into my plans and accomplish my purposes. Let me not waver from His ways.

**Monday**   *Read Isaiah 47*   **My Haughtiness**

All my boastings are vain, and all my confidence, if my life lacks love. None of my possessions shall save me, if I have not that possession. Where is my help, in which I relied? For love alone can summon aid in sore distress.

**Tuesday**   *Read Isaiah 48*   **My Peace**

Like a river flowing softly, and all its banks are full; like the sea, abundant in its waters; so had been my peace and my righteousness, if I had obeyed. So, with no lack and no doubt, if I had obeyed. Alas, for the proving of the truth that there is no peace, no smallest rivulet of peace, to the wicked!

**Wednesday**   *Read Isaiah 49*   **My Memorial**

I, even I, am graven upon God's hands! There upon His palms has He written my name, to remember me forever. Day by day He bears me in mind, and in the night He never forgets me. And I would forget Him!

**Thursday**   *Read Isaiah 50*   **My Tongue**

If there are thoughts of wisdom in my brain, if there are words of wisdom on my tongue, they are not for my brain or for my tongue. There, they would mildew. There, they would inwardly corrupt. They are for leaping forth. They are for sustaining the weary. They are for enlightening the world.

*WEEK 103*

**Friday**     *Read Isaiah 51*     **My Origin**

I am of the air; let me never forget that I was of the rock. I am of the sunshine; let me remember that I was of the darkness of the pit. It is so easy to forget. It is so easy to be ungrateful.

**Saturday**     *Read Isaiah 52*     **My Purity**

I bear the vessels of the Lord. Were it only the name of the Lord, that great thing I bear. And shall I hold it aloft, shining in beauty, radiant with silver and gold, and my hands that hold it to gaze are foul with mire? I must not even touch an unclean thing, I that bear this vessel of the Lord.

# WEEK 104

**Sunday**     *Read Isaiah 53*     **My Saviour**

He was a man of sorrows, that I might be a man of joy. He was wounded and heavy laden, that I might walk unburdened and unhurt. He was dumb that I might speak. He was smitten that I might be healed. Ah, shall He not see of the travail of His soul, and be satisfied in me?

**Monday**   *Read Isaiah 54*   **My Enlargement**

The Lord did not make me for a narrow tent! He bids me extend the canvas, spare not, lengthen the cords, and strengthen the stakes. He bids me stretch forth my life, build me more stately temples for my soul. And I still live in littleness!

**Tuesday**     *Read Isaiah 55*     **My Thoughts**

Surely God's ways are not my ways nor His thoughts my thoughts. Heaven-high above my ways and thoughts are His. But mine may rise into His. From the earth into His heavens, from smallness into largeness, and from futility into power and peace.

**Wednesday**   *Read Isaiah 56*   **My Sabbaths**

The crown of the week shall rest upon my head. The flower of the week shall be fragrant upon my bosom. The climax of the week shall round out my living. This day that the Lord loves shall be loved by me also, and shall enter into the strength of my soul.

**Thursday**     *Read Isaiah 57*     **My Sea**

My life is like a sea. Is it a troubled sea, or a sea at rest? Do its waters cast up mire and dirt, or shells of beauty and food for service? Are its waters fresh or turbid? Oh, enter Thou into the sea of my life, God of purity and power!

*WEEK 104*

### Friday  *Read Isaiah 58*  **My Fast**

Endow all my religion, O God, with reality. Let my fastings be clothed with beauty and garlanded with joy,—beauty of brightened eyes, joy of comforted lives. Let my religion reach outward as well as upward. So shall it be inward as well.

### Saturday  *Read Isaiah 59*  **My Helper**

Do I think that God is crippled? Do I deem that God is deaf? Shall He that fashioned the hand be unready to help? He that formed the ear, shall He not hear? Hush your foolish complainings, O my soul. What is it but impiety to doubt the answering of prayer?

# WEEK 105

**Sunday**   *Read Isaiah 60*   **My Glory**

My light has come; my glory has risen upon me; the shining of its splendor is about my head, its radiance attends my path. Men see it, and rejoice. I see it, and wonder. It is all because I have opened my door, and the Lord of Glory has entered in.

**Monday**   *Read Isaiah 61*   **My Preaching**

Because there is a good tidings, it is mine to proclaim it. Because there is a vengeance, it is mine to warn of it. Because there is a comfort, it is mine to give it. Because there are priests of the Lord, it is mine to be called by that name. Mine, and all men's.

**Tuesday**   *Read Isaiah 62*   **My Watch**

I can see the evil afar. The good also I can see afar. Blessed be God, that my eyes are keen, that the horror of great darkness is not upon them. And what shall I do with these seeing eyes? Shall I not forth upon the walls? Shall I not bear witness of the things I see? Shall I not justify the generous Giver?

**Wed**   *Read Isaiah 63*   **My Winepress**

There is One that has trodden the winepress alone; but I need never do it. He is ever my partner, though all men fail me. Forth bursts the red flood, the wine is made abundantly, labor is transformed into singing, because I do not tread the winepress alone.

**Thursday**   *Read Isaiah 64*   **My Fading**

Yes, we all fade as a leaf, until we lie in the ground. But not all leaves fade in the same way. Some moulder in unsightly blotches. Some curl up and wither. And some, in a splendor of gold and crimson, flame for days upon the branch, before they form upon the ground a carpet of glory. That last be my fading, O God of the leaf, when my time comes to fall from the tree of mortality.

**Friday** *Read Isaiah 65* **My Answer**

I am quick to hear the call of men, were a ruler to call, or a rich man, a famous man, or the voice of the people. I am quick to call, and alert to answer. Shall I be laggard when the Lord calls me, He that made men, He beneath whose finger the mightiest of earth are as insects?

**Saturday** *Read Isaiah 66* **My Comfort**

My Father in heaven, yea, and my Mother in heaven! Strength as from a father, and comforting as from a mother! Nothing is to lack in God —the broad breast, the tender arms, the gentle voice, the kisses on forehead and lips. As one whom his mother comforteth, so the Lord will comfort me.

# WEEK 106

### Sunday  *Read Jeremiah 1*  **My Mouth**

Thy hand upon my mouth, O Thou God of speech! My tongue trembles and stammers. I fall back from before the truth. I fear before men. Ah, be my fear directed toward Thee the rather! Touch Thou my mouth, and bid me speak Thy words.

### Monday  *Read Jeremiah 2*  **My Forgetting**

I do not forget the adornments of my body, but I neglect the jewels of my soul. I am not unmindful of the bath, till it comes to the cleansing of my heart. I would not go with ragged garments, but I suffer the nakedness of my soul to stand revealed. Oh, when shall I learn proportions, and when shall I keep house in my heart?

### Tuesday  *Read Jeremiah 3*  **My Treachery**

Base as the basest of human treacheries, baser than the treachery of man to wife and wife to husband, is it to play false to God. For He is more to us than husband or wife, or father or mother or any dear one.

### Wed  *Read Jeremiah 4*  **My Desolation**

There is a wilderness that grows within my soul, a place of stones and brambles, a place of barrenness and heat, a place of terror and pain. It is the place where God is not, and I fashioned it myself. I drove out the trees. I pulled up the grass. I drained the rivers of waters. Lo, I am desolate, O God; and it is I that wrought the desolation.

### Thursday  *Read Jeremiah 5*  **My Desire**

If my life is foul with sin, it is because I love to have it so. No fate thrust it upon me. No compulsion binds it upon me. No smith rivets my chains. I hug them to my bosom. I cry out when men would take them away. Let me not deceive myself: I do not hate my sin.

**Friday** *Read Jeremiah 6* **My Self-Deceit**

I often cry to my soul, Peace, Peace, when there is no peace. I often, when I would not think to cheat others, plot to cheat myself. I paint upon the sky my own mirages, and raise my own visions to deceive my eyes. Oh, the desperate folly of one that will not be honest with himself!

**Saturday** *Read Jeremiah 7* **My Trust**

A word cannot save me. A name cannot save me. A title cannot save me. Though I prattle forever of holiness, holiness, holiness, I am not thereby less impure. Though I cry daily, The temple of the Lord, The temple of the Lord, The temple of the Lord, I am none the more in the temple, nor the temple in me. O God of realities, lead me into the meaning of words!

# WEEK 107

**Sunday**  *Read Jeremiah 8*  **My Physician**

It is well to know when one is sick. It is better to know where there is medicine. But best of all is it to know where there is a physician. Ah, my soul, fevered and worn, there is balm in Gilead, there is a Physician there! He will touch you with His hand, and the fever will leave you.

**Monday**  *Read Jeremiah 9*  **My Tears**

I weep enough, but do I weep wisely enough? I have tears a-plenty, but are they well bestowed? Not when they are bestowed upon myself, upon my petty woes, my more foolish fears; but well, when they are bestowed upon my people, the slain by sin.

**Tuesday**  *Read Jeremiah 10*  **My Way**

Too often, alas! my way is in myself. Too often I direct my own steps. And then my way becomes a byway and my steps fall into the morass. Then I fall, and there is none to lift me up. Oh, that my way were directed! Oh, that I might cease from self-wandering!

**Wednesday**  *Read Jeremiah 11*  **My Cry**

When my cry to God is unanswered, it is never because God does not hear. It is because I do not hear the answer, or because, by reason of my sins, there can be no answer. For my sins block often the way of my prayers, and my iniquities are a barrier before advancing good.

**Thursday**  *Read Jeremiah 12*  **My Reasoning**

The Lord knows, He fully understands, yet will He be informed by His suppliants, yet will He listen to our pleas and be moved by our dull reasoning. In any way we may approach God, however stupid, so it be sincere. And God will be at the end of the way.

## WEEK 107

**Friday**   *Read Jeremiah 13*   **My Spots**

If I am a leopard, a spotted leopard I must be. No washing can remove the spots, no medicine can cleanse me from them, if they are leopard spots. There is a washing, that can cleanse. There is a Physician, that can purify. But by long evil there becomes a leopard, and the leopard spots at length—remain.

**Saturday**   *Read Jeremiah 14*   **My Famine**

It is not a famine of food, but of joy; not of water, but of love. That famine eateth sorely. That drought parcheth inwardly. And it is in sight of the Water of Life, in very touch with the Bread of Life. The supreme folly of earth is this famine of the soul.

## WEEK 108

**Sunday**  *Read Jeremiah 15*  **My Food**

I make my meals upon Thy words, O God. I eat them, I feed upon them, they enter into bone and muscle, they run with my blood, they leap with me, they are my strength all the day. They never fail me, but are become a feast in the wilderness, and a full table in the midst of the sea.

**Monday**  *Read Jeremiah 16*  **My Argument**

If I will not hear the argument of love, the Lord will cause me to hear the reasoning of terror. If my memory of Egypt fails, I shall have the fresh remembrance of Babylon. For the Lord will press Himself upon me; yea, with words that I must hear, and in some fashion deal with.

**Tuesday**  *Read Jeremiah 17*  **My Self-Deceit**

I can fool others, but far better can I fool myself. I can dissemble to others, but I can be a perfect dissembler to myself. I can hide to myself. I can paint my own face, and look in the mirror and say, Behold, how fair! I can even fall in love with myself.

**Wednesday**  *Read Jeremiah 18*  **My Pit**

All around me are pits for my soul. My enemies have dug them, and laid pleasant branches over the mouths of them, and drawn pleasant paths to them, and hidden behind them the enticements of song. Yes, and still I see them to be pits, and know that my enemies are there in ambush. Yes, and still I walk into them!

**Thursday**  *Read Jeremiah 19*  **My Breaking**

As a potter's vessel, thrown upon the ground, a heap of worthless shards, so shall I be, my Judge, unless I heed Thy words. As a potter's vessel, turned perfectly on the wheel and fired perfectly in the oven, to grace the table or the shelf, so shall I be, my Judge, if I follow Thy hand and am obedient to Thy turning.

### Friday  *Read Jeremiah 20*  **My Persecution**

What though all the world rise up against me, since the Lord has not risen up against me? What though my feet are fast in the stocks, so long as my thought is free to roam? What avails the persecution of man against the protection of God?

### Saturday  *Read Jeremiah 21*  **My Opponent**

If the Lord march against me, I am indeed undone! Before other advances I may set up a barricade, but none against His. Against other weapons I may raise a fort, but none against His. Oh, woe to me if the Lord march against me!

# WEEK 109

**Sunday**  *Read Jeremiah 22*  **My Injustice**

All wealth of mine that is not wealth for others also, is loss to me. All my pleasures that are sorrows for others shall become griefs to me. Every injustice of mine to others shall rebound upon my own head. Oh, Thou God of all righteousness, Thou perfect Judge, be Thou the director of my life!

**Monday**  *Read Jeremiah 23*  **My Hiding**

How many secret places have I sought, to hide from the Lord! I have concealed myself in self-love, I have lurked in hypocrisies, I have covered myself with sophistries, and I have retreated behind all evasions. But God has been everywhere I have gone, and beneath all covers I have seen His piercing eye.

**Tuesday**  *Read Jeremiah 24*  **My Basket**

In which basket shall I lie, among the good figs, or the bad figs? among those whose lives are sound and healthy, sweet and wholesome, or among those of inward pollution and outward disgrace? There is no third basket.

**Wednesday**  *Read Jeremiah 25*  **My Cup**

The Lord has a cup for me; one of two cups for me. One is the wine of His love. The other is the wine of His fury. I must drink the one or the other, and I must drink it all. I am reaching out my hand to take the one or the other. He will not give me both. He will not let me choose. He will give me one cup or the other. Which shall it be?

**Thursday**  *Read Jeremiah 26*  **My Turning**

The Lord's repentance is not like man's repentance. That God may repent Him of His purposed evil, man must turn from the evil he

*WEEK 109*

has done. God cannot, with all His power, turn from the ways of wrath till man turns from the ways of iniquity. Thus even the way of the Almighty is in my hands.

**Friday** *Read Jeremiah 27* **My Choice**

Life possible—and to choose death! freedom, —and to choose serfdom! blessedness—and to choose misery! No insanity so foolish as the insanity of the wicked. No folly so insane as the folly of those that despise their God.

**Saturday** *Read Jeremiah 28* **My Prophecy**

Whether pleasing or displeasing, grant me courage, O God, to speak Thy words. Whether easy or hard, whether the way of persecution or of popularity, let me speak the truth to all men as I see the truth for all men, and let me know no word that is not of the truth. For Thou, O God, art the Truth.

# WEEK 110

**Sunday**　　*Read Jeremiah 29*　　**My Search**

What is worth finding, save my God? What is worth seeking, save what is worth finding? My search is for folly, and half my striving is after emptiness. O God, teach me the value of things, and lead me to pursue the true values.

**Monday**　　*Read Jeremiah 30*　　**My Lovers**

I will count my lovers, not by their words but by their memories. I will reckon my friends, not by their promises but by their completions. If they forget me, I will forget even my love for them. But there is a Friend that never forgets, a Lover who loves everlastingly.

**Tuesday**　*Read Jeremiah 31*　**My Knowledge**

Why am I taught of the Lord but to know the Lord? To what avail are all these books and sermons, these witnessings heard and these evidences seen, the books of the Lord, written and growing? I should be far past hearing and seeing. I should know, and I should know that I know.

**Wed**　　*Read Jeremiah 32*　　**My Confidence**

All I have shall be cast upon the chance of the Lord's victory. All I am shall be hazarded on the Lord's side. Fields to buy, they shall be bought. Armies to fight, they shall be met. Nations to face, they shall be confronted, and God's power will overcome them. There is no risk, on the Lord's side.

**Thurs**　　*Read Jeremiah 33*　　**My Abundance**

What is the abundance I seek? A plenty of gold and goods. What is the plenty God holds out? An abundance of peace and truth. And the plenty I seek is scarcity, but God alone

*WEEK 110*

abounds. Oh, that I may cease from my unwisdom!

**Friday** *Read Jeremiah 34* **My Liberty**

The liberty I refuse to others shall be a chain about my own neck. It shall be a liberty to the sword, a title to the pestilence, a freedom for famine! There is no liberty to me, if I will not enfranchise others!

**Sat** *Read Jeremiah 35* **My Obedience**

Be the obedience of others my disgrace, if I am not also obedient. Be the grandeur of the law my shame, if I disobey the law. Be every possibility of nobility that I miss a swift certainty of ignominy. Oh, to do the words of the law, fully, freely, and forever!

# WEEK 111

**Sunday**  *Read Jeremiah 36*  **My Pen-Knife**

There are other knives than those made of metal which may cut leaves from Holy Writ, and thrust them into the fire. Indifference will do it, and carelessness, and indolence, and infidelity, and selfishness, and absorption in worldly cares. Ah, let me keep my pen-knife in its sheath!

**Monday**  *Read Jeremiah 37*  **My Enemies**

They charge me falsely. They put me in prison. Prisons of contempt. Prisons of ridicule. Prisons of deprivation and loss. What of it? What of it? Do not they imprison my God with me, since the charges are false? And when God is in the prison, in it are the liberties of all fair lands.

**Tuesday**  *Read Jeremiah 38*  **My Dungeon**

It is dark and foul. The air is a horror. I sink in abominable mire. It is the dungeon of my own evil thoughts, and there is no other dungeon for me in all the earth. Oh, for an Ebed-melech, to let down any rags and lift me out into the pureness and sunshine again! And my Ebed-melech is ever at hand.

**Wed**  *Read Jeremiah 39*  **My Captivity**

My captivity, if it is ever accomplished, will be wrought out by myself. My own guns will be trained against my walls, my own mines will blow them up from beneath, my own forces will storm the breaches, and my own chains will be passed around my body. Let me ascribe to no one else, on earth or below it, the deeds I do with my own brain and spirit.

**Thur**  *Read Jeremiah 40*  **My Dwelling-Place**

If I speak God's words and do God's will, I may dwell as I please in God's land. All its val-

*WEEK 111*

leys of peace are open before me, all its hills of power. Its fruitful orchards are mine, and its living waters. There is no confining of my pleasures, no stinting of my will, if my pleasurable will is to do the will of God.

**Friday** *Read Jeremiah 41* **My Stores**

I may buy off my life from my foe. My stores may purchase peace and safety for my body. But what store can I lay up, what treasury can I fill, that I may buy my soul's safety and peace? None; ah, none! But a ransom is ready, and I shall be bought.

**Saturday** *Read Jeremiah 42* **My Fear**

If I flee from my fear, it shall overtake me. If I pursue peace and safety, they shall flee from me and escape. If I would save my life, I shall lose it. My fear brings with it the evil that it dreads. O my soul, rest thou in the Lord! O my soul, bide thou blessedly at home.

# WEEK 112

**Sunday**   *Read Jeremiah 43*   **My Refuge**

If it is not the refuge that the Lord appoints, I shall hide there wholly in vain. Though the land is far to which I flee, though its armies swarm about me and its walls span all frontiers, it is no refuge for me. But if the Lord appoints me to the open desert, the unwalled plain, that is my refuge, and there I may not be touched.

**Monday**   *Read Jeremiah 44*   **My Prosperity**

In my prosperity I forgot the Lord and turned to the gods of this world. Shall I therefore say that those gods brought me prosperity? No, for they could not maintain me in it. Now that I am fallen into adversity, it is of the Lord; and He who brought me low is He who can lift me again, into all the prosperity from which I have fallen.

**Tuesday**   *Read Jeremiah 45*   **My Greatness**

Seekest thou great things for thyself? O soul, seek them not! Let the Lord seek them for thee. Let the Lord build thy house, let Him fashion thy crown. The greatness that He seeks for thee shall be thine; but the greatness that thou dost seek for thyself, no least part of it shall ever be thine.

**Wednesday**   *Read Jeremiah 46*   **My Stand**

If the Lord drive me, surely I shall not stand; but if men drive me, and not the Lord, certainly I shall not be driven, but shall stand unshaken. Oh, in my heart of hearts to be sure of this! Oh, to have an unshaken confidence in my God!

**Thursday**   *Read Jeremiah 47*   **My Sword**

If I wield the sword of the Lord, if He has given it into my hand, though it is heavy to hold, though I groan at the swinging of it and its hiss through the air, yet it must never go to the scab-

*WEEK 112*

bard till the Lord says, "Rest, and be quiet."
Alas for any peace that is not the Lord's peace!

**Friday** *Read Jeremiah 48* **My Negligence**

Ah, yes: cursed be he that doeth the work of the Lord negligently! The curse is not from the Lord, but from the neglected work. It shall rise up against me, if I am the sluggard. It shall drive a dagger to my soul.

**Sat** *Read Jeremiah 49* **My Deep Dwelling**

Dwell deep, O my soul! Dwell truly deep, O my soul! Pierce to the heart of the world. Enter into the secret of affairs. Know that the heart of things is God. There is no deep beyond His depth, no centre around which He moves. Reach Him, O my soul, and you have reached the Ultimate.

# WEEK 113

**Sunday**  *Read Jeremiah 50*  **My Flight**

As I am bidden, I will flee out of the midst of Babylon, I will go forth out of the land of the Chaldeans. Their ways shall not be my ways nor their desires my desires. Those that the Lord is wroth against must not be my friends; they must not fail to be my foes.

**Mon**  *Read Jeremiah 51*  **My Drunkenness**

The world offers me a golden cup, full of sparkling wine. Its fumes leap out and enwrap my brain. I am promised all happiness. I dream of all power. I stagger with pride. I am besotted with folly. O my God, when shall I have the manliness to strike this golden cup, and forbid it my lips forever?

**Tuesday**  *Read Jeremiah 52*  **My Allowance**

I am a king. Do I accept an underthrone in serfdom? I own a realm. Am I gladly receiving a change of prison garments? All wealth is mine. Am I shamefully grateful for an allowance from my captors? Oh, final ignominy of sin, that the royal soul forgets its rights!

**Wednesday**  *Read Lam. 1*  **My Heedlessness**

"Is it nothing to you, all ye that pass by?" Am I also among the heedless throng? Have I no ears for the moaning of Christ's brothers, no eyes to see their wretchedness? However their misery came, surely it is here; and I am here; and Christ is here. Is it nothing to me, while it is so much to Him?

**Thurs**  *Read Lamentations 2*  **My Enemy**

The Lord may become my enemy! No fate such as that, to be feared and to be avoided. His pity, even, may cease toward me, and the stream of His love be turned away from me, and

*WEEK 113*

all help fail. Oh, may this, the one sorrow of heaven, happen no more upon the earth. At least, let it not ever come to me, or to those whom I can save from it.

**Friday** *Read Lamentations 3* **My Mercies**

They are new every morning, Thy mercies toward me. Great is Thy faithfulness, O my God. They hold me from the fire of Thy anger, that I may not be consumed with my sins. They maintain me in the sunshine of Thy love, that I may grow and rejoice all the day.

**Sat** *Read Lamentations 4* **My Fine Gold**

Has my fine gold become as clay? Is it suffering the sad transformation? Let me guard against the coarsening of my life! Let me see to it that my purest and best is kept at its best and purest.

# WEEK 114

**Sunday**  *Read Lamentations 5*  **My Turning**

Turn Thou me, O Lord, and I shall be turned. Not in my own wisdom or strength can I turn from any evil. It is too strong for me. Its allurement debauches my will. I am as an infant in its hands. But an infant, O God, that reaches out its hands to Thee.

**Monday**  *Read Ezekiel 1*  **My Spirit**

Whither my spirit leads, all the wheels of my life will follow. I can lead myself. No other can lead myself. No other in all the universes can conduct my powers. Ah, but some other can guide *me*, the me that guides my powers!

**Tuesday**  *Read Ezekiel 2*  **My Fear**

If the Lord bid me speak, I will speak, though all men speak against me. I will arise at the august command, I will stand upon my feet, I will bear me like a man! For it is other than a man that commands me, other than all men and all worlds. There shall be in my heart no fear, no fear but of Him.

**Wednesday**  *Read Ezekiel 3*  **My Food**

Do I really feed upon God's word? Is it in my mouth, or only upon the table? Am I hungry for it, or indifferent to it? Is it an ornament rather than a food, an exterior rather than a component? O Christ, be to me truly the Bread of life! Be to me truly the Water of life!

**Thursday**  *Read Ezekiel 4*  **My Bread**

If I do not the Lord's will, my staff of bread shall be broken. That upon which I lean, the strength of my body and the power of my mind, shall be broken. And my joy shall be broken with it. Thou alone canst restore it, Thou Staff of men, Thou Bread of life!

*WEEK 114*

**Friday**   *Read Ezekiel 5*   **My Reproach**

Let me know what will come upon me, if I do not obey the divine behest. Let me see my shame afar off, that I may avoid that way, that I may flee from it and never know it. For it is a reproach hardly to be shaken off, it is a sword, it is a fire, it will enter the heart of my life and destroy it forever.

**Saturday**   *Read Ezekiel 6*   **My Waste**

The waste places of my life; alas, the deserts and desolations of my life, the places that should glow with blossoms and are barren, that should wave with verdure and are bare! To be a wilderness when one might be a garden! Does my life tend that way? Is my life running to waste?

# WEEK 115

**Sunday**     *Read Ezekiel 7*     **My Ways**

Truly the Lord will bring my ways upon me. Like chains rolled up around me and holding me close, He will gather up the long coiling courses of my iniquity; or, like garlands and wreaths, tokens of grace and glory, He will lay upon me the flowery pathways of past worthiness. What are these ways of mine that the Lord will bring upon me; ah, what?

**Monday**     *Read Ezekiel 8*     **My Thoughts**

What fills my chambers of imagery? Are they temples of beauty, or dens of vileness? Is God there worshipped, or lust? When some day those chambers are thrown open to the gaze of men and angels, shall I be humbly proud, or unutterably ashamed? O God, cleanse my mind! O God, beautify my mind!

**Tuesday**     *Read Ezekiel 9*     **My Mark**

Has the man with the inkhorn set his mark upon my forehead? When the sword of just retribution is drawn, when the fire of righteous wrath flames abroad, will it pierce my soul, will it devour my joy? Oh, Thy mark upon my forehead, Lord, that all men and angels may see it!

**Wednesday**     *Read Ezekiel 10*     **My Service**

As the spirits of the heavens obey Thee, Infinite One, and the spirits of the great deep, spirits of fire and of earth, wheel within wheel of Thy creatures, glory involving glory of Thy serviceable realm, so let me serve Thee with the whole heart, power upon power, joy upon joy, grace upon grace!

**Thursday**     *Read Ezekiel 11*     **My Sanctuary**

Thou art my sanctuary, O God, in a strange land. And though an exile, yet I am at home.

since I may enter my sanctuary, and find my Father there! It is a land of detestable things and all abominations; but in this sanctuary is pureness of heart.

**Friday**  *Read Ezekiel 12*  **My Removing**

Let me also, like the prophet of old, prepare my stuff for removing. In the sight of all men let me live as for another country, as an immigrant ready to start. Let me find here no continuing city, but carry my possessions ever with me for embarkation.

**Saturday**  *Read Ezekiel 13*  **My Visions**

Sometimes my visions are vain visions, mirages born of empty desires. Sometimes I prophesy out of my own heart, and deceive myself and others. And then I lead myself into morasses, and blindly lead others who are blind as I. Oh, for clearness of sight! Oh, for soundness of purpose! And they are to be found in God alone.

# WEEK 116

### Sunday   Read Ezekiel 14   My Comforting

Am I of the remnant, of those that will comfort others in the time of their trouble, when dire distress comes upon men because of their sin? Is my life a rock upon which drowning men may lay their hands? Is my life a light, toward which lost men may grope?

### Monday   Read Ezekiel 15   My Use

Am I as a vine, or as an oak? Can God use me for walls of His temple? for strength? for protection? Am I broad, stanch, substantial? Or am I pliant as a vine, and worthless as a burned branch of the vine? Not in my own vain thoughts, not in the partial thoughts of others, but in the veritable thought of God, what is the use of me?

### Tuesday   Read Ezekiel 16   My Ingratitude

No picture that can be painted, not even that of the adulterous wife of a faithful husband, is too black for my ingratitude. What could be done for man that has not been done for me? What could be done by man, of foul thanklessness and crude ingratitude, that has not been done by me? And yet the Lord has not given me up!

### Wednesday   Read Ezekiel 17   My Planting

The Lord of Plantations has set me in the soil. He will have His way with me, as is His right. He will bring down the high tree, and let it not rebel. He will exalt the low tree, and let it not be proud. He will dry up the green tree, and it may not revive. He will make the dry tree flourish, and it must not vaunt itself. For all fortunes are of the Lord, and all fortunes are just.

### Thursday   Read Ezekiel 18   My Inheritance

Truly I receive much from my forefathers, and they that come after me will receive much from

*WEEK 116*

me; much, both of good and evil. But I am to live my own life and make my own destiny, as are they also to do. My inheritance is mine, it is not I. It is tools, and not destiny.

**Friday** *Read Ezekiel 19* **My Failures**

There are many that are disappointed when I fail, for many are they that love me and have hopes for me. They mourn over my captivity, they faint in my sickness, they die in my death. I am not living for myself, but for all these also.

**Saturday** *Read Ezekiel 20* **My Life**

In Thy judgments is life, O God. In them I live, and from no other source do I draw my existence. Thy judgments are the springtide, blossoming in beauty; they are the autumn, golden with harvest. Thy judgments are a great arm, mighty to strike down, mighty to uphold. By Thy judgments, O God, I live forever.

# WEEK 117

**Sunday**   *Read Ezekiel 21*   **My Overturning**

God will overturn, overturn, overturn, will leave no fortune upright and no life established, till He is exalted in the life—He whose right it is to rule therein. There is no safety to the wicked. There is no confidence except in obedience to the Lord.

**Monday**   *Read Ezekiel 22*   **My Dross**

What can I wish but that my dross should be consumed, that I should be pure gold, for use and for beauty? Ah, but if I am all dross? If the furnace consumes me utterly? What am I building into my character against that stern testing?

**Tuesday**   *Read Ezekiel 23*   **My Defiling**

There is no evil that is not recompensed in sorrow. There is no impure outgoing that is not repaid by sad and ruinous incoming. God's justice is not to be escaped or diminished. Where were the race of men, if God's justice could be lessened or escaped?

**Wed**   *Read Ezekiel 24*   **My Endurance**

When God's justice smites with a sword, when the stroke of His righteousness falls, it is not for me to cry aloud, nor even to mourn before men, though my nearest and dearest is stricken down. All such sighing is a complaint, and all such mourning is an upbraiding of God.

**Thursday**   *Read Ezekiel 25*   **My Punishment**

God is an avenging God. I want Him to avenge me of that which harms my dear ones and me. Why should I complain when His vengeance falls upon me, if I do harm to others and to their dear ones? Shall not the Lord be impartial? Shall not the Judge hold even scales?

*WEEK 117*

**Friday** *Read Ezekiel 26* **My Replenishing**

Am I like Tyre, that said, " I shall be replenished, now that she is laid waste"? Do I find my fortune in others' misfortune, and build my blessings on others' bane? Let me know, then, of a surety, that no one in all the world can suffer loss without my suffering loss. Let me know that the system of the world is one.

**Saturday** *Read Ezekiel 27* **My Riches**

If my tower is ill founded, the higher it rises, it is uplifted but to the more awful fall. If my house is built upon a volcano, the more wealth I crowd within it, only the richer will be the lava. If in any way my prosperity is commingled with iniquity, the greater it is, the greater is the ruin I am devising for myself.

# WEEK 118

**Sunday**   *Read Ezekiel 28*   **My Pride**

Because my heart was lifted up, therefore it was struck down. Because my vanity was inflated, therefore it was pierced. Because I raised myself in foolish conceit above my fellows, therefore I am placed beneath their feet, and men trample upon me. There is a vice that punishes itself. That vice is pride.

**Monday**   *Read Ezekiel 29*   **My Staff**

Israel leaned upon Egypt, and it was a staff of reed. Upon what am I leaning? Does that on which I rest bend beneath my weight? Does it bend and will it break? Is it of man and so of weakness? Or is it of God, and so as firm as the everlasting powers, as rigid as the laws of the universe?

**Tuesday**   *Read Ezekiel 30*   **My Arms**

The Lord breaks the arms of those that oppose Him. The Lord strengthens the arms of His friends. The Lord smites the sword from the arms of His enemies. The Lord upholds the arms of those that trust in Him. If my arms are strong, it is of the Lord. If my arms are weak, it is of myself.

**Wednesday** *Read Ezekiel 31* **My Branches**

I am as a tree, planted by the rivers of water. If my branches grow long and thick, it is not of me; it is of the air and the water. If my shadow is good for rest, if birds nestle in my boughs, it is not of me; it is of the sunshine and the rain. Let me grow, but not in my own strength; let me grow in the strength of the Lord.

**Thursday**   *Read Ezekiel 32*   **My Darkness**

There come times, to me as to Egypt, when the Lord makes all the bright lights of heaven dark

*WEEK 118*

over me. It is that my soul may be light, and not that it may be dark. It is not that I may not see, but that I may not see the world, and that I may see God.

**Friday** *Read Ezekiel 33* **My Warning**

Those that warn me are many. The Lord has a myriad ways of guarding me. The Lord will not be blameworthy if I fall. They that warn me will not be blameworthy. The trumpets call here, they call there, and I lie upon my bed.

**Sat** *Read Ezekiel 34* **My Greediness**

I am one of the Lord's great flock. Where I feed, others also are to feed. Where I drink, there are many to drink. If I tread down the grass that I do not feed upon, and muddy with my feet the waters for others, what am I but a thief, a common thief? For all greed is theft.

# WEEK 119

**Sunday**  *Read Ezekiel 35*  **My Magnifying**

How vast the difference, whether I magnify myself against the Lord, or magnify the Lord, to the forgetting of myself! The first is the desolation of Mount Seir, the second is the exaltation of Mount Zion. For whosoever exalts the Lord shall himself be exalted, even to the heavens.

**Monday**  *Read Ezekiel 36*  **My New Heart**

That is what I need, O God,—a new heart. Not a new house, nor a new fortune, nor new garments; not new knowledge nor new philosophy; not new achievements even. No; what I need is new power of achievement, new capacity to enjoy, to bless and be blessed. What I need is a new heart.

**Tuesday**  *Read Ezekiel 37*  **My Revival**

Dry bones, in very truth, is all my life, O God. A life of disjointed plans, of fleshless purpose, of brainless pleasures. The mere skeleton of life, compared with what it might be, and should be. Touch my life, O God, with Thy reviving finger, and all these dry bones shall live.

**Wednesday**  *Read Ezekiel 38*  **My Security**

Those whom the Lord protects shall dwell securely, all of them. There is no security in walls or fortresses. There is no security in wealth or worldly power and wisdom. There is no security in anything that has been made, but in the Maker. In Him let me rest my confidence.

**Thursday**  *Read Ezekiel 39*  **My Revenge**

Let my revenge be a part of God's revenge upon His enemies. Let it be no more. Let it be no less. Let it reach as far as God's revenge reaches, and let it extend no whit farther. Then shall my revenge be safe, and then shall my revenge be holy.

**Friday** *Read Ezekiel 40* **My City**

I will build in my heart a city of God. Its every measurement shall be familiar to me. All its directions shall be known to me, its every outline. I will dream of its perfections. I will gloat over its coming glories. And the vision of it shall abide with me until it is realized.

**Saturday** *Read Ezekiel 41* **My Temple**

I will rear a temple for my God. Though it be only in my longings, only in my dreams, the temple shall be built; and the dream shall become substantial, piece by piece. It shall be conceived of God within my soul, each part of it formed by His creative Spirit. And if it is thus conceived and fashioned, no fear but it shall come to birth.

# WEEK 120

**Sunday**  *Read Ezekiel 42*  **My Holy Places**

In all my life planning I must leave room for the holy places. Those spaces are more valuable than the work-shops of my life, richer than the treasure chambers, wiser than the library. They are places of withdrawal from the world, places of meeting with God. O my God, meet me there every day!

**Monday**  *Read Ezekiel 43*  **My Glorification**

My house is not glorified till the glory of the Lord has entered it. The glory of beauty may be there, yet it is not glorified. The glory of power may be there, and all the glitter of wealth, yet it is not glorified. But when the glory of the Lord enters its holy places, then my house shall shine as the sun.

**Tuesday**  *Read Ezekiel 44*  **My Ministering**

Whatever I do for the Lord—and should not all my deeds be for the Lord?—shall be done with a pure heart and clean hands. Oh, let me not venture otherwise into the presence of His purity and power! My service shall be service for a King, done in royal fashion and with kingly intent.

**Wednesday**  *Read Ezekiel 45*  **My Measures**

I must see to my standards. Whatever I measure out to men must be dealt forth out of true measures. It may be time or thought or any form of service. Whatever it is, let it be just weight, full quantity, pressed down, heaped up, running over.

**Thursday**  *Read Ezekiel 46*  **My Offerings**

Gifts for the Lord must be fit gifts. They must be such as He desires. They must be regularly presented. Such be my service, O God most

*WEEK 120*

worthy! Such be my offerings, due and desired! Let me not neglect them, nor stint them, nor cheat myself in seeking to cheat Thee!

**Friday** *Read Ezekiel 47* **My Evangelism**

That wonderful river should flow from my life, for I, I also, am a temple of the living God, and forth from my life should flow a fountain of living water. It should increase as it flows, broadening and deepening. It should reach to every nation. And everything should live, whithersoever those waters come.

**Saturday** *Read Ezekiel 48* **My Portion**

Share and share alike, equal in breadth, straight across the land of blessedness,—so shall fare the people of God! And if my neighbor's lot is fairer than mine let me rejoice. If it is more fruitful, let me be sincerely glad.

# WEEK 121

**Sunday**     *Read Daniel 1*     **My Fare**

Let my food be pulse and water, O God of temperance and power! I would be strong in will to resist the temptations of the senses, that I may be strong in body to do Thy will. Grant Thy help for this, my Father.

**Monday**     *Read Daniel 2*     **My Insight**

Things which man's wisdom cannot understand, Thou wilt reveal to the simple. It is not in the minds Thou hast created to pierce the mysteries of the universe, but it is in them to receive Thy revelation of all mysteries. Oh, let me do Thy will, that I may know Thy doctrine!

**Tuesday**     *Read Daniel 3*     **My Furnace**

When I bow down to God, and will not bow down to mammon, a furnace is kindled for me, and hot anger rages against me. It is a real furnace, and no mirage. It is a genuine peril, and no fancy. But from the midst of the fire moves the God of the fire, and stands by my side! Whom or what shall I ever fear?

**Wednesday**     *Read Daniel 4*     **My Seeming**

I do not go upon hands and knees and eat grass with the brutes, but often my soul goes upon all fours and wallows in the sty. What to me that I look like a man if inwardly I am a beast?

**Thursday**     *Read Daniel 5*     **My Warning**

I have a kingdom. Though it is small, it is all mine. Though it is poor, I am rich in it. I did not earn it or deserve it, but it was given me, and without my desert. Ah, let me see no warning over against it, no writing on the wall! I will acknowledge the Lord at all times, and His praise shall continually be in my mouth.

*WEEK 121*

**Friday**     *Read Daniel 6*     **My Lions**

There are lions in the way of doing God's will. They howl against me. They gnash their teeth upon my resolutions. They snarl upon my prayers. But I will continue to pray. And I will continue in the path. For I will remember how the lions slink away before God's sons advancing, and how they fawn about his feet who does God's will.

**Saturday**     *Read Daniel 7*     **My Fate**

Shall I be one of the saints, the judges of all the earth? or one of the evil beings that are judged? Am I to sit on a throne, or lie at the bottom of a pit? Which is to be my fate, of glory or shame, of misery or blessedness? Ah, my fate is in my own hands this day.

# WEEK 122

**Sunday**     *Read Daniel 8*     **My Sorrow**

When I hear of the woes of the world, do I faint like Daniel? Am I sick, as he was? When I perceive evil tendencies in the times, is my heart grieved as at a personal loss? How far, in reality, is the Kingdom of God my kingdom, and God's cause my cause?

**Monday**     *Read Daniel 9*     **My Confession**

If I should begin my confessions, and carry them through to the end, where should I begin and where should I make an end? For they must be as many as my days and as long as my years. I confess myself a sinner before Thee, O God who dost know all my sins. Yea, Thou dost know them better than I know them myself.

**Tuesday**     *Read Daniel 10*     **My Strength**

When I consider with whom I have to do, then my heart faints within me. When I remember whom I have offended, against whom I am in rebellion, who it is that stands before me as a Judge, my tongue is stricken and my spirit falls to dust. What strength have I in Thy presence, O my God, unless it be given me by Thyself?

**Wednesday**     *Read Daniel 11*     **My Exploits**

God has great deeds for me to do. I do not know what they are, because I do not know Him closely; but I do know Him, and that He has great plans for me. Oh, let me come to know Him better, that I may enter into His great plans for me, and, in His strength, carry them out!

**Thursday**     *Read Daniel 12*     **My Shining**

I wish to shine on earth, in these fleeting years of time. Ah, what folly to disregard the everlasting brilliance! I must be wise in the wisdom of God. In that wisdom I must turn men to God. That is the secret, the twofold blessed secret, of eternal shining.

### Friday       *Read Hosea 1*       My Name

Is my name Ammi, or Lo-ammi, God's, or not-God's? Not, What do men call me? but What does God call me? What is the new name, the character-name, the name of revealing, that will be conferred upon me in the land of open vision and frank naming?

### Saturday    *Read Hosea 2*    My Door of Hope

Dark though my life has been, it need no longer be dark. Hopeless though my future seem, it need no longer be hopeless. No, not an instant longer. The door of hope is at hand. Its knob is only a step before me. It is not locked. It is open. Some one stands there, beckoning to me.

# WEEK 123

**Sunday**   *Read Hosea 3*   **My Respite**

I need not fear: I shall have all chances for repentance. God will even hold me from my sinning by force at times, that when released I may not return to it. Oh, the patient planning of my Teacher! How doubly sinful to disappoint Him!

**Monday**   *Read Hosea 4*   **My Permission**

If I am thoroughly joined to my idols, the Lord will leave me alone. I am allowed to sin to the full, to heap up the measure of the divine wrath. Oh, fearful opportunity! Oh, terrible license!

**Tuesday**   *Read Hosea 5*   **My Search**

Though I go with flocks and herds to seek the Lord, and though I plan altars full of sacrifices, if my will is not sacrificed, if my heart goes not with me, then shall I seek the Lord in vain. Alas, to seek Him in vain who never turns from any sincere approach!

**Wednesday**   *Read Hosea 6*   **My Following**

I cannot know the Lord unless I follow on to know Him. Not in an hour or a day am I to know Him, whom all angels in all eternity can study without fully learning. It is an everlasting pursuit, this knowing God. How good that my God cannot be known in a day!

**Thursday**   *Read Hosea 7*   **My Beleaguers**

I am beset. I am surrounded. Turn one way, and enemies face me. Turn another way, and I am walled in by foes. Ah, it is my own doings that thus beset me about. Ah, it is my own miserable past that thus imprisons my present.

**Friday**   *Read Hosea 8*   **My Reaping**

I, who have sown the wind, do I think to reap other than the whirlwind? The seeds that lie in

*WEEK 123*

the furrows are even now peering above the soil. Has soil a transforming power? Will it change wind to sunshine?

**Saturday**  *Read Hosea 9*  **My Bread**

Have I so used my possessions that I cannot use them for God? Have my flocks been for my maw, so that they cannot lie upon the altar? Has my bread been for my appetite, so that it cannot be devoted to my God? Are my goods so selfishly mine that they can no longer serve my highest uses?

# WEEK 124

**Sunday**   *Read Hosea 10*   **My Time**

Verily it is time for me to seek the Lord. Long time have I sought other gods. Long time have I learned what they can do for me—what they can *not* do for me. The time of punishment has come. The time of disillusion has come. The time of death draws near. Surely, it is time, sad and shameful time, to seek the Lord.

**Monday**   *Read Hosea 11*   **My Bands**

Well might the Lord have led me with the cords of a wild beast, but He has drawn me ever with the cords of a man. Well might He have bound me with bands of terror, but He has constrained me with the bands of love. And yet, ah, wretch that I am! I rebel against His gracious guidance!

**Tuesday**   *Read Hosea 12*   **My Memorial**

Be my memorial the Lord, as He was the memorial of Israel! Let my life be so joined with His designs, my honor so associated with His glory, that there may be no separation of the two. I would merge my memory in the history of the Kingdom of God.

**Wednesday**   *Read Hosea 13*   **My Grave**

What place can be a grave for me? What death can have terror for me? Where is the sting of death and where its victory? There is no grave to him who lives with the Ever-Living; and there is no defeat, even by death, for him who dwells with God.

**Thursday**   *Read Hosea 14*   **My Return**

With words, for they are all that I have. With sacrifices of my lips, for I possess no other flocks. With humility and repentance and with fitting speech I will return to my God. For I am a prodigal, and I have spent all else in the far country.

**Friday** *Read Joel 1* **My Famine**

When I am without Thee, O God, I am without all things. I have no food without Thee, and all my fields are bare. I have no flock without Thee, and all my folds are empty. It is desolation without Thee, and yet I go running after the pestilence, and consort with the plague!

**Saturday** *Read Joel 2* **My Visions**

Why have I eyes, but to see more than is visible? Why am I on the earth, but to peer beyond the earth? Why am I in this life, but to know further than this life? O Lord, open Thou mine eyes! O God, enlighten my understanding!

# WEEK 125

**Sunday** *Read Joel 3* **My Valley**

"Multitudes, multitudes in the valley of decision!" And I there among them. I with my evil past. I with my gloomy future. I with my tainted present. Ah, but my Saviour is there, too. And therefore Hope is there.

**Monday** *Read Amos 1* **My Transgressions**

They are three, yea, four! They have been heaped up so long that God will not turn away the punishment. It will burn as a fire. It will weigh as a chain. It will devour the palaces of my peace. But God is in that fire.

**Tuesday** *Read Amos 2* **My Flight**

Am I swift? Flight shall perish from me. In the day of the Lord's wrath, of little avail are feet or wings. Though I took the wings of the morning, though my retreat were beyond the sea, it would be as if I moved not.

**Wednesday** *Read Amos 3* **My Prophecies**

I would not speak my own words in any speech. I would wait till God has spoken, and then repeat His words after Him. For my words are emptiness, and all their syllables are vain.

**Thursday** *Read Amos 4* **My Preparation**

I am preparing my food for the morrow and my clothing for the next season. I am preparing my work ahead of me, and the work I shall set others to doing. I am preparing to meet men, and show them my works and myself. But there is one preparation I am forgetting to make. Prepare to meet thy God, O my soul!

**Friday** *Read Amos 5* **My Enjoyment**

The houses I have built, shall I live in them? The vineyards I have planted, shall I eat of them?

## WEEK 125

The work I have done, shall I reap the rewards? Yes, if it was the Lord's work; but only in the Lord's time and only in the Lord's place. Would I have it in any other time or place?

**Saturday** *Read Amos 6* **My Ease**

I have a bed, but woe to me if I lie on it! Couches have I, but woe to me if I use them! There is no time for rest. There is only time for work. In work shall be my rest and my ease, all the days of my life!

# WEEK 126

**Sunday**   *Read Amos 7*   **My Opponents**

When men rise up against me, let me remember that they are only men. When they bid me be silent, let me inquire only what God would have me speak. When they threaten death, let me not forget that God offers life.

**Monday**   *Read Amos 8*   **My Famine**

I am hungry, and I do not understand what food I want. I am thirsty, and I forget what fountain will quench my thirst. I feed upon air, I drink the wind, I spurn bread and abhor water. The famine is in my soul; it is not in God's world around me.

**Tuesday**   *Read Amos 9*   **My Sifting**

God is sifting my life, as in a sieve. He shakes it back and forth, passions and powers and possessions, hopes and fears, ambitions and failures, what I am and what I might be. Back and forth He shakes it all, and not one grain of true wheat is allowed to fall to the ground.

**Wednesday**   *Read Obadiah*   **My Pride**

I have dwelt in the clefts of the rock, and have asked, " Who shall bring me down to the ground?" And the Lord has laid me low. I have mounted on high with the eagle, and made my nest with the stars, and the Lord has reached and taken me. No pride is safe from Jehovah; but all humility is His delight.

**Thursday**   *Read Jonah 1*   **My Flight**

I thought to escape duty, and a harder duty followed me. I would run away from God, and God piloted the vessel on which I sailed. I drew myself into concealment, and I drew Jehovah in with me. There is no fleeing from Thee, O God! My very flight is a summons to Thee.

## WEEK 126

**Friday**  *Read Jonah 2*   **My Repentance**

Out of the depths I cried to God. His waves and His billows were over me. His storms were round about me. I was afraid of His wrath. But I had learned to be even more afraid of myself. From my inner storms I turned to Him, even in His anger; and I found a haven of peace.

**Saturday** *Read Jonah 3* **My Proclamation**

Let me declare the will of the Lord. Though I am small and the city is very great. Though I am feeble and my enemies are very strong. Though my wisdom falters and my foes are shrewd. Let me proclaim the will of the Lord and all men shall fall down before it.

# WEEK 127

### Sunday     Read Jonah 4     My Gourd

How much more kind is God than men! He is patient while men strike, long-suffering while men berate. He is not too proud to forgive. He relaxes His penalties without fear for His authority. The vast sphere of the universe, and all therein, is my gourd to teach me the goodness of God.

### Monday     Read Micah 1     My Witness

It is the Lord, who will witness for me or against me. If for me, though all men and angels condemn me, I shall be safe and honored. If against me, though the universal voice applaud me, I shall go down to the everlasting shame.

### Tuesday     Read Micah 2     My Haughtiness

Where is my warrant for my pride? Why do I walk haughtily, the time being evil? Have I not sinned enough to bow my head? Should not my transgressions bend me to the dust?

### Wednesday     Read Micah 3     My Prophecy

Are my words weighty words? Yea, if the Lord be upon them. But if only I am borne thereon, any zephyr may carry them, any zephyr may blow them away. It is a great thing to speak the words of the Lord. There is no greater fortune to the sons of men.

### Thursday     Read Micah 4     My Security

Who shall make me afraid? The Lord's word is my bulwark! What attack shall confound me? Jehovah's promise is my fortress! My home is an impregnable castle though only a hut, if it is God's home as well as mine.

*WEEK 127*

### Friday  Read Micah 5  My Supremacy

But little among the thousands am I, as Bethlehem among the cities; but though I were as Nineveh I am nothing, and though I were as Babylon I am emptiness. Cometh the Lord from my life? That shall greaten it! Spring His deeds from my dust? They shall be my glory!

### Saturday  Read Micah 6  My Requirements

They are three heavy things that the Lord requires of me,—justice, and mercy, and humility! Heavy, because they require nothing of me but love. Heavy, because they mean only unselfishness. Heavy, because they would be so easy to one in whom dwelt the Spirit of Christ!

# WEEK 128

**Sunday**   *Read Micah 7*   **My Waiting**

I will bear the indignation of God. I will not chafe against His penalties. They are deserved penalties. It is an inevitable indignation. I will wait till He Himself plead my cause. I will wait, for the divine indignation will speak for me, and the divine penalty will be my advocate!

**Monday**   *Read Nahum 1*   **My Strong Hold**

The Lord is my strong hold. The strength of all that come against me is of Him, and subject to His permission. He that holds me holds them from me. What folly are the poor defences I contrive against them!

**Tuesday**   *Read Nahum 2*   **My Overthrow**

If the Lord come up against me, farewell to my proud possessions! They melt away like morning vapor, or like shadows before the sun. My jewels dissolve, my houses crumble, my robes vanish. Woe to me and mine, in the day when the Lord comes up against me!

**Wednesday**   *Read Nahum 3*   **My Warnings**

These whom the Lord has overthrown—let me consider: Am I better than they? Are my sins less? Is my pride less? Is my obedience greater than theirs? If they fell under deserved penalty, how shall I escape?

**Thursday**   *Read Habakkuk 1*   **My Gods**

Am I one whose might is my god? Do I sacrifice to my net and burn incense to my drag? Is my work my deity, do my achievements fill my pantheon? Yea, I need no wooden image to know the guilt and folly of the idolater!

**Friday**   *Read Habakkuk 2*   **My Faith**

Let it be my livelihood, my faith; that whereby I get goodly gain, and day's wages as the year is

*WEEK 128*

long. Let it be my life, my faith; that of which I breathe, that on which I feed, my pulse-beat, my vivifying joy. I am not just, but I am justified; and in that faith I live.

**Sat**  *Read Habbakuk 3*  **My High Places**

I will not live in the valley while I may live on the mountain. I will not mourn while I may rejoice. I will not rear my mountain, for it is already uplifted. I will not climb my mountain, for the Lord will place me on its summit.

# WEEK 129

**Sunday**  *Read Zephaniah 1*  **My Silence**

In the presence of the Lord I am to hold my peace. When His decree goes forth, my very heart is to be acquiescence. When He upbraids, I am to make no reply. My condemnation is fed by my complaint.

**Mon**  *Read Zephaniah 2*  **My Carelessness**

Am I one that says in his heart, "I am, and there is none else beside me"? Is my soul the joyous city that dwells carelessly? Am I heedless of others, reckless of myself, scornful of my God? Then shall my life become a desolation, a place for beasts to lie down in!

**Tuesday**  *Read Zephaniah 3*  **My Language**

When shall mine be the pure language, that calls upon the name of the Lord? When shall mine be the fruitful language, that issues in consenting service of God? No other speech is worthy of Thy son, O my Father! Thy name includes all that is high, and beautiful, and strong. Be Thy name my language forever.

**Wednesday**  *Read Haggai 1*  **My Building**

If my wealth is for myself, it is kept in a bag with holes. If my house is for myself, it will not shelter me. It is never a time to dwell in ceiled houses while the Lord's house lies waste. And the house of the Lord is love.

**Thursday**  *Read Haggai 2*  **My Courage**

I have no courage in me. My heart is not in me. I would not have my heart in me; I would rest it on the Lord. Jehovah shall be my courage and my strength. When I am my own courage, it is as water.

**Friday**  *Read Zechariah 1*  **My Comfort**

Though I am distressed, my prosperity shall

yet spread abroad. Though I am in despair, the Lord will yet comfort me. Though I am outcast, the King of kings will yet choose me, even me. And in the assurance of what is to come I will now lift up my head.

**Saturday** *Read Zechariah 2* **My Glory**

The Lord shall be the glory in the midst of my life. It shall be a burning glory, purifying all that is base. It shall be a shining glory, beautifying all that is ugly. It shall be an enlarging glory, ennobling all that is small and mean. All this will the Lord be to me.

## WEEK 130

**Sunday**  *Read Zechariah 3*  **My Rescue**

Surely I was a brand in the fire. The flames leaped upon me. Passions devoured me. They breathed hot breath against me, and my soul entered the horror of death. But surely I am a brand from the burning. A Hand has been reached forth. It has taken me from the fire. Soiled, black, charred,—ah, the beautiful white Hand!

**Monday**  *Read Zechariah 4*  **My Golden Oil**

When I run by my might, how am I distanced! When I fight by my power, how am I overthrown! When I shine by my light, how I flicker and go out! Feed Thou me, mysterious flowing Olive Tree! Not by my might or power, but by the might and power of Thy Spirit, O Thou only Strength of men.

**Tuesday**  *Read Zechariah 5*  **My Ephah**

When shall my wickedness be cast into a measure, and be borne away? When shall a weight of lead be cast upon it, to bury it forever? Ah, when I will! For the ephah is ready, and the weight has been provided.

**Wednesday**  *Read Zechariah 6*  **My Crown**

If I am to wear a crown, the Lord is fashioning it. The crowns I am wearing now shall fall to dust. The earth made them and the earth retains them. There are crowns that fall from heaven, and carry their crowned ones thither again.

**Thursday**  *Read Zechariah 7*  **My Fast**

Did I fast, and oppress the widow? Did I pray, and withhold compassion? Did I sing anthems, and imagine evil against my brother?

## WEEK 130

Therefore is my fast become a curse, and my prayer a pestilence, and my song a hissing in the ear.

### Friday   *Read Zechariah 8*   My Neighbor

Before the Lord can enter my house, I must enter the house of my neighbor. Truth I must take with me, and peace and good will. Then may God enter my house; but He enters no house that loves no neighbor.

### Saturday   *Read Zechariah 9*   My Prison

I am a prisoner, but a prisoner of hope! Deep is my dungeon, but not too deep for the sun. I have dwelt there long, and may dwell there longer, but I shall not be there forever. And when I look back, it will be upon the dark entrance of Paradise!

# WEEK 131

**Sun** *Read Zechariah 10* **My Remembering**

I will remember Jehovah in far countries. Far from His house, I will make a sanctuary among the heathen. Far from His peace, I will remember Him in the tumult of battle. Far from His joy, I will not forget Him though wretchedness surround me. And in the remembrance will be joy, and peace, and home.

**Monday** *Read Zechariah 11* **My Sheep**

Though I think I have no sheep, yet I have some. Others look up to me, others depend upon me. No man goes utterly lonely through the world. Am I the worthless shepherd, whose are the woes? or the faithful shepherd, whose are the joys of the flock and of their Owner?

**Tuesday** *Read Zechariah 12* **My Look**

Straight through the loving heart of my Father my sins have pierced. The blood of His anguish has flowed. The horror of my iniquity has been upon Him. Ah, that one look upon Him whom I have pierced! It will burn in my mind forever.

**Wed** *Read Zechariah 13* **My Fountain**

Foul indeed am I, and full of all uncleanness. It is not enough to wash me without when I am filthy within. The Fountain must be within me, and it must not merely lave me. Yes; and the Fountain will spring up within me at a wish.

**Thursday** *Read Zechariah 14* **My Evening**

I care not for the day, if the sun break forth in the evening. Let the last sky be cloudless, and the whole day is fair. So shall it be with me, according to Thy word, O God. After all storms and darkness, at evening time there shall be light.

*WEEK 131*

**Friday**   *Read Malachi 1*   **My Offerings**

The best for the Best! The best of my time, and not a hurried fragment hastily torn away. The best of my talent, and not what is unmarketable. The best of my goods, and not the worm-eaten. The best for the Best! Anything less leads to the worst.

**Saturday**   *Read Malachi 2*   **My Brothers**

The next man I meet has my Father for his own. The same love of God yearns out for him that awaits me. The same heaven, the same hell, are possible for him. Why, then, do I not fly to my brother? Why do we not walk together, at least a little way?

# WEEK 132

### Sunday     Read Malachi 3     My Tithes

My possessions are not mine. If I call them my possessions in my heart, it is because they have come to possess me. All that I have is the Lord's; and shall He not have His will with His own? What is the whole tithe but the whole? And if God return nine tithes, how liberal is He!

### Monday     Read Malachi 4     My Healing

Upon the first chapter of the Old Testament the sun arises, and upon the last the Sun of Righteousness. Between the two chapters how much of sin, how much of terrible warning! But in the last chapter is healing. My healing, as well as for the Israelites, for upon me also the Sun has risen.

### Tuesday     Read Matthew 1     My Immanuel

The Sun of Righteousness, no longer prophesied, has come indeed! Out of dawning, it is full day! With healing in His wings, He shall save His people from their sins. God with us! *My* God with *me!*

### Wednesday     Read Matthew 2     My Offerings

The offerings for which Malachi pleaded before he prophesied the coming of Christ, here, now that Christ is come, we see poured out by the wise men. Wise men indeed were they, and wise shall I be if I follow them, kneeling at Jesus' feet with my glad gifts.

### Thursday     Read Matthew 3     My Repentance

So closely is the Bible knit together that at the entrance to the New Testament stands the incarnation of the Old Testament. O that my life may heed the message of the Baptist! For there is only one door to the Door, and that is sincere repentance, leading to repentant deeds.

*WEEK 132*

**Friday**   *Read Matthew 4*   **My Testing**

Not only in the wilderness, but in the palace, comes the devil to me; and where he comes is wilderness. My temptations are not those of Jesus, yet they are the same. For all temptation is to forget others and seek self. From that temptation, O my unselfish Saviour, bring me into Thy salvation.

**Saturday**  *Read Matthew 5*  **My Blessedness**

When He that made blessedness points to humility as the highest gain, shall I pursue pride? When He exalts purity, shall I endure a stain? When He commends mercy, shall I be hard of heart? or mourning, shall I shrink from dark pathways? Is it because I, who am unhappy, am wiser than the Creator of all joy?

# WEEK 133

**Sunday**   *Read Matthew 6*   **My Hypocrisy**

I do not think myself a hypocrite. Does any one think himself a hypocrite? But the question is, Does God know me to be a hypocrite? And the test is, Would I be willing that all men should know me as He knows me? Ah, would I?

**Monday**   *Read Matthew 7*   **My Foundation**

Is my house built on the rock or on the sand? Will it endure the tempests that are sure to come? Will it remain stanch when swept by the dark waters of death? Do I reach down to what is solid, and am I comforted, daytime and nighttime, by the Great Certainty?

**Tuesday**   *Read Matthew 8*   **My Demons**

Yes, I too am possessed of demons. They lead me with them to solitary places. They tear my soul. They cause me to do shameful things, and separate me from my kind. But Thou, O Christ, art greater than my demons; even a legion of them is less than Thy least whisper.

**Wednesday**   *Read Matthew 9*   **My Touch**

If I but touch the hem of Christ's garment with the hand of faith, I shall be made whole. If I clasp Him and cling to Him with the hand of unfaith or of half-faith, it is nothing. Oh, to believe my beliefs!

**Thursday**   *Read Matthew 10*   **My Mission**

If Christ sends me forth (and Christ does send me forth), He will go with me. What I carry will not matter, in my purse or in my hand. How I am received will not matter, whether with praise or a blow. I shall go with Christ, and I shall go to success.

### Friday  Read Matthew 11  My Yoke

The trouble is, I am bearing my own yoke. I have chosen it. I have fashioned it to my shoulders. I have fixed the burden on it. And it is weighing me to the earth. Oh, let me throw it off! Lay upon me, O Christ, Thy yoke, which is easy, and Thy burden, which is light.

### Saturday  Read Matthew 12  My Sabbaths

Do I truly yield up to Christ one-seventh of my time? He made the Sabbath for me; am I using it, not for myself, but for the world? not for the eternities, but the temporalities? He made the Sabbath. Should not He best know how to use it?

# WEEK 134

### Sunday  Read Matthew 13  My Receiving

How good is God to me! How He pours forth His bounty, like the myriad seeds of the summer! It is no question of seed, it is a question of soil. Is my heart ready to receive God's gifts? Is my life eager and swift to use them?

### Monday  Read Matthew 14  My Daring

Waves dash around me, as they rose and fell before Peter. Waves of trouble. Waves of fear. Waves of passion. I can walk upon them, if I will, for my Lord bids me to. Or I can sink in them, if my faith fails, though the Lord is standing by. Ah, which shall it be, on my Gennesaret?

### Tuesday  Read Matthew 15  My Persistence

When Jesus repulses me, as He repelled the Syro-phœnician, it is not to drive me away, but to draw me near. It is to spur my resolution, test my courage, and render me more worthy of my desires. Let me not complain, then, at the divine delays. They are divine invitations.

### Wednesday  Read Matt. 16  My Self-Seeking

My mistakes are only one, and that is all-comprehensive. It is in following self instead of Christ. It is in seeking gain and not God. What I find, when I seek gain, is only my wretched self. What I find, when I seek God, is eternal gain.

### Thursday  Read Matthew 17  My Demon

Why cannot I cast him out? For the same reason that kept the disciples from healing the epileptic. Because I have not faith. No faith, not even a mustard-seed of faith, for that would be enough. O Christ, be Thou my faith, as Thou wilt be. Then shall I get rid of my demon.

*WEEK 134*

### Friday  Read Matthew 18  My Stumbling

Let me clear my path before me! Evil desires, unholy passions, worldly ambitions, faithless worries, let them all be cleared from my path. If anything is an occasion of stumbling, however dear, however familiar, let me cast it from me. A clear path, from earth to heaven! Can any rejected joy equal that?

### Saturday  Read Matthew 19  My Riches

To leave all and follow Christ,—be that my bank account! To give gladly and freely,—be that my treasury! I would be rich, but with the enduring riches. Oh, make me a millionaire of heaven, Thou heavenly Treasurer, though I become a pauper on earth!

# WEEK 135

**Sunday**  *Read Matthew 20*  **My Vineyard**

I have a work to do, a corner of the vineyard to till. God has a reward to give. If he choose to give it for past work, for belated work, the greater His glory and the more my grief. I receive the pay. Ah, yes; but I have not done the work.

**Monday**  *Read Matthew 21*  **My Triumph**

When Christ, the Lord, next goes on a triumph, shall I be of His retinue? Shall I have a share in His plaudits? Shall I be admitted to His joy? For no Calvary is to follow that triumph. No cross is to attend that crown. It is to be all glory, and forever.

**Tues**  *Read Matt. 22*  **My Wedding Garment**

Service is not enough, though the service be ever so faithful. No service suffices without soul. It is never enough to lavish time without thought, nor thought without love, nor love without joy. It is never enough to go to the wedding, if one goes as to a workshop.

**Wednesday**  *Read Matt. 23*  **My Hypocrisy**

I am what I am within, and not what I am outwardly. It is easy to cheat myself with my mirror. It is easy to see myself reflected in men's praises, and approve myself and fall in love with myself. But that is not I, not at all I. I am what I am within.

**Thursday**  *Read Matt. 24*  **My Expectation**

Men live jokingly over a mine that may any day explode. Men feast amid the falling cinders of an active volcano. Men saunter through streets that quiver with earthquakes. Ah, the folly of those that live to the day, and take no thought for the hereafter!

*WEEK 135*

**Friday**   *Read Matthew 25*   **My Talents**

It is not how many talents I have, but what I do with what I have. It is not what gain I make with my talents, but what attempt I make to increase them. God will not hold me accountable for what is not of man; he will hold me accountable for my desire.

**Saturday**   *Read Matt. 26*   **My Gethsemane**

To feel one's self abandoned by man. To feel one's self an outcast from love. To be unvalued, unpraised, neglected, scorned. To see the heavens black overhead. To hear no echo of my prayer. To be alone in eternity. That is to enter Gethsemane. This is the triumph of faith, not to be alone in Gethsemane. To say, Christ also has been here; therefore, though I cannot see Him, He is here with me.

## WEEK 136

**Sunday**     *Read Matthew 27*     **My Cross**

I crucified with Christ? What nail has yet pierced my body or my soul? Upon what rack of agony have I yet been stretched, even an hour, for the love of man? What darkness has been thrust upon me by the hatred of enemies,— enemies made by my righteous zeal? I crucified with Christ? Nay; I have not yet crept to the foot of Calvary.

**Monday**   *Read Matthew 28*   **My Comrade**

Lo, He is with me alway. To the end of the world He is with me, to the end of all worlds, if I am one of His disciples. Do I rejoice in the gladness of His presence? Do I realize my glorious partnership? Why, all life should be a sunrise in the joy of it!

**Tuesday**     *Read Mark 1*     **My Fishing**

A fisher of men! For what am I fishing? Is it for gold dollars? Is it for a laurel wreath? Is it for costly raiment? Or is the end of my search, the real longing of my soul, my brother's heart? What is my toil for, truly? And is Christ in the boat with me?

**Wednesday**     *Read Mark 2*     **My Palsy**

I am borne of four; yea, of more than four. What friends, what countless holy influences, carry me Christward! And I need Him so, with my palsied soul! Yet ever I shake them all off, and flee from the house where the Healer is. Ah, my palsy itself has become dear to me!

**Thursday**   *Read Mark 3*   **My Discipleship**

Twelve? Nay; twelve hundred; twelve hundred million! My Lord appointed the Twelve

*WEEK 136*

just to show how He appoints all, how He appoints me. It is the highest honor of earth and heaven, and it is veritably mine.

**Friday**      *Read Mark 4*      **My Fear**

To be sure, the wind rages, and the lightning flashes, and the waves run high. To be sure, the boat tosses, and seems about to swamp. But Christ is in the boat, and fear is folly. Christ is in the boat, and it is as safe as any couch upon the land.

**Saturday**      *Read Mark 5*      **My Solitude**

Why do I go apart from men? Is it to meet God, or devils? Is it to build myself up, or to tear myself down? Is it to pray or to rage in frenzy? Ah, let me know that I certainly am not what I am in the throng, but what I am in the desert.

# WEEK 137

**Sunday**  *Read Mark 6*  **My Witnessing**

I am not called to bear witness before a king like John the Baptist; but I am to bear witness for a king. I may not be called to lay down my life in the way he laid down his, but I am called to lay down my life. God grant me his courage for his sacrifice!

**Monday**  *Read Mark 7*  **My Hand-Washing**

I would have clean hands; but let me not call my hands clean, though they be white as snow, if they obey a filthy heart. I would carry about a pure body; but let me count the least defilement of my soul as more deplorable far than a body whelmed in the mire. May I be washed, within and without, in the Fountain of Life!

**Tuesday**  *Read Mark 8*  **My Profit**

As I rise in the morning, I will say, "To-day let me seek the true gain." As I fall asleep at night, I will say, "Come, now; let me reckon up my true gains." Not the winning of goods, but the bestowing of blessings. Not the receipt of praise, but the strengthening of character.

**Wednesday**  *Read Mark 9*  **My Maiming**

If my goods cause me to stumble in the Christian path, I must count it a gain to give them away. If my talents cause me to stumble, I must know that I am more talented when I forget them utterly. Whatever I do not use for the Master masters me, and I am better off without it, till I can master it.

**Thursday**  *Read Mark 10*  **My Glory**

Is what I wish a share in the Saviour's glory, or in the love and self-sacrifice that make the glory? Do I seek the crown without the cross, Olivet without Calvary? Then I am one of those endlessly foolish ones that expect something out of nothing; nay, the greatest thing of all the universe out of the least thing in all the universe.

**Fri** *Read Mark 11* **My Money-Changing**

Am I one of those whom Christ would drive from His Father's temple with a scourge? Yes, if I take into that temple my own self-interest, though only the gloating over a successful bargain, though only the planning for a bargain on the morrow. For the temple is for God and man, and not for self. It is for eternity, and the things of eternity, and not for bubble-blowing.

**Saturday** *Read Mark 12* **My Mite**

Let me give as the poor widow gave! If I give as she gave, I shall have nothing left. If I give as she gave, I shall have all things gained. She entered, bearing her whole livelihood. She went away, bearing life, which is better than livelihood.

# WEEK 138

**Sunday**   *Read Mark 13*   **My Endurance**

There will be much to endure,—wars and rumors of wars, fightings within and without, fears and tumults and hatreds and despair. But nothing will befall me that I cannot endure, with Christ; and if I endure to the end, I shall be saved. An endurance how brief, for a salvation endless and entire!

**Monday**   *Read Mark 14*   **My Forsaking**

If they all forsook Him and fled, may not I? Am I stronger than Peter the rock? Am I wiser than James? Am I more alert than Andrew and Philip? Am I more loving than John? Am I readier and more self-denying than Matthew? If they forsook Him, must not I fear that I shall forsake Him, and guard myself in that fear at every point?

**Tuesday**   *Read Mark 15*   **My King**

He was the King of the Jews, of those who had denied Him, and given Him up. He was the King of the Romans, of those who were crucifying Him, unjustly and cruelly. He was King of the Greeks, who were looking on, in the enjoyment of a new sensation. He was the King of all the unborn ages. Yea, my King, Lord of my body and soul, of all I am and have, hung there on the awful cross!

**Wednesday**   *Read Mark 16*   **My Risen Life**

When they, the early disciples, had entered into the joy and power of the resurrection, they went forth everywhere preaching Christ, mysterious attestations attending their words. And all, ever since, who have entered into the joy and power of the resurrection have proved that en-

*WEEK 138*

trance by the same going forth. Oh, be mine the risen life, and no longer the cell life of the worm!

**Thursday** *Read Luke 1* **My Magnificat**

Let my soul magnify the Lord, for the Lord has magnified me! He has greatened me and exalted me and overpassed my hopes with His bounty. I cannot overpass Him or enlarge Him, but I can magnify my love for Him, and my service, and my praise. O my soul, magnify the Lord!

**Friday** *Read Luke 2* **My Good Tidings**

"Good tidings of great joy," and "to all people." News. Most joyful news. To all. Then to me. Have I really received it? Why, then, am I not joyful?

**Saturday** *Read Luke 3* **My Repentance**

I have only one evidence of repentance, and that is the fruits of repentance. I have tried others. I have presented the feeling of repentance, but that has been rejected. And the words of repentance, but they have been refused. Ah, the deeds of repentance! They have brought peace to my soul.

# WEEK 139.

**Sunday**　　Read Luke 4　　**My Temptation**

My Lord would not have suffered His temptations if they had not been my temptations also. He conquered them to show me how I may conquer them: by resistance of evil; by hatred of sin, in thought as well as deed; by prayer; by the sword of the Spirit, the invincible Word!

**Monday**　　Read Luke 5　　**My Friends**

All around me are those that need my Saviour. They are sick, and He is the Physician. They are ignorant, and He is the Teacher. They are lost, and He is the Good Shepherd. I know the way to Him, and they do not. How am I worse than the ugliest churl if I do not help to carry them to Him, yea, even though I must break through roofs to lower them at His feet?

**Tuesday**　　Read Luke 6　　**My Appointment**

What an eternal honor it would be, to have one's name enrolled among those Twelve! What twelve names, among the sons of men, have received a more glorious privilege? Ah, none; but every name that has confessed Jesus to be Lord has a privilege as glorious. My name, even mine, may stand among the ever-widening Twelve!

**Wednesday**　　Read Luke 7　　**My Doubts**

When I share the doubts of John, in his moody prison, let me go forth with John's messengers and see Jesus at work. Let me see Christianity opening blind eyes, raising up the lame, cleansing the leper, raising the dead! In the sunshine of that joy my doubts will melt away.

**Thursday**　　Read Luke 8　　**My Storms**

Tempests arise in my soul more terrible than any on the Sea of Galilee. I am not as fearful of

*WEEK 139*

them as I should be, and yet I am fearful. But I am not often so terrified as to be driven to the One who alone can still them, the One who is with me in the boat.

**Friday**  *Read Luke 9*  **My Life**

Let me once clearly know what my life is, and I shall begin to live! But I follow a no-life, a mirage, a sham of a life, and deem myself to be living. Could I lose that life, it would be my life's chief gain.

**Saturday**  *Read Luke 10*  **My Neighbor**

My neighbor is he who has fallen among thieves. Yes, and my neighbors are the priest and the Levite, who passed by on the other side. Perhaps they are in sorer need of me than the wounded man, for their hurts are in a deeper, more difficult part. My neighbor is he that needs me, in any way, body or soul.

# WEEK 140

**Sunday**   *Read Luke 11*   **My Request**

What do I desire of the Lord? Is it something that He can grant? Yes, always. For what I really desire is not the wild and foolish thing that often springs to my lips, and that He would no more give me than a kind father would give poison to his child that cried for it. What I really desire is the joy and peace that my Father is always eager for me to have.

**Monday**   *Read Luke 12*   **My Anxiety**

How do I most surely disclose the folly of my heart? By my foolish fears. I have God for my Father, and tremble like a forlorn orphan. I have all the wealth of the universe, and go ragged like a pauper. When shall I believe my beliefs and confide in my confidence?

**Tuesday**   *Read Luke 13*   **My Leaven**

Is the leaven of the Word really hidden in my heart? If it is, let me look to my life. It cannot remain without a witness of itself. It cannot tarry in one place. It must permeate. It must become my life, my self.

**Wednesday**   *Read Luke 14*   **My Promotion**

What seat do I occupy at the feast of life? Am I in the lower seats, and discontented? Am I in the lower seats, and there in the expectation that I shall be asked to go up higher? There is no virtue in that. But am I in the lower seats because I really think that I belong there? Because I honor others and distrust myself? Then I may some day be invited higher.

**Thursday**   *Read Luke 15*   **My Joy**

What constitutes my pleasure? Eating and drinking and wearing and getting and owning?

*WEEK 140*

In none of these things can I have fellowship with the joy of my Lord. His joy is in what others eat and drink and wear and get and own. Can I attune my joy to His?

**Friday**      *Read Luke 16*      **My Fidelity**

A key is a small thing, but it opens a large thing. No test is a small thing that determines our fitness for a large thing. And every act of life is a test, and every lot in life is an examination, and the humblest life on earth, if well lived, may become the passport into the sublimest kingdom of eternity.

**Saturday**      *Read Luke 17*      **My Profit**

I am an unprofitable servant. At the best, my service yields no surplus, nothing over and above my duty. I can no more than earn my living, I can make no profit for my Master. Oh, may that Master look leniently on His slave!

# WEEK 141

**Sunday**  *Read Luke 18*  **My Importunity**

O my Judge! O my Physician! With an eagerness more than any wronged, more than any sick, I come to Thee. Thou hast all I need, and in over-abundance. And Thou hast this that I need most of all, the willingness to give. Thou dost ask only the asking. Thou eager and I eager, shall not I receive?

**Monday**  *Read Luke 19*  **My Colt**

My Master sends to me for many things. "The Lord hath need of them," the messengers say. "And I also, I have need of them," say I. Ah, fool that I am, not to know that what the Lord borrows He returns tenfold!

**Tuesday**  *Read Luke 20*  **My Tribute**

I render to Cæsar the things that are Cæsar's, and to God things that are God's; but do I render to God *all* that is His? And do I not render to Cæsar far more than is his? It is so easy to stint heaven, and it is so hard to stint earth!

**Wednesday**  *Read Luke 21*  **My Mites**

Shall I give the widow's mites? That is, shall I give my all? It would not be a small sum, as was hers; and yet, large or small, it must be my all to equal hers. Oh, how pitiful are my gifts, after all! How little do they cost me, and how foolishly I overestimate them! May the Holy Spirit show me myself, and in opening my eyes may He open my purse.

**Thursday**  *Read Luke 22*  **My Pitcher**

Whatever my task, though it be only drawing water from the well, it may be the token for the messengers of the Most High. By my perform-

*WEEK 141*

ance of it I shall be known to be the Lord's. In the doing of it will come my highest honor, my connection with the noblest renown.

**Friday** *Read Luke 23* **My Herod**

My Herod is the one on whom I throw, or try to throw, the tasks that God has given me to do, the problems that God has given me to solve. It is all emptiness, for no one can do my work for me, or solve my perplexities, but I pretend it to myself. Any excuse will deceive me, and I think that God is deceived when I am!

**Saturday** *Read Luke 24* **My Stupidity**

The Lord is by my side, and I do not see Him. He talks with me as I walk, and I do not hear Him. He prepares food for me, and I do not thank Him. I see only common men and hear only common sounds. Ah, when shall I open my eyes, and when shall I unstop my ears?

# WEEK 142

**Sunday**　　　*Read John 1*　　　**My Light**

The true Light has shone upon me, as upon every one that has come into the world. But, seeing, have I seen it? As it shines in and through the light of the sun, and all things that have been made, do I foolishly see the natural light and catch no gleam of the Light behind the light? That is to be blind indeed.

**Monday**　*Read John 2*　**My Money-Changing**

I do not set up a bank in the house of God, or open my ledger there before men's eyes; but what, before the eyes of God, do I bring into the sacred precincts? What greeds, what ambitions, what worries, what animosities! Were Christ to come again with the whip of cords, would He lash backs alone, and not also souls?

**Tuesday**　　　*Read John 3*　　　**My New Birth**

I am in this beautiful world of God's. Am I also in the far more beautiful kingdom of God? I belong to the world that passes away—ah, how rapidly! Do I belong to the world that endures—ah, how happily and surely? Let me, in the midst of all my toiling and getting, remember that there is nothing more important to me than this.

**Wednesday**　　*Read John 4*　　**My Thirst**

I know the waters of earth. I have drunk of the well of pleasure, the well of knowledge, of other wells as promising. And I am as thirsty as before. But there is a well from which I have never gone thirsty away, a well whose water reaches to the innermost longings, and satisfies them wholly. O Jesus Christ, my Joy and my Portion forever!

*WEEK 142*

**Thursday** *Read John 5* **My Waiting**

He had waited thirty-eight years for the Healer, —that sick man by the pool of Bethesda; but it was all as a day, after the Lord had cured him! And I, if the Lord bids me wait in my sorrows and trials the rest of my life,—yet there will come a time when He will take me by the hand, and bid me arise, and all my grief will be forgotten in that hour.

**Friday** *Read John 6* **My Bread**

I eat; but what do I eat? I eat; but I am not fed. The bread I eat is not the true bread, the living bread, the life of the Living One. I eat ashes, and call it bread; yes, and beg for more ashes, and moan because I have not enough.

**Saturday** *Read John 7* **My Will**

Do I know Christ's teachings, know them inwardly, rejoicingly, powerfully? Alas, no! but only, or chiefly, with the mind. It is because I do not will Christ's will. When His will is my will, His wisdom also will be mine, and will shine in all my living.

# WEEK 143

**Sunday**     *Read John 8*     **My Freedom**

I am to know the truth, and the truth is to make me free. If, then, I feel myself constrained and in bondage to anything, it is because I do not know the truth. I may know it with the head and not with the heart. I may know it with the heart and not with the life. At any rate, I do not know it.

**Monday**     *Read John 9*     **My Certainty**

Sceptics may seek to confuse me, but they shall not confuse me. Worldlings may ridicule me, but they shall not disturb me. One thing I know, and that knowledge cannot be shaken: that once I was blind, but now I see. I was blind to the best things in time and eternity, and now, in all their glory, they have entered into my life.

**Tuesday**     *Read John 10*     **My Door**

Am I seeking other doors than the one Door? other entrances to joy? other portals to power? other ways to wisdom? If I am, let me turn from them with scorn, knowing how empty is the hope they hold out. For there is no door but one, to all that I wish to reach.

**Wednesday**  *Read John 11*  **My Resurrection**

Out of the deaths I die daily, my Resurrection, O my Lord! Out of my fears of the death to come, my Resurrection, O Christ! Out of all danger of the eternal death, my Resurrection, O my Saviour!

**Thursday**     *Read John 12*     **My Spikenard**

It is not much I have that is precious and fragrant; but how happy I am that I have anything that is at all fit to pour out at my Saviour's feet!

*WEEK 143*

The cost? It is a privilege! The trouble? It is a joy! The sneers of men? They are my crown!

**Friday**      *Read John 13*      **My Basin**

In what way am I following my Lord's example, and washing the feet of my brothers, as He bade me? What is my basin? What is the towel wherewith I gird myself? Though I possess many goods, that basin shall be my most valued possession. Though my garments are many and rich, I shall have no garment so highly esteemed.

**Saturday**      *Read John 14*      **My Worries**

Every worry is a direct trangression of my Lord's command not to let my heart be troubled. It is an admission that I do not believe in God, or in my Saviour. It is a proof that the Comforter whom Christ sends is not with me. It is a denial of my faith, a negation of my religion.

# WEEK 144

**Sunday**  *Read John 15*  **My Source**

I am a branch. That I cannot avoid. But of what vine am I a branch? Of the True Vine, or the false vine? Of the vine whose sap flows eternally and pure, or of the vine whose sap will soon dry up and the stalk wither away?

**Monday**  *Read John 16*  **My Comforter**

He is the Comforter of the nations, yet He deigns to comfort my distresses. He is the support of Paul and Luther and all men of might, yet He condescends to my feebleness, and does not call it condescension. God of very God, one of the blessed Trinity, and yet mine!

**Tuesday**  *Read John 17*  **My Glory**

If even Christ is glorified in His followers, glorified with the glory which He had with the Father before the world was, then surely Christ's followers are glorified with Christ. Ah, to seek the petty glory of the world, the transitory applause of time, when this eternal renown is within my reach!

**Wednesday**  *Read John 18*  **My Denial**

Not in saying that I do not know Christ; I would not say that; but in saying that I know Him, and then not knowing Him. Not in denying my Lord, but in confessing Him, and falsely. In that is my peril. For between a traitorous denial and a hypocritical confession there is little to choose.

**Thursday**  *Read John 19*  **My Calvary**

It is there that I should be, if sin had its way with me. It is there that I should suffer, if my punishment were what I deserve. I am not there, because He was there. I am not suffering, I shall not suffer, because He suffered; nay, because He suffers still!

### Friday      Read John 20      My Doubts

I have had my doubts, but the blood from the cross has washed them all away. I have had questions, but the wounds in His hands and feet have answered them all. If I am ever sceptical, it is because I am far from Christ. When He is with me, I know! I know!

### Saturday      Read John 21      My Proof

If I would show my Lord how I love Him—as I would—let me show Him how I love those whom He loves. Let me take His place, so far as I can take His place, and do the things that He would do. Let me minister in His stead and in His name. That will be proof to Him that I love Him, and all the proof He needs.

# WEEK 145

**Sunday**    *Read Acts 1*    **My Power**

If Christ promises power, the power will come; but it will come in the way Christ promises, and at the time He names. If I seek from the world, from my own wisdom, from my friends, the power that Christ promises to send through the Holy Spirit, I shall seek forever in vain.

**Monday**    *Read Acts 2*    **My Pentecost**

Perhaps with the rushing of a mighty wind, perhaps with the still, small voice. Perhaps with flaming tongues of fire, perhaps in midnight darkness. What care I how it comes, if only it does come? if only the power of the Holy Spirit rests upon me, and enables me to work for God?

**Tuesday**    *Read Acts 3*    **My Gifts**

Silver and gold, if I have it, and if silver and gold are needed by any man; not always, however, silver and gold. Often a kind word is the best of silver, and a warm handshake is the richest of gold. My wealth, whatever it is, to his need, whatever that is—this must be the rule of my giving.

**Wednesday**    *Read Acts 4*    **My Goods**

Shall I follow the example of the early Christians, and hold whatever I have at the call of my brothers in Christ? Yes, if it is also the call of Christ! Not every call of man is to be heeded, for man's own sake; but every call of the Master is to be heeded for the Master's sake, and for man's.

**Thursday**    *Read Acts 5*    **My Withholding**

When am I akin to Ananias? Whenever, having dedicated to Christ my all, as I did when I joined Christ's church, I hold back from His ser-

*WEEK 145*

vice and refuse to His request any part of my all. Then I am brother to Ananias, and his fate, whatever befalls my outward body, befalls the body of my soul.

**Friday**      *Read Acts 6*      **My Serving**

Whether I am a deacon or not, have I not some deacon's work to do? Yes, while there are poor I know, while there are hungry I can feed, while there are weak I can strengthen. If each Christian is a king and a priest unto God, certainly each Christian is also a deacon.

**Saturday**      *Read Acts 7*      **My Witnessing**

In the face of flying stones? Sometimes flying jibes are as hard and cut as deeply. Before pressing throngs of angry foes? Sometimes indifferent friends are opposition quite as harmful. But however God appoints, in quiet ways or tragic, I am to bear witness with my life, as Stephen bore witness with his; and it is to be to the death,—in ten minutes, or twenty years.

# WEEK 146

**Sunday**   *Read Acts 8*   **My Chariot**

Along some road of life a chariot is moving, and I am to draw near to the charioteer and explain to him the Word. I am not wise to explain it, but it will be given me in that hour what I shall say. How shall I know which chariot, of all that are moving along the road, is my chariot? Ah, if I approach the wrong one, no harm will be done!

**Monday**   *Read Acts 9*   **My Vision**

God grant me, on every Damascus road, a vision of the Lord whom I am persecuting! God show me, whenever I harm any of Christ's followers, Whom it is that I am harming! God cause me to fail, whenever my success would injure the Kingdom of Christ!

**Tuesday**   *Read Acts 10*   **My Prejudice**

If there is a man upon earth whom I call common and unclean, may the Lord cleanse me of that uncleanness in my soul! Lift me, O Christ, into that rare charity which loves all men, and sees in every man something to honor.

**Wednesday**   *Read Acts 11*   **My Cleaving**

If "with purpose of heart" I "cleave unto the Lord," all good things will cleave to me. That purpose will animate all other purposes, and give strength to all my living. All my perseverance will be made more persistent by it, and it will lead me into the success I crave.

**Thursday**   *Read Acts 12*   **My Chain**

Prison walls are around me, and prison chains are upon me. That they are not walls of stone or chains of iron makes no difference in my dire captivity. Chains of the spirit are as fearful as

## WEEK 146

chains of the body, and the walls that Satan builds are as terrible as any made by mortal mason. But He that opened the doors for Peter can open for me this severer prison.

**Friday** *Read Acts 13* **My Blindness**

If I am an Elymas, let me suffer the merciful fate which he suffered. Far better be blind from the sun for a season than blind forever from the Sun of Righteousness. Far better be led about this world by the hand, than cast hand and foot out of the heavenly world.

**Saturday** *Read Acts 14* **My Sacrifices**

How do men sacrifice to me? Whenever they bestow upon me any credit that belongs to God, as for any gift that He has given me, or any talent that He has bestowed upon me. Let me not receive honor from men. Woe unto me when all men speak well of me! Woe unto me when I fall under that most subtle of all temptations, and accept credit for what is not at all mine.

# WEEK 147

**Sunday**   *Read Acts 15*   **My Preferences**

I will learn to distinguish essentials of faith from non-essentials of form. I will learn my brother's wisdom and I will remember my own frequent folly. I will prove all things, the views and methods I dislike as well as those I like. And I will hold fast to the good.

**Monday**   *Read Acts 16*   **My Macedonian**

He may not live across the seas. He may not live in another city. He may live in my own town; nay, in my own house. And for years he may have been calling upon me to help him. O thou missionary God, help me to hear and heed all calls for help!

**Tuesday**   *Read Acts 17*   **My Unknown God**

Is my God an unknown God? Do I worship Him ignorantly? Is He a stranger to me, or half a stranger? How little time I give to communion with Him! I could not get acquainted with a petty man in so slight a time; how can I expect to know so easily the Lord of heaven and earth?

**Wednesday**   *Read Acts 18*   **My Confidence**

When God, for whom I speak, bids me not to fear nor to hold my peace, then fear is mistrust of Him, and silence is disobedience to Him. What fear is so great as the fear I should have of disobeying my God?

**Thursday**   *Read Acts 19*   **My Profit**

Shall I follow Christ so long as it costs me nothing, and leave Christ as soon as my purse is lightened? Ah, what is in Christ's purse! When I leave Him, I leave the silver and gold of all the earth, and the cattle upon a thousand hills!

## WEEK 147

**Friday**   *Read Acts 20*   **My Giving**

Let me so give as to show that I really believe it to be happier than receiving. Let me not ask to receive anything except larger opportunities of giving. Christ was the largest giver of all time, and He said that giving is more blessed than receiving. He knows.

**Saturday**   *Read Acts 21*   **My Readiness**

Prison or death, or any other fate that men call misfortune—let me be ready for it all, if God sees best to send it. I will not call it misfortune, if God sends it, or allow others to pity me. It is the best of good fortune, whatever it is, if it is the lot which God has picked out for me.

# WEEK 148

### Sunday    Read Acts 22    My Citizenship

Am I a citizen of the Kingdom? Am I proud of it? Do I rely upon that citizenship for my safety? Do I depend upon it for my joy? Have I other honors of which I am more proud? Are there other allegiances that bind me more closely?

### Monday    Read Acts 23    My Cheer

If I am giving testimony for my Master, let me count that fact my passport of safety. Let it be my good cheer, that, as I have testified for Him thus far, I am to testify for Him farther, even as far and as long as His Kingdom needs me. And longer than that I do not want to speak in this world.

### Tuesday    Read Acts 24    My Conscience

Ah, but it needs endeavor, strenuous exercise, urgent will and purpose, to have a conscience always void of offence toward God and toward men! By no lax dallying is that great boon to be won. Not for an instant is it to be held subsidiary to other aims. My conscience is a jealous mistress. Ah, but a beautiful one!

### Wednesday    Read Acts 25    My Appeal

Not to Cæsar, not to any man, shall be my appeal. But let me not say this, and then in my heart, or with my desires and envies and fears, make such an appeal to men and the affairs and powers of men. Let me hold my life serenely above what men can do or say to me.

### Thursday    Read Acts 26    My Visions

Heavenly visions, indeed! They have been visions of my Saviour, glorified, loving, mighty, my Master, my Guide, my everlasting King!

*WEEK 148*

They have held me entranced; and then I have gone away and straightway forgotten them, and straightway belied my nobler self. How often, oh, how often, I have been disobedient to the heavenly vision!

**Friday**     *Read Acts 27*     **My Belief**

When God comes to me, in any storm of life, and tells me that all is well with me and with those that are in the ship with me, and bids me be of good cheer,—how often He does thus come; as often as the storms themselves come!—let me say with Paul, "I believe God, and it shall be even so." What, otherwise, is the use of hearing God at all?

**Saturday**     *Read Acts 28*     **My Vipers**

Out of any fire one is liable to come and fasten upon my hand. Vipers of falsehood and calumny. Vipers of misgiving and worry. Vipers of harshness. Vipers of injustice. The woods are full of vipers, upon all shores! And I am to hold myself calm. And I am to shake them off into the fire. And I am to take no harm.

# WEEK 149

**Sunday**  *Read Romans 1*  **My Pride**

Be it my glory, to glory in the right things. Be it my shame, to be ashamed of the things that are right. If I do not glory in Christ, how can Christ ever glory in me? If I am ashamed of the gospel, how shall I by the gospel be rejected!

**Monday**  *Read Romans 2*  **My Legality**

If I do not in my heart the deeds of the law, what avails it that my body does them? The Judge of the law is not outside, but His throne is within my soul. How long shall I befool myself with looking upon my exterior life, and forgetting the evil within?

**Tuesday**  *Read Romans 3*  **My Justification**

Verily I have sinned, and fallen short of God's glory. What have I done but sin? But I have not fallen short of God's grace. I am unjust, but He is the Justifier. I am evil, through and through; but He, through and through, is Love.

**Wed**  *Read Romans 4*  **My Resurrection**

I have been buried in sin, as Christ in the grave. But He, when He rose, stretched forth His hand to me, and lo! I am risen with Him, I from my grave as He from His. It is a better resurrection, this of mine, than that of Lazarus.

**Thursday**  *Read Romans 5*  **My Peace**

Since I am freed from the dead body of sin, why do I not move freely? Since I am ransomed from darkness, why do I not sing in the light? Shall the child of the King despond, now that he has found the King's palace and the King?

*WEEK 149*

### Friday    Read Romans 6    My Service

I must serve. It is not mine to command, however I feign it. Shall I serve an evil master, or the Just One? For I must serve, but I can choose my master.

### Saturday    Read Romans 7    My Will

I will the good. I will the bad. I mourn over my folly. I rejoice in it. I shrink from wickedness. I long for a chance at it. Alas, my pitiful will, how weak it is, how pliant, how fluctuating! and how it needs to be guided and upheld by the just and mighty will of God!

# WEEK 150

### Sunday  Read Romans 8  My Helper

If God is for me—nay, *since* God is for me—who can be against me? What foe within, of all foes the most deadly and insidious, since He is within? And what foe without, however bold and insolent, since He is the Lord of heaven and earth?

### Monday  Read Romans 9  My Free Will

I am surrounded by a thousand opportunities and incitements to goodness. God means me to be good. But He also means me to choose goodness, not to have it forced upon me. It is His will that I shall be able to fall as well as rise. How am I recompensing His trust in me?

### Tuesday  Read Romans 10  My Listening

If belief comes of hearing, and salvation comes of believing, surely I am saved. I have heard very much; I have heard the whole gospel. Ah, but have *I* heard it, or only my ears? Has my soul listened? Has my life listened? Such hearing only is for salvation.

### Wednesday  Read Romans 11  My Fear

When I vaunt myself and am puffed up, with conceit of goodness or pride of attainment, let me look at those that have fallen. So much better than I, so much wiser and stronger than I, and yet they have fallen! And if they, why not I? Ah, let me humble myself before God!

### Thurs  Read Rom. 12  My Transformation

From fear to trust, from flesh to spirit, from envy to content, from weakness to power, from folly to wisdom, from ugliness to beauty, from sorrow to joy, from earth to heaven! Indeed I must be renewed for this transformation, and no one but the Infinite Father can effect it.

### Friday    *Read Romans 13*    My Debt

Though no man loves me, I am in a love-debt to all men; but Christ loves me with a love greater than the love of all the world, and all the world is His, and He bids me join Him in His love of all the world. Ah, but this is a blessed way of paying the endless debt I owe to Christ!

### Saturday    *Read Romans 14*    My Judging

I am not to judge any one, save one alone,—myself. I can know myself very poorly, and yet I can know myself better than I know any one else. I can know myself well enough to be ashamed to judge any one else!

# WEEK 151

### Sunday   Read Romans 15   My Pleasure

Do I take my pleasure with my Saviour? If I do, I take my pleasure in the pleasure of others. Is my satisfaction a lonely one? Then it will not be satisfaction very long.

### Monday  Read Rom. 16  My Fellow Workers

I am the stronger for all the strong men about me. My toil is the happier for all their cheerful labor. The swing of their activity carries me with it. Blessed be God, for all the comrade workers He has given me!

### Tuesday   Read First Cor. 1   My Wisdom

Let me not seek to be wise above my Lord. What unwisdom is more foolish than to vaunt one's self above the God of wisdom? When I would teach, let me first learn; and when I would learn, let me first empty myself of pride.

### Wednesday   Read First Cor. 2   My Mind

To have the mind of Christ! Ah, what honor, what glory, is so mysteriously exalted? To think God's thoughts after Him in human science—that is wonderful; but to think with the mind of God —that is the climax of faith.

### Thurs   Read First Cor. 3   My Foundation

Whether I know it or not, daily and hourly I am building my life. I am building it upon something,—gold or hay, silver or stubble. Some day it is to be tested, building and foundation and all. Ah, what of the trivial affairs that occupy me is to be compared with this affair about which I think so little?

### Friday   Read First Cor. 4   My Stewardship

Only one thing is required of me,—faithfulness to the task and powers entrusted to me. Not

*WEEK 151*

faithfulness to-morrow, but to-day. Not fidelity to an ideal, but the actual. Not loyalty to some impossible vision, but loyalty to the duty of the hour.

**Saturday** *Read First Cor. 5* **My Purity**

How easy is contamination! How little of evil leaven will leaven the whole lump of my life! How necessary is daily purifying, hourly watchfulness, instant readiness to repel the assaults of the devil!

# WEEK 152

### Sunday    *Read First Cor. 6*    **My Body**

My body a temple of the Holy Spirit of God! How impossible that seems, knowing all the evil that is in me! How possible it seems, knowing all the mercy that is in God!

### Monday    *Read First Cor. 7*    **My World**

It is my world. All things are mine, in Christ, the maker of all things. But it is a bubble world, though it is mine, and Christ's. Its fashion passes away. I will use it while it lasts, but it shall not use me.

### Tuesday    *Read First Cor. 8*    **My Liberty**

Grant, O God of my conscience, in whom I walk freely and boldly, that my freedom enslave not any one, and my boldness put not any to shame. Help me to live not as alone, but always as by the side of my brother; who may in many ways be stronger than I, but in some ways also weaker than I.

### Wednesday    *Read First Cor. 9*    **My Reward**

I have a right to my reward; but let me look carefully what reward I shall claim. It must not be a lower reward when I may claim the higher. It must not be a temporal reward if that would shut out the eternal recompense.

### Thursday    *Read First Cor. 10*    **My Escape**

Am I tempted? Is it hard to withstand? Am I almost persuaded to evil? In the temptation itself is hidden a way of escape, if I will seize upon it. I need not look to another hour; my salvation is in this very moment, this time of my testing and weakness.

*WEEK 152*

**Fri** *Read First Cor. 11* **My Remembrance**

When I bethink myself that Christ desired me to remember Him, how am I exalted! That I, a dust-grain of His universe, should take thought of Him! And then, when I bethink myself how empty is my life of that remembrance, how am I filled with shame and remorse!

**Saturday** *Read First Cor. 12* **My Gifts**

I cannot speak, but I can pray. I cannot evangelize, but I can testify. I cannot teach, but I can give. Something is given me; shall I fail to use it because it is not everything?

## WEEK 153

**Sunday** *Read First Cor. 13* **My Love**

What is my love? Is it the desire to be served, or to serve? Is it jealous absorption, or eager self-giving? Does it suffer long, or make others suffer long? Is it unfailing, or fluctuating? There is a love that is greater than even faith and hope. There is a love that is hardly to be called a grace at all. Which is mine?

**Monday** *Read First Cor. 14* **My Edifying**

I am not so unwise but I have some wisdom that will help others. I am not so weak but there is some one whom I can strengthen. My life is not so ruinous but there is some life that I can build up. And I shall best build up my own life if I seek ever to build up the lives of other men.

**Tuesday** *Read First Cor. 15* **My Victory**

If Christ has conquered death for me, why do I make His conquest of no effect through my fear and dread? If death has a sting for me, my own death or the death of my beloved, then Christ, so far as I am concerned, has not conquered death. Ah, is it not, rather, that He has not yet conquered me?

**Wed** *Read First Cor. 16* **My Stanchness**

I can quit me like a man, I can be strong, but only as I watch unceasingly, only as I stand fast in the faith. If, even in the faith, I stand unsteadily; if, even in the faith, I keep a poor guard against the allurements of the world and its sore temptations, I shall not acquit myself as a man, but as a child and a weakling.

**Thurs** *Read Second Cor. 1* **My Consistency**

In God shall be my yea and my nay and my Amen. If I agree always with Him, I shall not

*WEEK 153*

mind that I do not always agree with myself. He shall be my consistency, before my conscience and before men.

**Friday**   *Read Second Cor. 2*   **My Savor**

If I am of God, I shall be a test to other men, a standard, a praise or a condemnation. I shall not judge them, but God within me will judge them. The Christ-life will judge them. Do I shrink from this, as if it separated me from others? Nay, it joins me with Him, and with His!

**Sat**   *Read II. Cor. 3*   **My Transformation**

How shall I become Christlike? By looking upon Christ. Not by any deeds of mine, but by my love. I do not become like Christ by imitation, but by association. This is because it is not I that makes the transformation—how impossible for me!—but Christ, of His great love.

# WEEK 154

**Sunday** *Read Second Cor. 4* **My Affliction**

It is a light affliction, though it seems heavy at the time. It is light, because my Saviour carries it with me. It is but for a moment, though it seems sadly long. It is transitory, because though it lasted all my life, it would last only an instant in eternity.

**Monday** *Read Second Cor. 5* **My Newness**

If at any time I grow tired of my life, if it seems stale and unprofitable, let me know in that hour that I have wandered from Christ. For if I live with Him and in Him and He with me and in me, all will be new in my life from day to day. Everything will be fresh and interesting.

**Tuesday** *Read Second Cor. 6* **My Alliances**

Am I unequally yoked with any unbeliever? In society, in business, in pleasure, do I seek with eagerness the company of God's people? When I seek out the unbeliever, is it that I may turn him to belief? Let me rejoice in God's people. even as I rejoice in God.

**Wednesday** *Read II. Cor. 7* **My Contrition**

I am not to rejoice in all kinds of sorrow. There is a sorrow for worldly things which does despite to my Father in heaven. But there is a godly sorrow for sin, working repentance, in which I am to rejoice, and will rejoice. The experience is not pleasant, any more than the surgeon's knife; but the health is sweet.

**Thursday** *Read II. Cor. 8* **My Liberality**

Let not mine be the gathering that impoverishes, but the scattering that increases. Let me learn so to give as to grow. May the spirit of the great Giver animate me. Let me be a faithful steward, that mine may be the mastership of what I have. For I know that there is no having by hoarding.

**Friday**  *Read II. Cor. 9*  **My Thankfulness**

It is an unspeakable gift; but I am to try to speak it. It passes knowledge, but I am to try to measure it. Not all tongues in all time could tell it, but my tongue, in this present time, is to tell it. For if only eternity can express it, then surely it is time to begin the gratitude!

**Saturday**  *Read II. Cor. 10*  **My Glorying**

If I boast, let me glory in the Lord. Let it be a vaunting of what God has done for me and through me. Indeed, what else have I, of which to boast? What else has any man? If I glory in anything as if it were my own, I condemn myself in my boasting.

# WEEK 155

**Sunday** *Read Second Cor. 11* **My Perils**

Let me make my perils, my sorrows, my sufferings, occasions of glorying, even as Paul did with his. They are tokens that God thinks me worth testing. Or, they are even evidences that God deems me able to bear the most undoubted witness to His power, the witness that is borne in trials. Either way, they are my highest honor.

**Monday** *Read II. Cor. 12* **My Weakness**

Thorns in the flesh? Yes, many of them! Who has not? But such thorns as Paul had,—ah, how few of us have them! Thorns by patient courage encrusted with jewels. Thorns by wise insight become agents of healing. Thorns by union with the Lord Jesus Christ become crowns, even such as He wore upon the cross.

**Tuesday** *Read Second Cor. 13* **My Testing**

Need I wait for the testing of the Lord? Why may I not test my faith myself? Why may I not put myself to the proof in all the ways of hardship and endurance that God could use? Shall I build a character and not try the building to see whether it will stand the stress of the elements, the strain of time?

**Wed** *Read Galatians 1* **My Popularity**

Am I seeking to please men, or God? Can I not please both? Perhaps; but I cannot try to please both. My desire must be solely toward God, or it is not toward Him at all. I cannot serve God and mammon, for both are jealous; and God is rightly jealous.

**Thursday** *Read Galatians 2* **My Crucifixion**

If I have been crucified with Christ, I can no longer live to the world. If I am living to the world, I have not been crucified with Christ. I have not entered into His sorrow. I have not entered into His joy. I have no part in his triumphs. I am not living in His world at all.

**Friday** *Read Galatians 3* **My Faith**

How great need have I to be made just! How deeply is wrong become a part of me! How impossible I find it to eradicate that wickedness! I have tried every way but the one way that is efficacious. I have tried every agent but the One that can do it; that has done it, for uncounted millions. O Lord, increase my faith!

**Saturday** *Read Galatians 4* **My Bondage**

Let me not, having known Christ, the splendors and the joys of His gospel, turn back again to the weak and beggarly rudiments of the world. Let not the ransomed slave seek again his chains. Let me recognize my liberty, let me glory in my privileges, let me use my new powers. Let me not turn my back on Canaan and long after the fleshpots of Egypt.

# WEEK 156

**Sunday**   *Read Galatians 5*   **My Fruits**

If I am bearing the fruits of the Spirit, shall not I know it? Better, will not all around me know it? And if I fear that I am not bearing the fruits of the Spirit, that fear is quite sure to be justified in a barren life. Ah, let me be rooted and grounded in the love of God and man!

**Monday**   *Read Galatians 6*   **My Burden**

I am to bear my own burden. I am to bear the burdens of my fellow beings. I am to let them bear my burdens! I am to live my own life. I am to live in the lives of others. I am to let others live in my life. Helping and being helped,— ah, how much that sums up the Christian life!

**Tuesday**   *Read Ephesians 1*   **My Revelation**

What I know of God and of all good things I know not of myself. It is God who has opened the windows of my soul and let in all the light I see. If I would know more, I must be more acquainted with God. I must withdraw myself into the recesses of God's Spirit, if I would range abroad among the glories of His worlds.

**Wednesday**   *Read Ephesians 2*   **My Building**

What is the eternal edifice I am rearing for my soul to dwell in? Is it the hut of my foolish desires? Is it the leaning tower of my selfish ambitions? Is it the subterranean storehouse of my base greed? Ah, let me build with God and His saints, that my home may be a palace of heaven!

**Thursday**   *Read Ephesians 3*   **My Strength**

My power is in what is within and not what is outside. My power is in what is given me and not in what I get for myself. I am strengthened not by possessions that can be handled and weapons that can be felt, but by the Spirit of the living God. I belong to the unseen forces—that is, when my earthly passions subside and I am of any force at all.

**Friday**   *Read Ephesians 4*   **My Stature**

No man is a dwarf. No man but may grow. No man but may grow to the highest. No man farthest from God but may come nearest to God. No depth but may become highest height. And I, even I, may attain to the measure of the stature of the fulness of Christ!

**Saturday**   *Read Ephesians 5*   **My Time**

My minutes are golden, my hours are great diamonds. Every day is a crown, and every year is a king's ransom! It is by these hours and days and years that I am to buy up my kingdom. Alas, if I am a beggar still, I know where my kingdom has gone!

# WEEK 157

**Sunday**   *Read Ephesians 6*   **My Armor**

I must have some armor, for the assault of evil is fierce. I must have some armor, for I am weak. Shall it be bravado? pride? philosophy? Ah, how flimsy protection do they afford! and how secure is my shelter within the armor provided by the Captain of all salvation!

**Monday**   *Read Philippians 1*   **My Life**

If my life is Christ, as was Paul's, then life is gain to me, and death is gain to me, and nothing can ever be loss to me. To be Christ's is to be Prosperity's, and Safety's, and Joy's. And if my life does not mean this to me, it means nothing to me that is worth while.

**Tuesday**   *Read Philippians 2*   **My Salvation**

How can I work out my own salvation? Is not all salvation of Christ? Yes, and it is He that works out my salvation, in me and through me. He sets up anew His cross in my life. He ascends it again; and lo! I hang there with Him!

**Wednesday**   *Read Philippians 3*   **My Goal**

I have many goals; let me have but one goal. Mine is a crowded past; let me forget it all. Mine is an ambition-filled future; let me simplify it all. My calling makes many demands upon me; I will subordinate them all. I have only one calling, and that calling has only one goal: to be like Christ.

**Thurs**   *Read Philippians 4*   **My Thoughts**

I am not responsible for anything so much as for my thoughts. It needs not wealth to buy good thoughts. It needs not station or authority

*WEEK 157*

to exile bad thoughts. The best of all the universe is freely open to me here, if I will.

**Friday** *Read Colossians 1* **My Reconciling**

How I have fought against the Father! By what outrages have I tried Him! What taunts have I flung against Him! How have I despised His wrath! Surely if any one ever needed an advocate, it is I. And surely if any one ever had an Advocate, that one is also I.

**Saturday** *Read Colossians 2* **My Wisdom**

Continually I find myself seeking wisdom elsewhere than in Christ. Continually I look for wisdom from my own contriving, or from the devices of men. But Christ alone is wise. I have known it, I have proved it; and why do I go about my living as if I knew it not?

# WEEK 158

**Sunday**  *Read Colossians 3*  **My Longings**

I am what I desire. I throw myself into my ambitions. If they are worthy, they make me worthy. If they are ignoble, before long I also become ignoble. If they are attached to the fleeting things of earth, it is impossible for me to grow into fitness for the endless life.

**Monday**  *Read Colossians 4*  **My Speech**

Gracious and salty! Is my speech what the speech of a child of God should be? Is it loving? Is it true? Is it kind? Is it bold? Does it leave its hearers happier? Does it leave them stronger? Does it leave them with a merrier light in the eye and with a more cheerful heart?

**Tuesday**  *Read First Thess. 1*  **My Example**

In spite of myself, and even contrary to my desire and earnest hope, my life becomes an example. Unworthy as I am, insignificant as I am, men copy me, women copy me, little children copy me, friends copy me, strangers copy me, and I am copied by those that never saw me, but copy from those that copy from me. And all this without my knowing it, or their knowing it!

**Wed**  *Read First Thess. 2*  **My Reputation**

Paul sought to please, not men, but God. In this lay his strength with both men and God. Men he could not please, fundamentally, except as he first tried to please God. God he could not please except as he placed God's desires first in his life. Is this, which was at the heart of Paul's life, at the heart of mine also?

**Thurs**  *Read First Thess. 3*  **My Firmness**

It is far from enough that I go over to the Lord's side. I must stand there steadfast. And

## WEEK 158

I must do more than stand there; I must work there. And I must do more than work there; I must win others to stand there and work there. So much is involved in coming out on the Lord's side!

**Friday**  *Read First Thess. 4*  **My Heaven**

Ever to be with the Lord! Let me seek no other heaven than that. Where He is, sin cannot enter. Where He is, sorrow cannot be. Where He is, are all that are worth knowing. Where He is, is the work that is worth doing. Where He is, there are powers unlimited, and pleasures for evermore.

**Sat**  *Read First Thess. 5*  **My Expectation**

Not in any brooding or melancholy, but in joyful anticipation, I would be ever expecting the end of my life, the end of the world. Let it come as a thief in the night, it shall not be night when it comes, nor shall the messenger be received but with outstretched arms and a happy smile.

# WEEK 159

**Sunday**  *Read II. Thess. 1*  **My Judgment**

Do I look forward with certainty to the coming great day of judgment when the flaming fire will be the wrath of my God upon all disobedient? when the light of shining peace will be the joy of my God in all obedient souls? Oh, let me live day by day in that fear and in that hope!

**Monday**  *Read II. Thess. 2*  **My Establishing**

It is possible for me to become so firm in the truth and in the practice of it that lies shall no longer turn me here and there, either the lies of man or of Satan or of my own foolish heart. And what peace will that be! What peace, and what power! Grant it, I pray Thee, through Thy grace, Lord Jesus!

**Tuesday**  *Read II. Thess. 3*  **My Patience**

"The love of God and the patience of Christ"! Love and patience—the active and the enduring, the outgoing power and the power at home! I shall be well equipped indeed if the Lord direct my heart into these two.

**Wednesday**  *Read I. Timothy 1*  **My Faith**

Why does Paul write so earnestly of "a faith unfeigned"? Because it is so easy to feign faith. It is so easy to cheat ourselves, and others also, into the belief that we have a faith that we have not, nor even the glimmerings of it. We test our other possessions, but we have no possession that so needs testing as our faith.

**Thursday**  *Read I. Timothy 2*  **My Mediator**

When the unseen God seems vague and far away, I have Christ, who is near, and has been seen of men. When the almighty God seems too awful for approach, I have Christ, who took little children in His arms. When the just God seems implacable in His wrath, I have Christ, who will forgive till seventy times seven.

**Friday**   *Read I. Timothy 3*   **My Bishopric**

To me, even to me, has God given a diocese. I have a company, large or small, over whom I am set as leader in holy things, as example and admonisher, as friend and protector and teacher. If I do not anything else, this is to be done. If I fail everywhere else, in this I dare not fail.

**Saturday**   *Read I. Timothy 4*   **My Profit**

I must take heed where I find my profit. For there is profit in many things, but there is great and eternal profit in few things. And if I get the lesser profit from the lesser things, I shall surely become a little man; but if I get the greater profit from the great things, I shall become a great soul.

# WEEK 160

### Sunday  Read 1 Timothy 5  My Household

If I care not for my own household, how am I worse than an unbeliever! Indeed, what belief have I in the great things of the gospel, if I do not desire them first for my own? How have I laid hold of eternity, if I have not laid hold of my dear ones for eternity?

### Monday  Read 1 Timothy 6  My Contentment

If I have money, it is life, to be used for the purposes of life. If I have not money, I may still have life, and all the uses of life. Godliness is gain. Godliness is wealth. Godliness is all the gain and all the wealth that a Christian dares to set his heart upon.

### Tuesday  Read 2 Timothy 1  My Confidence

If my belief rested in my own wisdom, it would indeed be hesitancy; but it is firmly based upon a Person, who is Wisdom itself. If my reliance were upon myself, it would indeed be fear; but I rely upon a Person, who is Strength itself. My confidence is based upon the Rock that underlies all rocks.

### Wednesday  Read 2 Tim. 2  My Hardship

I am a soldier on service. It is no hardship for a soldier to fight; that is his glory and his delight. It is no final hardship for a soldier to avoid the entanglements of the world that would keep him from fighting, however for the moment it may seem grievous. If that were a hardship, he would be no true soldier.

### Thursday  Read 2 Timothy 3  My Bible

Here is the inspired Volume. How do I know that it is inspired? Because it inspires me! Be-

*WEEK 160*

cause it is profitable more than any other book is, and in a way no other book is. Because it is complete for me. I have never found it wanting. I have never gone to it in vain. It is alone among books. It is the Word of God.

**Friday**   *Read 2 Timothy 4*   **My Course**

I am to fight, but not forever. I am to run, but the long course has an end. Battles are not forever. Strain and stress are not forever. Possible defeat is not forever to be struggled against. Peace comes at last. Victory comes at last. Crown comes at last. And it is only a little way ahead.

**Saturday**   *Read Titus 1*   **My Purity**

My heart makes my world. If it is defiled, my world is loathsome. If it is pure, my world shines white and beautiful. What I am is reflected back from everything I see. It is an easy and a comprehensive way to make a lovely world, this planting of God's loveliness within.

# WEEK 161

### Sunday     *Read Titus 2*     My Sobriety

This is a world, not for gloom, but for soberness. The issues of life are too tremendous for trifling. While eternity is at stake, shall I play with time? My heart shall be light, for Christ is with me in the way. My steps shall be steady, for Christ is at the end of the way.

### Monday     *Read Titus 3*     My Regeneration

How I need renewing in the spirit, a purifying from the world, a change of nature! How I need to be lifted up from the old life, to be lifted up so far that the old life will be out of sight, forgotten forever! And I cannot lift myself an inch from the earth. Ah, but I can be lifted up!

### Tuesday     *Read Philemon*     My Intercession

Christ is my Great Intercessor, but I also am to be an intercessor. I am to place myself between all that have wronged and all that have been wronged, and try to bring them together. Between men that have wronged and men that have been wronged; yes, and between men that have wronged and God who has been wronged. Let me strive for the beatitude of the peacemaker.

### Wednesday     *Read Hebrews 1*     My Angels

I shall think of them as accompanying me about all my ways, beautiful, great, pure spirits, strong to protect and uphold, wise to direct, loving to comfort. They have access to the Throne on high. They are mighty to help. Ah, but there is One that is greater than they all, wiser, and more loving. It is He that sitteth upon the Throne! It is He that is nearer than any angel.

*WEEK 161*

### Thursday   *Read Hebrews 2*   **My Opportunity**

If I do not use the chance I have, where and how, through all the length of ages, may I hope for another chance of salvation? I see how every refusal confirms me in refusal. When I make the Great Refusal, how will it not invincibly confirm me in refusal? Ah, but I shall not make it!

### Friday   *Read Hebrews 3*   **My Hardening**

Every yielding to temptation hardens my heart. Every seeking of evil hardens my heart. Every excuse for sin hardens my heart. Every longing after sin hardens my heart. Every association with evil-doers hardens my heart. Every minute spent away from my Saviour hardens my heart. And every hardening of my heart stamps upon it more and more deeply the eternal doom.

### Saturday   *Read Hebrews 4*   **My Rest**

Tossed about in the storm of passion and temptation, there is yet a haven for me. That haven is in the heart of Him who was tossed about in every storm that assails me, beaten against every rock that threatens me, swallowed up in every darkness that hangs over me like a pall. There is my rest, in the heart of Christ!

# WEEK 162

**Sunday**   *Read Hebrews 5*   **My High Priest**

I, who am bidden to help others, how greatly do I myself need help! How weak am I, who am to strengthen others, and how foolish, I who am to give others counsel! If I have not a High Priest, how can I be a priest? If I have not a Saviour, how can I save?

**Monday**   *Read Hebrews 6*   **My Anchor**

Everywhere sand! Sand, sand, drifting sand, in which no anchor holds! And the storms of life beat my boat about, while there is no harbor in sight. Ah, but I can throw my anchor upward! There is anchorage there that holds, and there is such mooring nowhere else.

**Tuesday**   *Read Hebrews 7*   **My Intercessor**

I need to be saved unto the uttermost. Yes, for I have sinned unto the uttermost. Yes, for I have wandered unto the uttermost. Nothing less than the highest can reach to my depths; and nothing less than the highest is given me for my Intercessor.

**Wednesday**   *Read Hebrews 8*   **My Covenant**

It shall be a new covenant, this that I make with the Most High. A new covenant, because I want a new life. A new covenant, because I have a new life, the old things being gone forever. A new covenant, because it is one newly made for me by my Saviour; for me, and for me only, among the sons of men.

**Thursday**   *Read Hebrews 9*   **My Conscience**

Does my conscience need to be "cleansed from dead works"? Yes, if it knows what I am doing and not what my Saviour has done; if it even

*WEEK 162*

grieves over my sins and does not rejoice over my salvation; still more if it exults over my good deeds and forgets my sins.

**Friday**  *Read Hebrews 10*  **My Wilfulness**

It is indeed a fearful thing to fall into the hands of the living God, but no more fearful than first to fall into the hands of my passions and sins. If I sin wilfully after I know my folly, there is the condemnation, and at once my penalty begins. For I have trodden under foot the Son of God.

**Saturday**  *Read Hebrews 11*  **My Faith**

Faith is possible for me,—not my own faith, but Christ's faith given to me. Then all these lives are possible for me,—lives of Abraham, and Jacob, and Moses, and Gideon, and Elijah; for they were what they were only because of their faith. Oh, I believe! Help Thou my unbelief!

# WEEK 163

**Sunday**　　*Read Hebrews 12*　　**My Witnesses**

Let me name any one of the millions of great and good men and women that have passed into the heavens. If he or she were here by my side, watching me, knowing my inmost thoughts, how different my life would be! But I am compassed about very really by just such a cloud of witnesses, and among them is the chief Seer of all!

**Monday**　　*Read Hebrews 13*　　**My Stranger**

It is my stranger, this one that needs me. He may not speak to me, yet he is my stranger. I may never see him again, yet he is my stranger. For he is Christ's stranger, and Christ speaks to me. He is Christ's stranger, and I shall see Christ again.

**Tuesday**　　*Read James 1*　　**My Temptation**

How shall I count my temptations all joy? They are hard for me, bitterly hard, in themselves and their results. Ah, but I do not see all of the results; only a little segment of the results. If I face the temptations with Christ to help me, at the end of them—far off, perhaps, but still at the end of them—is a crown, a crown of life.

**Wednesday**　　*Read James 2*　　**My Faith**

It is easy to think about my faith. It is easy to talk about my faith. It is very hard to live my faith, yet that is the only kind of faith that lasts beyond the thinking or the telling,—the kind of faith that is lived out. O Christ, Thou source of all faith, help me to that kind!

**Thursday**　　*Read James 3*　　**My Tongue**

Surely I trust too much to my tongue. I let it go unwatched, as if it had not a thousand times

*WEEK 163*

betrayed me. I do not discipline or train it, though its heedlessness has a thousand times brought me into trouble and grief. Nothing that I have or am so harms me, yet nothing else is given such liberty. O God, place Thy angel at the door of my mouth!

**Friday**     *Read James 4*     **My Resistance**

Has the devil fled from me? Nay, he is right by my side, ready with a thousand crafty temptations. But why is he there, seeking to persuade a child of God to devilish deeds? Alas, he is there because he is invited! When my soul resists him, he flees from me; but not when I resist him with one hand and beckon him with the other.

**Saturday**     *Read James 5*     **My Prayers**

It is the prayers of a righteous man that avail. It is not because of his righteousness that they avail, but they do avail. It is of God's righteousness that any prayers are heard, but it would not be God's righteousness if the prayers of the unrighteous were heard. O God, give me of Thy righteousness, that I may pray to Thee!

# WEEK 164

**Sunday**  *Read 1 Peter 1*  **My Sightlessness**

Not having seen Him, I yet love Him. How will it be when I can see Him! True, He is with me now. His breath is upon my brow. His words are in my ears. His hand directs me. His eye is upon me. But how much clearer are the words of men and the forms of men, and how different it will be when I see Him and hear Him even as now I see and hear my brothers on the earth!

**Monday**  *Read 1 Peter 2*  **My Patience**

Not to be patient when all things go well with me, or when my trials are as summer zephyrs; not to endure what a child might easily endure; not to face the light mists of the morning, which the sun will instantly scatter; but to be patient when the bitter troubles come, when sorrows that would cripple a giant hurl themselves against me, when the blackness of deepest night encompasses me,—that is the patience of Christ.

**Tuesday**  *Read 1 Peter 3*  **My Reasons**

It is well to have hope, of any kind, with whatever backing. But hope that is at the mercy of a sneer, or a doubt, or a crafty argument is poor hope. Let not such a hope be mine, but a hope that is sure and stedfast, firmly founded upon unshifting reason. If I cannot give a reason for my hope, it will not be my hope very long.

**Wednesday**  *Read 1 Peter 4*  **My Crisis**

The end is at hand. The end of all things temporal for me. The end of earthly life, and all its innumerable interests that so engage me. That the end is sure, I am certain. That it may come to-day, is also certain. That it will come when

## WEEK 164

I am not expecting it is most certain of all. O God, when it comes, may I be with Thee!

### Thursday    Read 1 Peter 5    My Care

Let me not know any care. Let me cast it all upon my Saviour. Let it be His care henceforth, and mine no longer. Not to burden Him, for it will be no burden. Indeed, it is His burden that I do not allow Him to carry it!

### Friday    Read 2 Peter 1    My Addition

From glory unto glory! From growth unto growth! If I am not growing, I am dwindling. If I am not going forward, I am going backward. If the Lord is not with me in greater blessing day after day, He is not really with me at all, and my blessings are daily melting away.

### Saturday    Read 2 Peter 2    My Deliverance

Temptations come to the godly, but the Lord knows how to deliver him out of them. Temptations come to the ungodly, but the Lord does not know how to deliver him out of them. Am I of God? Am I godly? Is my hand in God's, my reliance upon Him? Then alone shall the flood of temptation have no terrors for me, and I shall walk through it in safety.

# WEEK 165

**Sunday**  *Read 2 Peter 3*  **My Expectation**

I have great prospects; let me live a great life. I look forward to a mighty coming of my Lord, when all the heavens shall shine, and all the earth shall shout, and His grace and glory shall fill the universe. O my Lord, am I to be a part of it all, or an outcast out of it all?

**Monday**  *Read 1 John 1*  **My Fellowship**

By this shall I know whether I am companying with the Father or not,—by noting whether my life is full of light or full of darkness. By this shall I know whether I am companying with the Son or not,—by noting whether my life is full of love or full of selfishness.

**Tuesday**  *Read 1 John 2*  **My Advocate**

As a criminal turns to his lawyer, and rests in him all his hope of freedom and happiness for all years to come upon the earth, so do I, a sinner, look humbly and confidingly to my Advocate, and repose in Him my hope for earth and endless heaven. What have I, O Christ, now or hereafter, if Thou dost fail me? But Thou wilt not fail me.

**Wednesday**  *Read 1 John 3*  **My Love**

Let my love for God be the test of my obedience to God, for I shall love Him if I do His will. Let my love to men be the test of my love for God, for if I love Him, I shall love those whom He loves so deeply.

**Thursday**  *Read 1 John 4*  **My Boldness**

Am I afraid of God or of man? Then I do not love aright either God or man, for perfect love casts out fear. If I love God with all my soul, I shall not fear God's judgment, to-day or here-

*WEEK 165*

after. If I love mankind with all my soul, I shall not fear that man will harm me. Love is my shield and my fortress, my defence and my sufficiency; for God is Love.

**Friday** *Read 1 John 5* **My Overcoming**

I have much to overcome, perils of this world close around me; perils of the world to come, tempting fiends, the threatening horrors of eternal death. But I have a victory, ever at hand,—even my faith. Nay, not my faith, but the faith of Him who upholds my will and my hope, when the one falters and the other cannot see through the mists.

**Saturday** *Read 2 John* **My Abiding**

Let me know myself, not by what I say with my mouth or even by what I believe with my mind. Let me know myself by what I do in my life. That is to abide in Christ,—to continue in His works and ways, speaking His loving words and doing His loving deeds. All other abiding is fallacious.

# WEEK 166

**Sunday**   *Read 3 John*   **My Imitation**

It is so easy to imitate! I am not merely myself, but all whom I see. Much of their good lives in me, and much of their evil. I am safe, O God, only as I turn toward Thee this imitative power of mine; only as I see Thee the One altogether lovely, the One who alone is to be imitated.

**Monday**   *Read Jude*   **My Defilements**

I hate even the spotted garments. I loathe the defilements of sin. Why is it, then, that I ever seek after them? Why is it that I wear the garments of evil, and add to their pollutions? It is because I live without Thee, O Thou Pure One! Without Thee, who art able to set me in the presence of Thy glory without blemish, and with exceeding joy!

**Tuesday**   *Read Revelation 1*   **My Kingdom**

I am made to be a king unto God; nay, I am made to be a kingdom. I am the realm and its ruler. The kingdom reaches to the end of time. It is my life, which is to all eternity. Within it are the thrones of all powers, the palaces of all joys. Ah, let me not trifle with my inheritance!

**Wed**   *Read Revelation 2*   **My First Love**

Alas for me, if any day is better than the present day! My life is to be an ascent, and not in any part a descent. Each sunrise is to usher in a greater glory, each evening to set upon a deeper blessedness. Thy help, O my God, if this is not so with me!

**Thursday**   *Read Rev. 3*   **My Lukewarmness**

Some day, I shall not be careless or indifferent about the things of heaven. It will be when I know that earth is nearly over for me. How my zeal will burn, then! How keen will be my anxiety, then! How hot will be my regret, then! Ah, there will be no lukewarmness, in that day.

**Friday** *Read Revelation 4* **My Praise**

If God were an earthly potentate, and I had access to his presence, how carefully I would con his deeds, what phrases I would frame in which to praise them, how they would dwell in my memory and linger on my tongue! But since God is not an earthly ruler, but the King of all kings and Lord of all lords, how witless is my silence and my forgetfulness!

**Saturday** *Read Revelation 5* **My Saviour**

He was slain. He redeemed with His blood all creatures. The highest beings in the universe are full of His praises. All heaven rings with the song of His glory. He was slain for me. He redeemed me with His blood. And not all the songs of archangels can satisfy Him if my poor note is lacking.

# WEEK 167

### Sunday   *Read Revelation 6*   My Safety

The great day of God's wrath shall come. The great day of Christ's wrath shall come. In that day men will cry to the mountains to fall upon them and hide them. And where shall I find safety in that day? Where but at the side of Christ? Where but in the bosom of God?

### Mon   *Read Revelation 7*   My Tribulation

Sometimes it is great tribulation. Sometimes it seems impossible to endure it. Yet how slight it will seem, in that great day! And how glad I shall be that I endured it! Help me in the tribulation, O Christ of many sorrows; and help me out of it, in Thy good time.

### Tuesday   *Read Revelation 8*   My Prayers

It is fine to offer visible worship, to see the clouds of incense rising toward God as in the days of the temple; but God has a better loved temple in the trusting heart, and better loved incense in the trusting prayer. Let me be the priest of such a temple, day and night.

### Wednesday   *Read Revelation 9*   My Seal

Do I wear the seal of God in my forehead? Has God imprinted upon me that mysterious and potent sign, known and obeyed by all His servants, marking me His forever? Yes, if I have surrendered myself His; no, if I have not.

### Thursday   *Read Revelation 10*   My Time

There will come an end of time, for me and all men. There will come a season when time will be meaningless, lost, altogether swallowed up in eternity. Awful thought, that my use of these measured intervals determines my character

*WEEK 167*

throughout that dateless existence! Creator of time, be Thou my guide through Thy creation!

**Friday**   *Read Revelation 11*   **My Kingdom**

Let me espouse the eternal success. Let me join myself to the everlasting triumph. Let me become a citizen of the unending Kingdom. And when the petty kingdoms of this world seek to tempt away my allegiance, remind me, O God, of their swiftly approaching end, and of my own endlessness.

**Saturday**   *Read Revelation 12*   **My Life**

I have a life, which I am to love, even to the death. And I have a life which I am not to love, even to the death. The fleshly life, if I love it, will conduct me to death indeed. The life that is hid with Christ in God, if I love it, will conduct me to the life that is life indeed. O God, my Life, help me to hold to life!

# WEEK 168

**Sunday**  *Read Revelation 13*  **My Patience**

What will test my patience? The trying of my faith. For I shall see the wicked triumphing in the earth, waxing rich and powerful, while the good are poor and oppressed. Yet let me remember their end, and trust in my God.

**Monday**  *Read Revelation 14*  **My Death**

Every day of my life shall bethink itself of the last day of my life. On that day my works shall follow me, whithersoever I go, and nothing else shall follow me. Will they follow me into rest, the Sabbath rest of God's children? Or will they follow me into the toil and sorrow everlasting?

**Tuesday**  *Read Revelation 15*  **My Song**

If I am to sing in heaven the song of Moses and the Lamb, it is time I was practising it upon the earth. It is time I was praising God, and rejoicing in His righteousness, and tuning my soul to His. What shame would be mine if I must be dumb, my first day in heaven!

**Wed**  *Read Revelation 16*  **My Garments**

What are the garments over which I must watch against the last day, lest I walk naked, and men see my shame? They are the robes of Christ's righteousness, the beautiful garments of my salvation. I must not lay them aside. My eye and my heart must be upon them, even in the night time.

**Thursday**  *Read Revelation 17*  **My Victory**

The Lamb shall overcome all evil; and they that are with Him, called and chosen and faithful, they also shall overcome all evil. What glory, O Christ, to be taken up into Thy conquests! I

*WEEK 168*

that seek fame and rejoice in it, what other fame shall I dare to seek?

**Friday**   *Read Revelation 18*   **My Babylon**

When Babylon falls, shall I have any share of the fall? Will aught of me—of my possessions, my hope, my life—be involved in it? God grant that there may not be. God grant that I, and all mine, may stand wholly outside of that great ruin; that it may not be in any wise my Babylon.

**Sat**   *Read Revelation 19*   **My Hallelujahs**

Let me live a hallelujah life, getting ready for a hallelujah heaven. I must not be ashamed of the glad tidings. I must not be forgetful of the glad tidings. My words of the glad tidings must not be faint or few.

# WEEK 169

**Sunday**  *Read Revelation 20*   **My Record**

My record is now making in heaven. How it is making, is not mine to know, or to care about; only that it is making. It is a just record. It is a complete record. It is a loving record. In it are many things of which I am terribly ashamed. In it is one thing in which I glory. That one thing is the blood of Jesus Christ my Lord, cleansing it from every stain.

**Mon**  *Read Revelation 21*  **My Abiding Place**

It is an abiding place, this country and city to which I go. No uncertainties there, no partings, no changes but joyful ones. It is a happy place, no tears, no pain, no sin. It is a beautiful place, with beautiful scenes and beautiful faces and beautiful words and deeds, and nothing else. Blessed be my Lord, who has prepared such a place for me.

**Tuesday**  *Read Revelation 22*  **My "Come"**

"Let him that heareth say, Come." I have heard. From beginning to close of the wonderful Book I have heard but one voice, "Come! Come! Come! Come to Me, and be saved, and happy, and strong." Lord Jesus, I come. Come Thou to me. And through these words I have written upon Thy Word, O come Thou to many souls. Amen.